Early Confucian Ethics

Early Confucian Ethics

Concepts and Arguments

Kim-chong Chong

OPEN COURT

Chicago and La Salle, Illinois

To order books from Open Court, call 1-800-815-2280 or visit
www.opencourtbooks.com.

Open Court Publishing Company is a division of Carus Publishing Company.

© 2007 by Carus Publishing Company

First printing 2007

Printed and bound in the United States of America.

Library of Congress Cataloging-in-Publication Data

Chong, Kim Chong.
    Early Confucian ethics : concepts and arguments / Kim-chong Chong.
        p. cm.
    Summary: "Explores the ethical theories of three early Confucian thinkers,
Confucius, Mencius, and Xunzi"–Provided by publisher.
    Includes bibliographical references and index.
        ISBN-13: 978-0-8126-9585-4 (trade paper : alk. paper)
        ISBN-10: 0-8126-9585-2 (trade paper : alk. paper)
     1. Confucian ethics. I. Title.
        BJ117.C577 2006
        170.931–dc22

                          2006027570

Contents

Acknowledgments

In the process of writing this book, I have received help, encouragement, and friendship from many people. Before expressing my gratitude, let me first acknowledge the publishers of some previously published essays on which chapters 1, 2, 3, and 5 are based. I list these essays below and also indicate the revisions that have been made in this book. This is beside making the chapters cohere thematically and ensuring (as far as possible) the consistent use of terms.

Chapter 1, "The 'Basic Stuff': Confucius and the Ethics of Character" is based on "The Aesthetic Moral Personality: *Li*, *Yi*, *Wen*, and *Chih* in the *Analects*," *Monumenta Serica* 46 (1998). A similar version was published as "Confucius's Virtue Ethics," *Journal of Chinese Philosophy* 25 (1998). In the present chapter, I no longer discuss virtue ethics in comparison with Kantian and Aristotelian ethics. Instead, I describe Confucius's "character ethics," and make only one or two minimal references to Western ethics. Strictly speaking, "virtue ethics" is a term of art that can only be fully understood in terms of an ongoing debate in Western moral philosophy between different (Western) ethical traditions. Nevertheless, readers who are interested in how Confucius may contribute to an understanding of virtue ethics may still (hopefully) learn something from this chapter. I have broadened the discussion to take into account other interpretations of some concepts and passages in the *Analects*.

Chapter 2, "The Orientation and Practice of *Ren*" appeared as "The Practice of *Jen*," *Philosophy East and West* 49, no. 3 (July 1999). Apart from minor revisions and some new references, this chapter remains substantially the same. Chapter 3, "Debating Human Nature: Mencius and Gaozi" is based on "Mengzi and Gaozi on *Nei* and *Wai*" in *Mencius: Contexts and Interpretations*, ed. Alan K. L. Chan (Honolulu: University of Hawai'i Press, 2002). I now refer to a few more interpretations of the debate between Mencius and Gaozi and discuss some of them in detail. I have attempted to demonstrate more clearly the logical structure of a central part of Mencius's argument against Gaozi's reasons for saying that *ren* (understood as love) is "internal" and that *yi* (rightness, for example, in evincing respect) is "external." Mencius's argument is, in technical terms, a *reductio ad absurdum*. In other words, it shows the absurd consequences that arise from accepting the premises of a particular argument. To help readers appreciate this, I have displayed the argument in schematic form.

Chapter 5, "Xunzi's Critique of Mencius" originally appeared as "Xunzi's Systematic Critique of Mencius," *Philosophy East and West* 53, no. 2 (April

2003). This chapter remains substantially the same but I have now attached an "Appendix." Xunzi is fond of using counterfactual arguments of the form: "If p then q, not q, therefore not p." In the appendix, I show two instances of this, both concerning Xunzi's affirmation that morality and the laws have a certain rationale that can be known and practiced.

Chapter 6, "Situating Xunzi," appears in English for the first time. A Chinese translation of chapter 6 entitled 荀子與四種人性論觀點 was published in the *National Cheng Chi University (NCCU) Philosophical Journal* 11 (December 2003). I thank Masayuki Sato of National Taiwan University for commissioning and overseeing this translation which was done by 黃裕宜. A conference on "Chinese Philosophy in Analytical Perspectives" organized by the Department of Philosophy at NCCU in September 2005 helped me to develop further thoughts on Xunzi. Masayuki Sato and Lee Jer-shiarn of the National Yunlin University of Science and Technology also organized a conference on Xunzi in February 2006 that allowed me to extend my thoughts thus resulting in chapter 7, "Ritual Transformation: Emotion and Form."

The writing of this book can be said to have begun when I spent a rewarding sabbatical in 1990 at the Department of Philosophy, National Taiwan University (Taida). This was a defining moment in my life that shaped my subsequent work. I already knew Kuo Po-wen who had earlier taught in Singapore. He introduced me to Chen Wen-hsiu, Hsia Ch'ang-pu (Department of Chinese Literature), Huang Yih-mei, Lin Yih-jing, Lin Cheng-hung, Tsai Hsin-an, Yang Hui-nan, and Yang Shu-tung. Their warm friendship made me feel at home. 張永儁 (then Head of Department) and Tseng Hann-tong (曾漢塘) helped me to settle in. I attended the classes of Hsia Ch'ang-pu and Lin Yih-jing (林義正). Hsia Ch'ang Pu introduced me to his student 宋有炯 who read with me Zhu Xi's commentaries on the *Four Books*. Lin Yih-jing especially nurtured in me a deep appreciation of the scholarly complexities of Chinese Philosophy. I feel that what Confucius's favorite disciple Yan Hui says of his teaching in the *Lunyu* or *Analects* (9.11) applies here as well: "The more I look up at it the higher it appears. The more I bore into it the harder it becomes. I see it before me. Suddenly it is behind me." (仰之彌高，鑽之彌堅。瞻之在前，忽焉在後。)

I was happy and honored to be invited back to the Department of Philosophy at Taida as external reviewer on two occasions by Lin Yih-jing and Chan Wing-wah (陳榮華). In one of these visits, Chen Guu-ying made me feel welcome and I was encouraged by his support of my reading of Xunzi in a seminar. During these visits and at conferences, I got to know Fang Wan-chuan (Academia Sinica) better and he too has given encouraging comments on my work.

The research and writing for the book was done mainly at the National University of Singapore (NUS). The following former colleagues and friends have helped me in various ways. At the Philosophy Department, I express my fond regards to Mabel Eickemeyer, John Greenwood (now at City University of New York), Hui-chieh Loy, A. T. Nuyen, Saranindranath Tagore ("Bappa"), Sor-hoon Tan, C. L. Ten, and Cecilia Wee. At the Chinese Studies Department and the Chinese Language Center, there were three former colleagues from whom I learned: Dongfang Shao (now Curator and Head Librarian of the East Asia Library at Stanford University), Ning Chen, and Zhi Chen. They participated in the reading groups organized when Kwong-loi Shun was visiting for a year. I subsequently read parts of the *Han Feizi* with another reading group led by Yuet-keung Lo from Chinese Studies. Although I am no longer with the NUS, I am proud to have been a part of this unique blending of Eastern and Western philosophy by a group that Roger Ames has so nicely referred to as the "Singapore philosophers."

The research and writing for this book was completed at the Hong Kong University of Science and Technology (HKUST), which I joined in January 2004. Yiu-ming Fung, Karl Kao, Chang-tai Hung, and William Tay have all helped me to settle into the lovely campus environment of Clear Water Bay with their warmth, generosity, and support. Yiu-ming Fung and Simon Wong have also shared with me their stimulating papers on Xunzi, Mencius, and Gaozi. Two graduate students, Brian Kei-yeung Luk and John Chiu-tuen Chow, have been of tremendous assistance in checking the drafts of the book.

Throughout the years, I have learned much from discussions with Antonio Cua and Kwong-loi Shun. Their writings have inspired me, and I am grateful to them for their support in various ways. From them, I have experienced the meaning of the first passage in the *Analects*, "Is it not a pleasure, having learned something, to try it out at due intervals? Is it not a joy to have like-minded friends come from afar?"

I am also grateful to the following: Paul Goldin provided helpful comments on the first version of the manuscript of this book. John Kekes offered comments on an earlier version of chapter 1 (although he may not remember this). Donald Munro was warm and hospitable during my short sabbatical visit at Ann Arbor, Michigan. Chung-ying Cheng was responsible for publishing the paper in the *Journal of Chinese Philosophy* mentioned above. Judging from citations, it has become better known than the other version in *Monumenta Serica*. Roger Ames runs a tight ship at *Philosophy East and West*. He and his anonymous reviewers provided very pertinent comments and challenging criticisms on papers upon which two chapters of this book are based. These resulted in quite a few revisions and refinements. Bo Mou and Vincent Shen provided impetus for furthering my thoughts through commissioning papers for their projects. Kerri Mommer at Open Court assisted me greatly with very pertinent queries in the course of editing.

I have benefited from the works of all the scholars that I have either mentioned or discussed in the book, even when I have disagreed with them. But of course, as the Daoist philosopher Zhuangzi intimates, one's perspective is limited. From all those whom I have mentioned in these acknowledgments and in the book, I have learned to appreciate that "A scholar must be strong and resolute, for . . . the road is long." (*Analects* 8.7). In other words, the path of learning that I took in the process of writing this book has no end.

I dedicate this book to my wife, Kathy Cheng-mei Ku, a Buddhist scholar who more than embodies the spirit of a scholar just mentioned. Like embroidering an altar cloth, "She makes every flower as lovely as the graceful flowers of the field, as far as she is able, every star as sparkling as the glistening stars of the night" (Kierkegaard, "Preface" to *Purity of Heart is to Will One Thing*).

Kim-chong Chong
Clear Water Bay, Hong Kong
August 2006

Introduction

In this book I aim to provide a philosophical account of the ethical thought of the three early Confucian thinkers, Confucius (c. 551–479 B.C.E.), Mencius (c. 371–289 B.C.E.), and Xunzi (c. 298–238 B.C.E.). Confucius inspired a humanistic ethical outlook that was developed by Mencius and Xunzi. This development took place amidst the background of arguments against other thinkers or in response to their criticisms of the Confucian school. The school of Mozi, the Mohists, played a pivotal role here. For instance, Mencius had to respond to the challenge posed by the Mohists that love should not be confined to within the family, but should be extended equally and administered impartially. And Xunzi felt compelled to respond to Mozi's criticism that Confucian ritual practices were not only unnecessary and wasteful, but also based on mere convention. There was disagreement within the Confucian school itself as well, as shown by Xunzi's critique of Mencius. I trace the philosophical development of thought from Confucius to Xunzi against the background of these arguments, criticisms, and disagreements.

Given the dominant position of Mencius in the Confucian tradition, there have been tendencies to read both Confucius and Xunzi in Mencian terms. Thus, Mencius's belief that human nature is originally good has often been read into certain sayings of Confucius. It has also been held that Xunzi's claims that human nature is "evil" or "bad," on the one hand, and that people can be transformed and become good, on the other, are inconsistent. It has been argued that for the claim of transformation to be sound, Xunzi implicitly assumes Mencius's claim that human nature is originally good; in fact, certain statements of Xunzi's seem to admit this. Against this tendency to read Confucius and Xunzi in terms of Mencius, a major task in this book is to keep the thoughts of the three thinkers distinct. I will devote close attention to the central concepts and arguments as they appear in three early Confucian texts: the *Lunyu* 論語 or *Analects*, the *Mengzi* 孟子 or *Mencius*, and the *Xunzi* 荀子.[1]

There are two reasons for maintaining the integrity of the different positions. First, the assimilation of one thinker's original thought to another—such as reading Confucius through Mencian categories—may blind us to important aspects of the assimilated thinker's position. Maintaining the integrity of this thinker's position would help us to focus on what is importantly distinct. Second, it would also enable us to see how the concepts and arguments developed from one thinker to another under the pressure of having to respond to the views of philosophical opponents. The value concept of *ren* (commonly translated as "humanity," "human-heartedness," or "benevolence"), for instance, was emphasized by all three Confucian thinkers. But as we shall see, it is not a static or unitary concept and it developed in the context of philosophical debate.

In the course of the discussion, it will be necessary to consider some issues that have been a matter of controversy. Broadly speaking, there are two kinds of issues. The first is how some passages in the *Analects* are to be read. I shall put forward the claim that these passages—commonly thought to be incongruous—can be read in a way that is consistent with Confucius's ethical position. More than that, these readings help to reinforce the coherence of Confucius's ethical position, despite the accretional history of the *Analects*.[2] Second, there is the issue of the way both Mencius and Xunzi argued—or some would say, did not *argue*, in the logical sense that an argument involves. I shall claim that both Mencius and Xunzi provided cogent arguments in parts of their discourses on human nature. In displaying the logic and force of these arguments, I shall show that Mencius was not being (merely) rhetorical in his central debate with Gaozi, and Xunzi was not simply relying on definitions in his critique of Mencius. The examination of concepts and arguments that accompany my claims with respect to the two broad kinds of issues mentioned will form a central part of my elaboration of the three ethical philosophies.

In the first two chapters I describe the ethics of Confucius as found in the *Analects*. I show that Confucius's ethical philosophy can be categorized as a "character ethics," that is, it emphasizes the importance of character and motivational attitudes instead of the guidance of general principles. Although they are not organized or presented theoretically, the concepts that permeate and express Confucius's ethical concerns form a coherent ethical philosophy when we see their interconnections.

In chapter 1, "'The Basic Stuff': Confucius and the Ethics of Character," I analyze two interconnected pairs of concepts. These are *li* 禮 and *yi* 義, on the one hand, and *wen* 文 and *zhi* 質, on the other. While much attention has been focused on the relation between *li* and *ren* 仁 in the recent literature, comparatively less attention has been given to the two pairs just mentioned and the relationships between them. Taken together, both pairs of concepts spell out the requirements of what I refer to as the making of an "ethico-aesthetic" personality. Music and knowledge of the *shi* 詩 or the *Odes* are an essential part of the learning of *li* or the rites, and the emphasis that Confucius places on their integration within the lives of his individual disciples means the cultivation of a harmonious personality attuned to doing what is *yi* or appropriate, according to the ritual circumstance and with the proper attitudes. To be *wen* is to be cultured, in accordance with the rites, music, and the *Odes*. And to have *zhi* is to have a substantial character that is the result of a refined training involving all these aspects of *wen*.

I will spend some time on the analysis of *zhi*, since it has been translated as "basic stuff" or "native substance," and this has led to some speculation that Confucius, prior to Mencius, believed the goodness of human nature was a necessary base for self-cultivation, and that the rites and ritual behavior were an "adornment" of this base. Analysis of this issue involves interpreting a passage from the *Odes* cited in *Analects* 3.8. I shall argue for a reading that denies the necessity of taking *zhi* as a "native substance." My analysis of the four concepts and their interrelations culminates in a detailed reading of the long passage 11.26, where Confucius approves of Zengxi, who expresses his wish "to go bathing in the River Yi and enjoy the breeze on the Rain Altar, and then to go home chanting poetry." This passage is commonly believed to be a later insertion, and to some, it is too "Daoist" in flavor to fit coherently into Confucius's ethical thought. Even if it is true that this passage is a later insertion, I show that there is a way of reading it that both illuminates and is consistent with Confucius's ethical philosophy as described, in terms of the two pairs of concepts mentioned.

The concept *ren* is central to the *Analects*. I discuss this in chapter 2, "The Orientation and Practice of *Ren*." Once again, I argue against tendencies to read the term through the perspective of the *Mencius* and its theory of human nature. There is some evidence that Confucius's own disciples expected him to hold forth theoretically on a concept such as *ren* and were disappointed that he did not do so. This expectation provides a context for the remark in *Analects* 9.1, that he "rarely" discoursed on *ren*. Given that there are many occurrences of the concept in the text, commentators have regarded this as a paradoxical remark and tried to provide all kinds of explanations to resolve the paradox. One recent resolution holds that this passage is a later insertion of a Confucian school devoted to the concept of *li*.[3] Whether this is true or not, there need be no paradox once we realize that Confucius was concerned with the practice of *ren* and not its theoretical discourse. For Confucius, *ren* connotes an ideal ethical orientation from which one sees the ethical life as a never-ending task. In different contexts, being a *ren* person connotes having emotions, attitudes, and values such as affection and reverence for elders, earnestness or the doing of one's best for others, sincerity, genuine feeling, cautiousness in speech, and congruence between speech and action. In this regard, I refer to an internal relation between *ren* and *li*. There are two aspects to this relation. First, learning to be a *ren* person involves the institutional and educational structures of *li*. Second, the emotions, attitudes, and values that *ren* encompasses are more or less similar to those that have been spelled out independently as the spirit of *li* in chapter 1.

Chapter 3, "Debating Human Nature: Mencius and Gaozi," concerns the concept of *xing* 性 or the *nature* of humans. There have been different opinions about the validity of the moves made by Mencius in this debate. I take a fresh look at this debate. Gaozi initiates the debate by trying to show that there is no inherent direction to one's *xing*—just as the *qi* willow is pliable, and just as water can flow in the direction in which it is channeled, similarly, *xing* is pliable or may be channeled in any particular (moral) direction. Gaozi is saying that *ren yi* 仁義 or morality is not an inherent feature of human nature, but an external imposition. Mencius replies that just as water tends to flow downwards, there is no *xing* that is not good. This is not a promising start. But later in the debate, Mencius manages to pin Gaozi down in terms of the latter's use of *nei* 內 and *wai* 外, "internal" and "external." Gaozi claims that *ren* (understood in terms of love, say, for one's brother) is internal, while *yi* (understood in terms of doing the appropriate thing such as showing respect for an elder) is external. Most commentators have understood Mencius to be agreeing with Gaozi that *ren* is internal, while disagreeing that *yi* is external. I offer a different explanation. Mencius is asking, "What do you mean by 'external' [and by implication, 'internal' as well]?" Through a superb use of analogies, Mencius demonstrates how Gaozi's answers result in logical absurdities, and *a fortiori*, cannot intelligibly be applied to the concept of *yi*, and by extension, to *ren* as well.

By going on to show how Mencius himself applies the terms "internal" and "external" in other parts of the text, we can see that comparatively speaking, Gaozi has a very impoverished moral psychology. He is limited to an account of human desires as merely sensory and appetitive (for example, the desires for food and sex). Through various examples, Mencius shows that besides the sensory and appetitive desires, human beings have motivational resources (and hence, qualitatively different desires) that enable us to relate to each other in moral ways. Thus, there are actions that we may be either compelled to perform (under one set of circumstances), or may not bring ourselves to do (under another set). These are due to moral predispositions that spontaneously reveal themselves under the circumstances described. We may interpret Mencius to be stressing the potential for relationships between human beings and for our having attitudes to things in general that are not relations or attitudes of (sensory and appetitive) desire, but of compassion, shame, respect, and (a sense of) right and wrong. Mencius is asserting that each person has, in his or her heart-mind, sprouts of moral awareness in different modes. The sense of "internal" for Mencius therefore has a moral significance that spells out what it is, essentially, to be human.

In chapter 4, "Mencius on *Ren* and the Problem of 'Extending,'" I examine the different senses of *ren* in the *Mencius* corresponding to three different motivational sources and principles: compassion, social concern, and affectionate attachment (to family members). As may be expected, the latter two can come into conflict under some circumstances. Although Mencius gives priority to affectionate attachment, this does not imply that he would abandon social concern. We see this in how he deals with the hypothetical dilemma facing the legendary Emperor Shun in *Mencius* 7A:35. While there is some difficulty with how Mencius and the Confucians in general would deal with "extending" affectionate attachment, this is because we tend to think of "extending" both logically and conceptually: given the conceptual barrier between affectionate attachment and social concern (that is, they are different kinds of "love"), such "extending" would appear to be impossible. However, we tend to forget that for the early Confucians (and perhaps for the Neo-Confucians as well), this was more an empirical problem than a conceptual one. Thus, they have developed a whole ritual corpus linking the individual, family, and society. Social values and attitudes of reverence and respect, for example, are expressed through ritual and cultural forms at various levels and on various occasions.

The rituals are not merely regulatory or instrumental to social order, but constitutive. That is, they allow for the creation of social processes whereby the individual could be emotionally, culturally, and morally transformed — as we shall see in the processes involved in creating the social order that Xunzi describes. Also, as far as Mencius is concerned, *ren* as "compassion" is a motivational source that is quite separate from affectionate attachment and social concern. Mencius shows through his example of the child about to fall into a well that as human beings, we are capable of an "expanding" of the heart-mind (instead of logically "extending" one kind of love toward others). In other words, we have the spontaneous resources to react compassionately under certain circumstances, in such a way as to override other, more limited, motivational concerns. One lesson to be drawn from this discussion is that Mencius is a motivational pluralist. That is, there is more than one motivational source in human beings, and this is precisely the problem with the Mohists and the Yangists (the egoistic and perhaps Daoist school of Yang Zhu). They seem to emphasize only one motivational source. Referring to them, Mencius says, "One thing is singled out to the neglect of a hundred others."

Chapter 5, "Xunzi's Critique of Mencius," brings us to an internal disagreement within the Confucian school. In this chapter, I try to locate the precise nature of Xunzi's criticism of Mencius. Xunzi has been described as merely stipulating the difference between *xing* and *wei* 偽 (what is not given at birth, but constructed). Thus, he is said to base his disagreement with Mencius regarding human nature by merely stipulating that people are born with selfish desires, and that *ren yi* (morality) or *li yi* (ritual principles) are constructed. Another criticism of Xunzi is that if (as he is said to hold) human nature is *e* (pronounced "er" without emphasizing the "r") 惡 "evil," how does he explain the alleged ability of the sages to construct moral or ritual principles? Any such ability must — so it seems — rely on moral predispositions, so Xunzi seems, after all, committed to accepting Mencius's claim that there are such predispositions.

But these criticisms fail to appreciate arguments that can be found in the *Xunzi*. In his critique, Xunzi denies Mencius's assumption that we are all born with moral predispositions. He shows that it is fallacious to assume that the resources and processes that go into the making of moral and ritual principles must have the same structure as those principles. In this regard, Xunzi's distinction between *ke yi* 可以 and *neng* 能 or "capacity" and "ability" does more systematic work in Xunzi's critique than often realized. An understanding of the distinction enables us to see that the objection that Xunzi is committed to Mencius's claim that there are moral predispositions in the heart-mind begs the question. This is because the claim (which the objection to Xunzi unwittingly accepts) assumes that the formal and constitutive structure of morality *must* be an original part of human nature. The objection also misses the point of Xunzi's critique because, instead of stipulating that nature is "evil" and goodness constructed, Xunzi in fact provides a diagnosis of Mencius's underlying assumption in his theory of the original goodness of human nature. That is, Mencius is diagnosed as relying on a picture of a pristine organic state of the human being as constituting his or her nature, and it is a moot question whether there is such a state.

Another point that is made is one that is now increasingly noted. For Xunzi, the claim that nature is "evil" does not contradict anything he says about the capacity to learn and to act upon ritual principles.[4] Instead, the claim refers more to the bad collective consequences of not regulating and not refining people's desires.[5] Also, the term *e* does not refer to "evil" per se, but to the ugly, unconstituted state of desires. Ritual principles were designed by the sages to bring about order not by merely regulating people's desires and their behavior, but also through instituting processes of aesthetic refinement. In these ways, the ritual principles came to constitute new forms of behavior.

In chapter 6, "Situating Xunzi," I show that instead of the claim that nature is evil or bad, Xunzi's considered position is that nature has the capacity to become good or to become bad. This is in fact one of the four prevalent views of nature stated in the *Mencius*. Interestingly, the view that nature is bad (that is, the nature of everyone is bad) is not included as one of the four prevalent views. In *Mencius* 6A:6, Gongduzi (Mencius's disciple) enumerates these as follows: (1) Gaozi's view that it is neither good nor not-good; (2) Nature has the capacity to become either good or bad; (3) There are natures that are good, and those that are bad; and (4) Mencius's view that nature is good. When stating the second view, Gongduzi says, "Human nature can become good or it can become bad, and that is why with the rise of [certain benevolent kings], the people were given to goodness, while with the rise of [certain cruel and tyrannical kings], they were given to cruelty." Xunzi makes similar remarks, and asserts a counterfactual: the influence exerted by the rulers on the people would not have been possible, if it were not the case that people have the capacity to become good, or the capacity to become bad. This corresponds to the second view mentioned by Gongduzi above. I show how Xunzi both elaborates upon and develops this view.

Thus, Xunzi's conception of human nature is wider than is usually thought. Instead of focusing as Mencius does on the essential nature of human beings in terms of the concept of *xing*, Xunzi asks, "What makes human beings 'human beings'?" In this regard, he refers to certain facts about or the *qing* 情 of human beings. For Xunzi, *xing* is a biological concept that refers to what all persons are born with, namely, the basic sensory and appetitive desires. The *qing* of humans, on the other hand, refers to the fact that people also have wants and capacities that go beyond these basic desires. Thus, people want wealth, luxury, and a refined life. At the same time, these imply the need for security, and the capacities to make social distinctions, think long-term, to be prudent, and to establish ritual principles to secure all these. Although the contents of *xing* are essential to biological survival, they do not constitute the *essence* of humans.[6] The biological "raw material" (so to speak) of humans can be transformed because the *qing* of humans is such that people possess the capacities mentioned. Xunzi frequently contrasts the possession of various desires, and the species-capacity to make social distinctions. The term that he uses to refer to this capacity of the species is *yi* 義, which many writers mistakenly take to mean a sense of morality and justice in Mencius's terms. Social distinctions lead to the making and institutionalizing of ritual principles. At the level of the species, people are said to have both the capacity and ability to discern the rationale of the rites. At the individual level, however, people differ. This is the case in terms of the amount of effort they make to learn, and in terms of whether they want to or are prepared to learn.

When Xunzi talks of the transformation of nature or *xing*, what exactly does he mean? In view of the prevalent misconception that Xunzi holds that human beings are by nature evil or bad, it is commonly thought that this transformation must simply refer to the setting up of rules to curb the naturally evil or bad behavior of human beings. Thus, transformation or *hua* 化 must be a negative thing: it is the constraining of human behavior through the institutionalization of ritual and moral rules. In chapter 7, "Ritual Transformation," I argue that for Xunzi, transformation involves a positive molding of individual character through a process of nurture, cultivation, and refinement, and ultimately a striving for a balance between emotion and form. We may extrapolate Xunzi's idea of the making of social distinctions to go beyond the mere institutionalization of social hierarchies. Instead, Xunzi's understanding of social distinctions includes the apprehension of more subtle aesthetic and moral distinctions that are involved in transforming individual character.

This discussion of ritual transformation is situated in the context of Xunzi's reply to Mozi's argument that Confucian ritual practices are not only wasteful—they are at the same time merely conventional practices that go against the Confucians' own value of *ren*. Here, Mozi assumes that *ren* is a spontaneous feeling that stands independently of ritual practices. A central reply of Xunzi's is that emotion and form cannot be separated. What constitutes *ren* is not self-evident. Instead, it is given a structure through ritual forms. There are objective criteria of whether some action constitutes being *ren* or not. Sometimes, for instance, the neglect of the proper ritual behavior would mean a failure to be *ren*. And there are circumstances where, for instance, the conduct of warfare constitutes being *ren*. The claim of a separation between nature and convention, or between the feelings and forms of ritual is spurious. Xunzi's response to Mozi shows that the latter's conception of human beings is too narrow given that it is confined to the basic desires and needs. In stressing the satisfaction of basic needs such as food and housing and arguing that anything beyond these (such as Confucian ritual) is unnecessary and wasteful, Mozi confines human beings to the satisfaction of their biological nature. It is precisely the object of ritual principles to transform this biological nature. Xunzi shows that there are various dimensions of a distinctly human life that go beyond the basic biological needs, and this is summed up in his remark that "ritual is nurture" (*li zhe yang ye* 禮者養也).

Throughout the different chapters, I make various comparisons between the three thinkers. I bring these comparisons together and draw out some possible insights in the concluding chapter 8, "Three Conceptions of the Heart-Mind." We look at how each thinker uses the term *xin*, "heart-mind," and how this gives rise to a conception of humanity. Confucius's use of *xin* to denote various states of mind is consistent with the attitudes, emotions, and values that form the human expressions of *ren*. For Mencius, the *xin* or heart-mind distinguishes the human in terms of its morally predisposed sprouts. For Xunzi, it is the cognitive capacity of the heart-mind to discern the rationales of the ritual and moral principles, or in other words, to make social distinctions, that is human. The difference between Mencius and Xunzi can be put in the following way: for Mencius, the *dao* resides in the heart-mind, whereas for Xunzi, the *dao* resides in the world, and is discovered by the cognitive capacity of the heart-mind.

The evidence adduced for Mencius's theory of the heart-mind is thin. Nevertheless, Mencius provides keen insights into moral psychology, especially with regard to moral desires as being qualitatively different from the sensory and appetitive ones, and with regard to the limits of action and what cannot be tolerated. Xunzi's strength lies in his structured logical arguments, and in his description of ritual principles as constitutive processes that go into the making of a refined individual. We realize from Xunzi's account of these processes that they are not merely instruments of social order, but importantly, they are constitutive of a civilized and orderly form of human life, and at the same time, of aesthetically and ethically refined individuals. In this regard, the tenor of Xunzi's ethical philosophy is very different from that of his student, the Legalist philosopher Han Fei.

Despite their different conceptions of the heart-mind and their different descriptions of humanity, we should remember that both Mencius and Xunzi were inspired by Confucius, and tried to defend the centrality of *ren* against the criticisms of the opposing schools of thought. As a result, the concept of *ren* developed from the appropriate expressions of ethical attitudes and feelings to encompass a theory of the goodness of human nature in the case of Mencius, and the objective structuring of feelings and emotions according to ritual forms in the case of Xunzi.

I have emphasized that each of these philosophers should be understood in their own terms. Once this understanding is in place, however, there is no harm in reminding ourselves that both Mencius and Xunzi drew their intellectual inspiration from Confucius, although I would maintain that we should not read Confucius or Xunzi in Mencian terms. Thus, an appreciation of the human expressions of *ren* (as described in the first two chapters) leads to the realization that if the ritual processes are not to be regarded as merely being instrumental toward social order, then Xunzi's account of these processes as having constitutive value must assume the fundamental ethical significance of the human expressions. Similarly, Mencius would find it difficult to argue for the contents of the heart-mind without a prior picture of the ethically fundamental conception of the human expressions that is described in the *Analects*. I cite some passages in the *Mencius* where Mencius refers to some states of mind that indicate a concern with individual character. For instance, referring to Emperor Shun, Mencius says that he "followed the path of morality" instead of "putting morality into practice." This would be one indication of what I have referred to when discussing the ethical philosophy of Confucius, as the "immediacy of ethical commitment." That is, this is an instance of someone who acts in a morally integrated manner. Mencius, however, cannot resist putting this in the context of the predispositions of the heart-mind by saying that this is a feature of the difference between human beings and animals that the common person loses but which the noble person retains.

I have tried to be detailed in my readings of the *Lunyu*, the *Mengzi*, and the *Xunzi* (including consulting some of the Chinese commentaries). But another method that I have used is a philosophical one. By this I refer to the following endeavors, although these would be another way of expressing what I have already said above in terms of content.

First, I identify and demonstrate forms of argument. This is especially pertinent, I believe, to a philosophical understanding of the *Mencius* and the *Xunzi*. Compared to the *Analects*, both texts are more theoretically structured, so I have pursued the philosophical links and arguments that I have discerned in them. Perhaps it is now more widely accepted that Mencius and Xunzi were not merely being rhetorical or stipulative. I do not know if this is the case. Even if it is, the exact nature of their arguments—especially where these are cogent and sustained—needs to be demonstrated more clearly and this is what I have attempted to do in this book. This is not to say, however, that both the *Mencius* and the *Xunzi* can be read throughout in terms of the argument forms that I identify.

Second, even in the absence of theory and conscious argument, there may still be an ethical outlook and I attempt to identify it. As in the case of the

Analects, this outlook may seem fragmented and the pieces may not seem to hang together very well. Various philological explanations may then be given for this, and some of these may be important. Thus, I do not deny the importance of close sinological readings and relevant philological work. However, if one is convinced—as I am—that the ethical outlook is a coherent one, it would then be a philosophical task to reconstruct this outlook, and to explain how the various pieces together help to express it.

Finally, let me say something about some translated terms. I have largely followed the translations of D. C. Lau (for the *Lunyu* and the *Mencius*) and John Knoblock (for the *Xunzi*). However, I have avoided their use of "gentleman" or "superior man" for the ideal Confucian character, the *junzi* 君子. I have replaced this with "noble person." I have rendered its opposite, the *xiaoren* 小人, as "ignoble person" instead of "small man." For the term *ren* 人, instead of "man" I have used "person(s)," "people," "someone," "human(s)," and "human beings." I have done this too for some authors that I discuss although sometimes I have left their use of "man" alone, especially when, for example, the author is distinguishing it from "animals." On occasion, I have used "she" instead of "he" when referring to some representative person. I am aware that the use of gender-neutral terms and the occasional use of "she" might be found to be incongruous with the male-dominant or patriarchal society of the Confucian thinkers.[7] However, from a philosophical point of view, there is no reason to think that their use of the term *ren* 人 refers only to the male members of the human species. Interestingly, classical Chinese seems to be more gender-neutral than English. When, for instance, Mencius says that "a *ren* person loves others" (*ren zhe ai ren* 仁者愛人 4B:28), the particle *zhe* denotes the "person" who is *ren*. In English, *ren zhe* is often translated as, for example (depending on the reading of *ren* 仁), "benevolent man." In a subsequent Chinese sentence where reference is made to this *ren* person, the term *qi* would be used, and this is gender-neutral. On the other hand, an English translation of this would (perhaps unavoidably) use "he."

The "Basic Stuff": Confucius and the Ethics of Character

1

In the *Lunyu* 論語 or the *Analects*, Confucius says that "people are close to one another by nature *xing* 性. They diverge as a result of repeated practice *xi* 習" (*Analects* 17.2).[1] Nothing is specified here about what this nature is. Seen in the light of later discussions by Mencius, Xunzi, and others about whether human nature is (originally) good or bad, Confucius's remark that "people are close to one another by nature" is compatible with their having been "close" in terms of either having been good or bad. Similarly, they could also have diverged in different directions, good or bad. For us to even put what Confucius says in the context of the (original) goodness or badness of human nature, however, may be to assume too much. Confucius's use of the word *xi* in the above passage is significant. It is the word that is used in the opening remark of the *Analects*, where Confucius mentions the pleasure of practicing what one has *learned* at due times.[2] "*Xi*" is linked to learning, and in the context of self-cultivation, this connotes a process of *practicing* what one has learned in the sense of instilling in oneself certain virtuous habits. Seen in this light, Confucius may have meant in 17.2 that people are close to one another in their capacities to learn, but diverge because of their different efforts at practicing (or not practicing) what they have learned.

This denial that Confucius holds any particular conception of human nature has to take into account the fact that in the *Analects*, there are some references to the term *zhi* 質, which has been translated as "basic stuff" or "native substance." I shall contend that *zhi* in the *Analects* does not refer to some inborn substrate of moral goodness. Instead, it should be taken as referring to a substantial individual character that is the result of a process of self-cultivational learning. An intimate part of this process involves learning and behaving according to *li* 禮 or the rites, with an emphasis on the instilling of certain motivational attitudes. An explication of this whole process entails a discussion of *zhi* and its relation to the rites and other concepts such as *yi* 義 and *wen* 文. I shall leave these last two concepts untranslated for the moment, as they bear some discussion.

I shall show that embedded within the *Analects* is an account of *li* or the rites that allows for its modification, based on a certain spirit in which *li* is to be practiced. This encompasses certain attitudes integral to the concept of *li*, and *yi* may be said to describe the proper expressions and execution of *li* in the right spirit. The practice of *li* in its many forms serves also to shape character, motivating one to behave, desire, feel, and act in the required ways. The harmonious performance of *li* is in itself a thing of beauty. The many references to music and the *Odes* in the *Analects* in connection with the proper performance of *li* suggest that the intimate connection between aesthetics and *li* is seen as a motivational tool in the training of a person's character. This training gives rise to certain virtues to be described in the process of observing *li*. The person is refined or "*wen*-ed" so to speak, and the virtues acquired in the process constitute his having *zhi*. Of course, conceptually, one can still make a distinction between *wen* and *zhi* especially as this would allow for criticism of a failure of character, for instance, when there is a specious overrefinement. But in the final analysis, *wen* and *zhi* are complementary—we cannot fully understand one without the other. *Wen*, in other words, is not the adornment to be added to *zhi* or morality, the icing on the cake as it were, or something that one does at leisure. *Wen* and its manifestation in the practices of *li* constitute the training of what I would refer to as a certain ethico-aesthetic character.

Analects 3.8 and the "Basic Stuff"

We begin with a passage that is open to different interpretations, *Analects* 3.8:

> Zixia asked,
> "Her entrancing smile dimpling,
> Her beautiful eyes glancing,
> Patterns of colour upon plain silk (*su yi wei xuan xi* 素以為絢兮).
>
> What is the meaning of these lines?"
> The Master said, "The colours are put in after the white (*hui shi hou su* 繪事後素)."
> "Does the practice of the rites likewise come afterwards?"
> The Master said, "It is you, Shang, who have thrown light on the text for me. Only with a man like you can one discuss the *Odes*."

Confucius approves the thought of his disciple Zixia, that "the practice of the rites likewise come[s] afterwards." The question is, after what? What could be more basic than the rites? Here is one answer. The rites or *li* as a traditional repository of rules that guide behavior and interpersonal relations are subject to revision through principles. These determine the rightness of rules and are therefore more fundamental. If we see the rites not merely as rules but as practices involving various forms of ceremony which include a minutiae of rules, we can begin to see the analogy with color. The raw material upon which the drawing or painting rested was plain silk (*su* 素), and so the plain silk comes first, while the colors come afterward.[3] Analogously, knowledge of principles was required before one could apply the rites. Otherwise, the mere application of certain rules could amount to ingratiating oneself with another, just as the lady with the entrancing smile and glancing eyes may exude her charm.

This, in essence, is D. C. Lau's answer, as may be gathered from the "Introduction" to his translation.[4] The route to it explores two pairs of related concepts, *li* and *yi*, *wen* and *zhi*. *Zhi*, according to Lau, is easier to understand. It is simply "the basic stuff or native substance a thing or a person is made of." *Wen*, on the other hand, which Lau thinks is more difficult to grasp because of its far-ranging application, means roughly the following: adornment, refinement, accomplishment, good breeding, culture, literature, music, poetry, and so forth. As he says, *wen* may refer to "the beautiful qualities (a person) has acquired through education. Hence the contrast to *zhi*" (Lau 37). The contrast is between possessing moral qualities on the one hand, and adornment on the other.

As Lau has just explained it, however, *wen* is not difficult to understand. On the contrary, *zhi* is more puzzling. Here, Lau relies on a remark of Confucius's: "The noble person has morality as his basic stuff and by observing the rites puts it into practice" (15.18).[5] Lau translates *yi* as "morality," and states that the relation between *zhi* and *wen* "corresponds to" the relation between *yi* and *li* (Lau 38). Evidently, the practice of *li* is a cultural accomplishment and adornment (*wen*), or an expression of *wen*. Without its basis in *yi* ("morality") or *zhi* ("basic stuff"), however, the expression of *li* would be hollow. That is, it would be mere *wen* or an empty adornment.

According to Lau, *yi* has the following more specific meanings: (1) "right" as a moral quality of an act; (2) "duty" as an act one ought to perform; (3) "righteous" or "dutiful" as descriptive of an agent. Lau takes it as distinctive of *yi*, however, that it is act-based, i.e., the rightness of an action depends on its "being morally fitting in the circumstances and has little to do with the disposition or motive of the agent." An agent is described as "righteous" or "dutiful," derivatively, in this regard: "rightness is basically a character of acts and its application to agents is derivative. A person is righteous only insofar as he consistently does what is right" (Lau 26–27). *Yi*, according to Lau, is the underpinning of Confucius's moral system:

> Although Confucius does not state it explicitly, one cannot help getting the impression that he realizes that in the last resort *yi* is the standard by which all acts must be judged while there is no further standard by which *yi* itself can be judged. After all, even benevolence does not carry its own moral guarantee. "To love benevolence without loving learning is liable to lead to foolishness" (17.8). As we shall see, the object to be pursued in learning, in this context, is likely to have been the rites, and the rites, as rules of conduct, can, in the final analysis, only be based on *yi*. We can

say, then, that in Confucius's moral system, although benevolence occupies the more
central position, *yi* is, nevertheless, more basic. (Lau 27)

In effect, *yi* is the *zhi* or the basic stuff that comes before *li* or *wen*. Lau specifically talks of their relationship in terms of principles and rules. It is *yi* that
guarantees the rightness of *li*. Whether the rules "are right or not depends on
whether they measure up to the demands of rightness. Rightness, on the other
hand, is the standard by which all acts have, in the last resort, to be measured.
Thus there is an intimate relationship between *li* and *yi*" (Lau 49). Although
Lau qualifies this position by stating that principles require rules for their expression, it is nonetheless clear that rules in Confucius's ethics are said to be
subordinate to principles which establish their rightness.

Lau's analysis implicitly attributes to Confucius a duty-based ethics and its
central place as a decision procedure in the resolution of questions of rightness.
In this regard, rules and principles play an essential role. Indeed, the claim is
made that the "dialogue between rule and principle constitutes the essence of
Confucius's moral thinking" (Lau 50). This conclusion is based on the fact
that Confucius subjected existing precepts to fresh scrutiny. Circumstances
change, what was appropriate before may not be so now, rules may conflict,
and the mere observance of a rule may conflict with the spirit of the rule (Lau
49–50).

Although Lau is right that Confucius is not obstinate or pedantic in his
observance of the ritual rules, it is difficult to accept the idea that the relation
between *li* and *yi* constitutes a relation between rule and principle, in the way
that Lau describes.[6] That is, although there is something fundamental about *yi*,
this lies in the importance of certain attitudes (to be described later) that go to
make up a basic ethical character and orientation. Lau is not unaware of this.
However, his description of *yi* as a fundamental moral principle that is the final
arbiter of rightness and capable of overriding rules leads one to expect specifi-
cation of the principle. There is, however, no such principle or criterion either
in the *Analects* or in Lau's account.[7] Certainly, the mention of *yi* as "right" or
"duty" or "morality" does not as such provide a criterion. Similarly, the definition of *yi* as act-based and as being "morally fitting in the circumstances" does
not provide any criterion.

A second reading of 3.8 is possible, although this reading still relies on
the idea that the plain silk or the white comes first. That is, the plain silk upon
which the colors are laid connotes the "basic stuff" or "native substance." The
colors connote the rites that adorn or embellish the basic stuff. But in order
for the rites to have any effect, the basic stuff has to be there in the first place.
Edward Slingerland suggests this reading when he comments on 3.8: "Just as
all of the cosmetics in the world are of no avail if the basic lines of the face are
not pleasing, so is the refinement provided by ritual practice of no help to one
lacking in good native substance. It is this entailment that explains Confucius's

concern that cultural adornment be firmly rooted in its native substrate. . . ."[8]

There is more than one description of this "native substrate" in Slingerland's account. First, Slingerland refers to this as constituting some "basic emotions" that form the root of the ritual forms. For instance, that it is important not to lose touch with emotions such as grief when mourning, instead of being overly concerned with the formal details.[9] As we shall see, we can speak of the expression of certain emotional attitudes as being important to the rites without having to refer to any native substrate. But Slingerland supplements this with a second description, citing passages that would indicate "some kind of innate tendency toward the good"[10] or even that "innate orientation toward the good is a universal quality."[11] Slingerland is concerned to show that there is a "paradox of virtue" in the *Analects*: one must already be virtuous in order to acquire virtue.[12] Also, there is a tension in the *Analects* between what he calls the "adornment" metaphor, and the "craft" metaphor. In the former, the rites do not alter the native stuff, but instead can only be said to depend for their effectiveness on the prior existence of the native stuff. The craft metaphor, on the other hand, connotes a radical shaping of a material that has no particular prior mass or shape,[13] or that requires "violent reshaping of the original material."[14]

In describing these metaphors, Slingerland indicates the affinities with Mencius (human nature is originally good) and, at the same time, with Xunzi (goodness is the result of accumulated effort and not the result of any originally good material). Slingerland is not wrong in pointing to these affinities. It is possible to read the *Analects* in either a Mencian way, or in a Xunzian way. Whether it is legitimate to read the ethical philosophy of the *Analects* in either of these ways, however, is a further question. In this regard, I think that a focus on the term *zhi* as "basic stuff" or "native substance," and the conception of the rites as an embellishment or adornment can distort Confucius's ethical concerns. This brings us to a third reading of 3.8.

The Qing dynasty commentator, Dai Zhen, objects to the view of the rites as an adornment, commenting that "it is because (someone's) feelings have already become insincere that he can only regard outward adornment to be the purpose of the rites."[15] Instead of "The colors are put in after the white," Dai Zhen reads the words *hui shi hou su* (in 3.8) as "After laying on the colors, white is applied."[16] This refers to a technique where white is applied last, to bring out the distinctiveness of the colors of a painting. In other words, although one has to have some character in the first place, the rites are still required to refine one's character. This refinement is not an "adornment," but involves a process of learning. As Dai Zhen says:

Truthfulness and trust (*zhong xin* 忠信) emanate from a good character (*zhi mei* 質美). The sages, while discussing human conduct, definitely regarded truthfulness and trust to be important. But in the case of a man who has a fine character but not sufficient learning, when you come to consider how he has managed his affairs, you may find he has erred from ignorance and consequently has made mistakes in his conduct. In such a case, he may have done great harm to the Way, although there was nothing but truthfulness and trust in his heart. Those who err in what they do without realizing it and at the same time seek only to have a clear conscience are the type of persons who are truthful and trustful but have no love for learning, and this is where their mistake lies. From this we can see the importance of learning and the practice of the rites.[17]

Although Dai Zhen talks of a good character to begin with, he explicitly rejects any reference to the practice of the rites as "embellishing" or "adorning" (*shi mao* 飾貌). For him, this only arises when "a person's feelings are wearing thin and yet he continues to work on the appearance of things."[18] Instead, he emphasizes learning and practice in talking of the rites in the above passage. Elsewhere, but in the same context, he talks of the balanced regulation of feelings, becoming cultured and advancing oneself through ritual practice.[19] As Dai Zhen sees it, therefore, the "adornment metaphor" would be inappropriate to a description of the purpose of the rites as an educational and self-cultivational medium. One could say that for Dai Zhen, the rites play a more active and positive role in the formation and the improvement of character. Does this mean that he would endorse the "craft metaphor? This would not be right either, insofar as this is taken to mean the "violent reshaping" of any original material, or of giving shape to some "shapeless mass."

I suggest that the difficulties with using these metaphors can be avoided if we realize that a full explication of *zhi* requires a description of its interrelations with the other concepts that were mentioned in the beginning of this chapter. In the next section, I shall follow up on Dai Zhen's active and positive conception of the rites in the process of self-cultivation and the refinement of character by describing the role and function of *li* and its relation to *yi*, and the corresponding role and function of *wen* and its relation to *zhi*.

The Spirit of *Li*

We need to explore afresh the two pairs of concepts, *li-yi* and *wen-zhi* by contextualizing them. First, we must remind ourselves of various aspects of *li* in the *Analects*. I shall concentrate mainly on passages in Book 3. These tell us much about *li*: its application and abuses, its proper expression and understanding, and the attitudes and emotions involved.

Several passages note Confucius's displeasure at the arrogation of certain rites by some prominent families and personalities (3.1, 3.2, 3.6, 3.10, 3.22). Others inform us of Confucius's concern to understand the details of various rites. He confesses ignorance regarding the theory of a certain rite (3.11), and talks of the necessity of "supporting evidence" (3.9, 3.11, 3.15).

The rites pervade all areas of life, for example, in archery: "There is no contention between noble persons. The nearest to it is, perhaps, archery. In archery they bow and make way for one another as they go up and on coming down they drink together. Even the way they contend is noble" (3.7; see also, 3.16).

Certain expressions, values, and attitudes are essential to the performance of the rites. For example, Confucius asks, "What can a person do with *li* who is not *ren*? What can a person do with music who is not *ren*" (3.3)? "'Sacrifice as if present' is taken to mean 'sacrifice to the gods as if the gods were present.' The Master, however, said, 'Unless I take part in a sacrifice, it is as if I did not sacrifice'" (3.12). Asked about the basis of the rites, Confucius says, "A great question indeed! With the rites, it is better to err on the side of frugality than on the side of extravagance; in mourning, it is better to err on the side of grief than on the side of formality" (3.4).

Reverence is an important attitude. It takes precedence over frugality. Thus, Confucius approved the majority's use of ceremonial caps made of black silk instead of the linen prescribed by the rites, on the ground that it was more frugal. In another aspect of ceremony, however, he disagreed with the majority practice. It was prescribed that one should prostrate oneself before ascending the steps, while the majority did so only after ascending them. Confucius regarded this as irreverent (9.3). Confucius also warns against obsequiousness in performing the rites (3.18).

Finally, it is important to stress the intimate relation among the rites, the *Odes*, and music. Two passages indicate the need for aesthetic sensitivity. Referring to the first of the *Odes*, Confucius says, "In the *Guan Jü* 關雎 there is joy without wantonness, and sorrow without self-injury" (3.20). Discussing music with the Grand Musician of Lu 魯, he says, "This much can be known about music. It begins with playing in unison. When it gets into full swing, it is harmonious, clear and unbroken. In this way it reaches the conclusion" (3.23). Balance and harmony are integral to the rites and they constitute important virtues. Aesthetic discrimination provides sensitivity to the nuances of balance and harmony and such discriminatory ability is part of being a "complete person" (*cheng ren* 成人, see 14.12).

To sum up, the rites are an elaborate edifice of human conduct, priorities of relationships, gradations of rank, religious sacrifice, rulership, and so on. Fingarette has also drawn our attention to *li* as "holy rite," magically ensuring the performance of actions in all kinds of contexts that we take for granted (performative utterances), and in the context of rulership, ensuring order and action through the correct and imposing posture of the ruler.[20]

Confucius's questioning of the details of the rites and his confession of ignorance show their complexity, and the scholarship required for their understanding. There is no doubt that the rites constituted a deep and vast resource that could be used to regulate all aspects of life, and also to resolve any particular conflict that might arise. We are not told much about these conflicts but surely there is no one fundamental principle here. A reading of the *Analects* reveals the enunciation of different principles in different contexts.

Indeed, Confucius goes so far as to give what seems to be contradictory advice to different people. When asked by Zilu 子路 whether he should immediately practice what he has heard, his answer is negative, citing the reason that his father and elder brothers were still alive. He gives a positive answer to Ranyou 冉有, however, when asked the same question. Asked about this, his reply is that "Qiu 求 [Ranyou] holds himself back. It is for this reason that I tried to urge him on. You 由 [Zilu] has the energy of two men. It is for this reason that I tried to hold him back" (11.22).

It is possible to draw a principle for this stratagem of Confucius's. But to insist on this would be to distort the point of his action which is precisely a *strategy* designed to treat different people differently, given their characters. In any case, the enunciation of a principle here would still not show that Confucius had any fundamental principle. Thus, the example of frugality and reverence mentioned earlier shows that Confucius was concerned to balance different values and attitudes in different contexts.

What comes across very clearly, however, is Confucius's concern that the rites were not performed in the right spirit. He severely criticizes the dead performance of *li*: "Surely when one says 'The rites, the rites,' it is not enough merely to mean presents of jade and silk. Surely when one says 'Music, music,' it is not enough merely to mean bells and drums" (17.11). The tone here is irritable, angry, and despairing.

The expressions and attitudes described above are all crucial to the very meaning of the rites, not external to them. Thus, his objection to the arrogation of royal rites by some prominent individuals and families was an objection to a certain presumptuousness and even hubris. This is also evident in 3.6 where an improper sacrifice to the sacred Mount Tai 泰山 is considered by Confucius as an offense against Mount Tai. Similarly in 3.13 he says: "When you have offended against Heaven, there is nowhere you can turn to in your prayers." This presumptuousness and hubris was, in itself, a breach of the rites.

Being obsequious in performing the rites violates their solemnity and dignity. Lack of genuineness of feeling in ritual action negates its point. It is better to err on the side of grief, says Confucius, than on the side of formality (see above).

Respect or reverence is crucial to the spirit of the rites. This should not be sacrificed in the name of frugality (3.17: "Referring to Zigong 子貢, Confucius says, "you are loath to part with the price of the sheep, but I am loath to see the disappearance of the rite"). But at the same time, it is better to err on the side of frugality than extravagance for the latter in itself does not convey the spirit of the rites.

Aesthetic sensitivity and understanding are required in balancing these judgments. The passage from the *Odes* quoted in 3.8 shows this. Confucius is commending Zixia 子夏 for his understanding of the nuance of the passage and being able to relate it to the fundamentals of the rites. It is no coincidence that Confucius praises him for this.

The Relation between *Li* and *Yi*

Given this concern about learning and practicing the rites in the right spirit, what can be said to be the relation between *li* and *yi*? I would suggest that *yi* 義 constitutes doing what is right or proper, as specified by *li*. And essential to what is right or proper is the way this is carried out, that is, *yi* is the carrying out of the specifications of *li*, *in the spirit* of *li*. As we have seen, Confucius refers in 15.18 to *yi* as the *zhi* or the "basic stuff" of a noble person, and it is through the observance of the *li* or rites that it is put into practice. The above discussion has shown, however, that *li* is not just a prescribed set of rules, but that what is to be stressed are the emotions and attitudes that are expressed through the rules. As the "basic stuff" of the noble person, *yi* can be said to refer to something similar, incorporating the following attitudes: not having a frame of mind that is merely concerned with profit (4.16); being able to enjoy the simple material conditions of life, and at the same time, to be indifferent toward wealth and rank especially when they can only be got through improper means (7.16); and having moral courage (17.23). What is also striking is that for Confucius, *yi* is not something determinate. Thus, Confucius says, "In his dealings with the world the noble person is not invariably for or against anything. He is on the side of what is *yi*" (4.10). This is linked to another statement, "I have no preconceptions about the permissible and the impermissible" (18.8). Although *yi* has been translated as "right," "rightness," "righteousness," or "duty," it is for Confucius not a principle of rightness or duty. Instead, it constitutes a basic ethical orientation involving, in broad terms, the attitudes just described. Here, we see the point of the association in the *Zhongyong* 中庸 between *yi* and its homophone *yi* 宜, or (the performance of what is) suitable or appropriate.[21]

Wen and *Zhi*

What about the other pair of terms, *wen* and *zhi*? We should first dispel the idea that the latter may be an inborn quality of goodness or rightness. Lau states of 3.8 that "the refinement of observing the rites is inculcated in a person who is born with the right substance" (Lau 41). He also mentions being "born with good native substance," being "inclined towards doing what is right by nature," and that "it is essential that one should be versed in the way this inclination can be given refined expression" (Lau 38). Clearly, *yi* or *zhi* is suggested to be some inborn quality that gives rise to an inclination toward right action. But as we have seen, Lau also tends to talk of *yi* as a principle of action. Given that the rightness of any particular action is said to be based on a determinate moral principle of "right," it cannot at the same time be an inborn inclination. Even if this were not contradictory, it would not help our understanding of any so-called determinate moral principle to say that it arises out of some inborn substance. For this would leave it wholly mysterious as to what the substance is. But there is no mystery here if we do not neglect the importance of the training necessary for a noble person. Lau does not neglect this. However, he tends to divide the understanding of moral principles from it, as if they were two separate matters. As we shall see, this separation would be incompatible with Confucius's stress on the harmonization of motivational attitudes and action in the ethical context. But first, note that *zhi* need not refer to any native stuff or substance.

Let us look again at Lau's translation of 15.18: "The noble person has morality as his basic stuff and by observing the rites puts it into practice, by being modest gives it expression, and by being trustworthy in word brings it to completion. Such is a noble person indeed!" As noted earlier, Lau here translates *yi* as "morality," and this is said to constitute *zhi*, the "basic stuff."

A contemporary Chinese paraphrase renders this passage as follows: "A noble person (regarding his activities), *bases upon what is appropriate*, follows the rites in their operation, uses modest language in stating them, and has a sincere attitude in completing them. This way, is he truly a noble person!"[22] Although this literal translation (my own) is inelegant, it shows that *zhi* here need not connote any substance, but has the meaning of a "basis." In other words, *yi* is here said to be basic to action. This should remind us of the earlier discussion, where I argued that *yi* is the execution of *li*, in the spirit of *li*.

Consider next, 6.18: "When there is a preponderance of native substance over acquired refinement, the result will be churlishness (*zhi sheng wen ze ye* 質勝文則野). When there is a preponderance of acquired refinement over native substance, the result will be pedantry (*wen sheng zhi ze shi* 文勝質則史). Only a well-balanced admixture of these two will result in a noble person (*wen zhi bin bin ran hou junzi* 文質彬彬然後君子)."

The phrase *wen zhi bin bin* requires some explanation to bring out a very important aesthetic flavor. Beside "a well-balanced admixture" of refinement and substance, at the same time, it connotes a substantial elegance. *Zhi* here is paraphrased by Yang Bojun as *pu shi* 樸實 or being "plain and sincere."[23] The *wen* is that of the empty scholar, the pedant whose words float among the clouds—he is not quite sincere. An appropriate balance of the two qualities gives rise to the noble person, who is *wen zhi bin bin*. The complementarity of *wen* and *zhi* is stated in 12.8:

Ji Zicheng said, "The important thing about the noble person is the stuff (*zhi*) he is made of. What does he need refinement (*wen*) for?" Zigong commented, "It is a pity that you, sir, should have spoken so about the noble person. 'A team of horses cannot catch up with one's tongue.' The stuff is no different from refinement; refinement is no different from the stuff. The pelt of a tiger or a leopard, shorn of hair, is no different from that of a dog or a sheep."

A paraphrase of the analogy can be rendered like this: the difference between the leopard/tiger on the one hand, and the dog/sheep on the other, lies both in the stuff (*zhi*) they are made of, and in their fur, color and stripes (*wen*). If we shave off the fur, color, and stripes, then the hide of the leopard/tiger would be no different from the hide of the dog/sheep.

The meaning of the analogy can be said to be as follows: although *zhi* and *wen* are conceptually distinct, they should in practice be well-integrated. Remove *wen*, and there would be no difference between the noble person and the peasant. Thus explained, *zhi* is no longer mysterious.[24] It is, *in practice* (though not conceptually) inseparable from *wen*. The successful training of the individual gives him both *wen* and *zhi*, welded together as a character ideal—the noble person. This training covers many different aspects of art and life. It encompasses the rites, music, literature (the *Odes*), writing and mathematics, archery, and charioteering. In the emphasis on the practise of the rites within these various arts, we have the actual integration of both qualities.

A further understanding of *wen* and *zhi* requires placing them next to *li* and *yi*. The latter pair of concepts specify acting appropriately, while the former pair serves to assess character. The person who does what he should, elegantly, with the proper expressions and attitudes, is *wen* and *zhi*. The phrase *wen zhi bin bin*, as we have seen, may be ascribed to him.

Harmony and Motivational Attitudes

As I have explained it, *li* and *yi*, *wen* and *zhi* are closely inter-related concepts. If one mentions *yi* as basic, this is a stress on the motivational expression of *li*. *Wen* and *zhi* complement *li* and *yi*, being different aspects of the latter pair, and with the stress on character. The four concepts are intertwined such that the full explanation of one requires relating it to the others.

We may sum up the import of the above discussion of Confucius's ethics of character in the following way. There is a certain form necessary to action. This form is set by the rites. These specify not merely a set of rules, but a way of acting. A central requirement here is harmony although it should be noted that harmony is not treasured for its own sake, but is constrained by the rites. Harmony or *he* 和 is said by Youzi to be the most valuable aspect of the rites. At the same time (as quoted earlier), this harmony is regarded as the most beautiful of the "ways of the Former Kings," something "followed alike in matters great and small" (1.12). Instead of "harmony," Joel Kupperman has adopted a translation of *he* as "naturalness" that helps to explicate this passage. As Kupperman sees it, what is involved here is an educational training that results in a form of behavior that becomes natural for the person.[25]

The need for harmony, constrained by the rites, suggests a motivational problem. That is, Confucius was concerned with creating the motivation to act in accordance with *li*. As we have seen, one may be acting in accordance with *li* but in the absence of the necessary expressions and attitudes, one may not be doing so appropriately. Seen in this light, 15.18 gains a new significance. *Yi* may be said to be basic only in the sense that the correct motivational attitudes should be in place, and they are expressed in the performance of *li*, and sincerity or trustworthiness is required in bringing things to a completion, that is, to *act*. The end result is the harmonious person, one whose motivational attitudes are congruent with the rites, and elegantly expressed through them, in action.

Objection: Moral Priority of *Yi* and *Zhi*

One possible objection to the above account is as follows. While there may be etymological and traditional commentarial support for the interpretation that *yi* is the appropriate expression of certain attitudes in the performance of *li* (arising from the original context of religious ceremonies and later extended to moral contexts) this does not mean that *yi* has remained static. Instead, it has developed further into something more basic than *li* and also independent of *li*.

This is where, so the objection goes, we need to look more carefully at the relation between *wen* and *zhi*. As noted by Lau, this pair of concepts may be said to correspond to *li* and *yi*, respectively. There is evidence to show that *zhi* is more fundamental than *wen*. For a start, Confucius's response to Zixia's question about the meaning of the ode cited in 3.8 that "The colours are put in after the white," could be said to point to an incipient theory of human nature, later to be developed by Confucius's followers, especially Mencius. Seen in this light too, there is nothing mysterious about Lau's reference to the basic or native stuff as being "inborn." In this regard, both *yi* and *zhi* are not just another aspect of *li* and *wen*. They are more fundamental, principled elements of human nature that may stand opposed to or be taken to judge a person's practice of *li* or his possession of *wen*.

Thus, there are some passages in the *Analects* that imply a negative moral judgment against the quality of *wen*. Zixia himself (recognized for his expertise in the *Odes*) states, "When the ignoble person makes a mistake, he is sure to gloss over it" (19.8). This literally means that the ignoble person applies *wen* to cover up a mistake. And perhaps it is because of Zixia's preoccupation with *wen* that he is warned by Confucius, "Be a noble *ru* 儒, not an ignoble *ru*" (6.13). (Lau notes that originally *ru* probably referred to those "for whom the qualities of the scholar were more important than those of the warrior." It later denoted the Confucian school.) Furthermore, the following passage seems to suggest that *wen* is secondary to moral cultivation: "A young man should be a good son at home and an obedient young man abroad, sparing of speech but trustworthy in what he says . . . If he has any energy to spare from such action, let him devote it to making himself cultivated" (1.6), that is, devote it to the study of *wen*.

In sum, the emphasis given to the aesthetic in my earlier analysis could be held to be misplaced insofar as it ignores the priority of the moral. *Zhi* is not interchangeable with *wen* but may, instead, override it. A natural and inborn morality is foundational while cultural refinement is secondary. Correspondingly, *yi* may ultimately have become a determining principle of action, a deliberative principle applied to what constitutes right (ritual) action.

My first reply would be that although it is possible to construe both *yi* and *zhi* as the basis of a theory of human nature and the development of a more substantial theory of morality, this theory is certainly not present in the *Analects*. However, it could be pointed out that quite independently of this theory of human nature, and even consistently with seeing Confucius's ethics in aesthetic terms, it might be possible that the idea is already emerging in the *Analects*, that it may not be appropriate to follow *li* in certain circumstances. This opens up the possibility that *yi* might be linked up with this idea, so that sometimes not following *li* can be *yi*.[26] In other words, although in a positive sense *yi* may be a matter of following *li* in the proper spirit, this may not just involve the attitudes like reverence or grief, but also an awareness of the appropriateness of following *li*. However, on this conception of their relation, *yi* might also involve one's not following *li* in exigent situations. And this sense of what is appropriate need not be related to claims about the goodness of human nature, since it can itself be a product of training.

However, strictly speaking, there is no unambiguous evidence for this idea in the *Analects* itself, apart from a stress on 9.3. Certainly, the idea is clearer in relation to the *Mencius*. Thus, *Mencius* 4A:26 (where the emperor Shun married without telling his father) involves departing from a rule of *li* so as to preserve the spirit behind the rule while 4A:17 (holding the hand of one's sister-in-law in order to save her from drowning) involves departing from a rule of *li* on the basis of considerations not related to the rule.[27] Nevertheless, it is clear that one cannot properly extend this point about *yi* forming some kind of standard which judges *li*, without seeing how it is developed in the *Mencius*. I would prefer to say that in the *Analects*, there is a conception of the spirit of *li* in terms of motivational attitudes that enable one to judge ritual performances, and that *yi* is part of this cluster of motivational attitudes that forms the spirit of *li*.

In response to the second of the objections listed above, although it may be admitted that there are certain negative connotations of *wen*, this is consistent with the analysis that the four concepts are inter-related and inseparable (which is not to say that they are interchangeable), such that the proper balance of *li* and *yi*, *wen* and *zhi* should, ideally, result in harmony.

The third response emphasizes the following philosophical point. The word "morality" either inadequately expresses the dynamics of Confucius's ethics, or brings with it assumptions that may not serve our understanding of this ethics. One assumption, as we have seen, is that this is a duty-based morality, in the way that has been described by D.C. Lau. Against this, I have used the term "ethico-aesthetic" to stress the fact that Confucius's ethics is very much concerned with a self-cultivationist program in which one's motivational attitudes and one's actions are harmoniously integrated.

A brief reference to a problem in Western ethics will help us to see the significance of this issue. In a paper well known to (Anglo-American) moral philosophers, entitled "Moral Saints,"[28] the philosopher Susan Wolf complains that both the ethical theories of Kantianism and Consequentialism implicitly require us to be as good as possible, i.e. to be moral saints. This ideal, however, is not something that Wolf herself would care to aspire to. This is because it calls on us to neglect other aspects of our lives—artistic and other endeavors, spontaneous relations, etc., which we value but not necessarily in a moral sense. It could be argued that Wolf's claim that these theories imply a neglect of individual perfection is not well conceived. But whatever may be the case, one thing she is arguing for is that moral reasons are not necessarily overriding. A possible split exists therefore, between one's aesthetic personality and one's moral personality.

However, it is unclear that there must be such a split. And this brings us back to the nature of Confucius's ethics. One salient aspect of Confucius's ethics, we should note, is that it tries to avoid such a split. For Confucius, the aesthetic character is per force, an ethical one.[29] Part of the point of the ethico-aesthetical training is that one's emotions, motivations and attitudes are harmonized with reasons for acting, as spelled out within the rites. As we have seen, the dignified and graceful performance of the rites is, in itself, a thing of beauty. I know of no better illustration of this point in the *Analects* than the contrast of characters that appears in the longest passage of the text, 11.26. Although this passage has been cited and discussed by others,[30] I think there is more to be learned from it.

Interpretation of *Analects* 11.26

Before discussing this passage, we should note its overall context, involving an expression of *zhi* 志 (not to be confused with the *zhi* that has been translated "native stuff"). In the *Analects*, this word is used several times in conjunction with the preposition *yu* 於, for example, *zhi yu dao* (way 道 4.9, 7.6), *zhi yu xue* (learning 學 2.4), *zhi yu ren* (14.4). In these cases, *zhi* means setting one's heart-mind upon the way, learning, or ren. It is orienting oneself toward something, giving oneself an aim or direction. There are at least two occasions in which the participants are asked to "speak" (*yan* 言) their *zhi* (5.26, 11.26). Here, the sense seems to be to express what is close to one's heart-mind. The context in each case is one where Confucius is in a relaxed mood, accompanied by some of his disciples. The setting encourages uninhibited answers, as we shall see.

There is a close connection between the *Odes* and *yan*. The person who fails to study the *Odes* will be unable to *yan*, and this intimates not just speaking *per se*, but speech informed by general knowledge, subtleties, nuances, sensitivities, and deep-seated aims and feelings. In addition, it is said that knowing *yan* enables one to know people (20.3). The term here probably means "words," and one is said to know the person behind the words.

The *Odes* stimulate imagination, heighten observation, give rise to harmonious socialization, and enable one to complain (17.9). Music was inseparable from the *Odes*, and we find Confucius distinguishing between the tones and nuances of different forms of music, saying for instance that the music of Cheng was licentious (*yin* 淫), and associating this with glibness (*ning* 佞 15.11, 17.18, 3.20).

Thus, although the word *zhi* can be translated as aim or direction, or what the individual sets his heart-mind upon, it presupposes a background of education in order to form and express one's *zhi*. The expression of *zhi* seems to have been a shared practice. Such expressions allow for exploration of one's aspirations and affiliations, knowledge of self and others, exchange of ideas, criticism, contemplation, and self-examination. We know that the ability to interpret the *Odes*, to discover new or hidden meanings, and to use it to illuminate some aspects of the rites (3.8), was highly praised by Confucius. This ability must have been part of the determination of one's *zhi* and the development of character.

It is interesting to compare the *zhi* expressed by Zilu, Yan Hui, and Confucius in 5.26. Zilu is known for being brash, reckless, and immodest. His sentiment to share things with friends, and "have no regrets even if they become worn," perhaps unwittingly reflects not just generosity but bravado. Yan Hui's resolve not to "boast" of his own good points or to make a display of his efforts in helping others shows a moral concern that is, at the same time, somewhat self-conscious. In contrast to these two, Confucius's *zhi*, namely, to "bring peace to the old, to have trust in my friends, and to cherish the young," expresses directly his concerns without any tone of self-consciousness. Bringing peace to the old and cherishing the young are among the concerns of *ren*. Cherishing the young is also consistent with Confucius's educational mission. Trustworthiness (*xin* 信) is an important subject of his teaching (7.25). Thus, one's *zhi* can reveal something about oneself. It can also be more or less mature or committed, and may require modification and instantiate self-reflection. The expression of one's *zhi* is therefore a stage in the training of the elegant person, requiring development and consolidation.

In 11.26, Confucius, evidently in a relaxed mood, muses that his disciples are always complaining that others do not "know" them, i.e. appreciate their abilities. What would they do if perchance someone were to "know" them?

Zilu brashly answers: "If I were to administer a state of a thousand chariots, situated between powerful neighbours, troubled by armed invasions and by repeated famines, I could, within three years, give the people courage and a sense of direction." Confucius merely smiles and turns to Ranyou, who responds in a similar vein, ending modestly with, "As to the rites and music, I would leave that to abler noble persons." Gongxi Hua's response outdoes Ranyou's in modesty: "I do not say that I already have the ability, but I am ready to learn. On ceremonial occasions in the ancestral temple or in diplomatic gatherings, I should like to assist as a minor official in charge of protocol, properly dressed in my ceremonial cap and robes."

Confucius finally turns to Zengxi, who has evidently been playing the lute as the conversation was proceeding:

> After a few dying notes came the final chord, and then he stood up from his lute. "I differ from the other three in my choice."
>
> The Master said, "What harm is there in that? After all each man is stating what he has set his heart upon."
>
> "In late spring, after the spring clothes have been newly made, I should like, together with five or six adults and six or seven boys, to go bathing in the River Yi and enjoy the breeze on the Rain Altar, and then to go home chanting poetry."
>
> The Master sighed and said, "I am all in favour of Dian [Zengxi]."

Why does Confucius approve of Zengxi over the others? After all, are they not each (in their own way) specifying what they ought to do according to the rites? Remember our earlier question, namely, what could be more basic than the rites? One might think that the responses of Zilu, Ranyou, and Gongxi Hua are perfectly dutiful since they state the requirements of bringing peace and prosperity in accordance with the ritual ceremonies necessary to Confucius's prescription of social and political order. In addition, these three disciples are noted in the text for their administrative abilities (Zilu and Ranyou) and the intricacies of ritual procedure (Gongxi Hua).[31]

This is a problem that has vexed many traditional commentators and there have been many explanations.[32] I shall attempt an interpretation that is consistent with the account of the rites that I have given earlier. As Confucius tells the puzzled Zengxi when they are alone, he smiled at Zilu because governing a state requires attending to the rites, but his answer showed a dire lack of understanding of the rites because it lacked modesty (*qi yan bu rang* 其言不讓). This is an important answer for it indicates the ethical meaning of the rites for Confucius. Thus, they do not refer merely to ceremony, but embody certain attitudes and values. In the case of Zilu, a lack of understanding of ritual is betrayed in the immodest way he replied to the question of how he would administer a state.

The second disciple, Ranyou, is more modest when he says that he would leave the rites and music to "abler noble persons." Zengxi is therefore puzzled that Confucius does not seem to approve of Ranyou's answer, too. Zengxi asks,

"In the case of [Ranyou] was he not concerned with a state?" Confucius's answer indicates that this was precisely the point: "What can justify one in saying that sixty or seventy *li* square or indeed fifty or sixty *li* square do not deserve the name of 'state'?" In other words (to paraphrase), "Certainly, Ranyou was concerned with a state!" What is left unsaid, however, is that in wanting to leave the rites and music to others he has missed the essence not just of government, but of much else.

The third disciple Gongxi Hua is known for his grasp of the details of the rites, which includes court and diplomatic ceremonies, yet he offers to take a most minor role. Perhaps Confucius was unhappy with what he thought was a touch of obsequiousness here, or with the glib diplomatic language. On another occasion, Confucius had claimed not to be a sage and that the only thing that might be said of him was that he learned without flagging and taught without being weary. On that occasion, Gongxi Hua had replied, "This is precisely where we disciples are unable to learn from your example" (7.34). Such expressions may be perfectly suitable in a diplomatic gathering, but directed to his own Master in an informal setting, this sort of response may have been a touch too smooth. This is a fair deduction since there are several passages in the *Analects* where Confucius disapproves of glibness.

Zengxi's answer, by contrast, is a breath of fresh air. He is not a major disciple and critics might argue that Confucius's approval of his remarks should not be taken too seriously. Nonetheless, Zengxi's response does serve as a foil to the stilted and mechanical responses of the other three. (On another occasion Confucius himself says, "If anyone were to employ me, in a year's time I would have brought things to a satisfactory state, and after three years I should have results to show for it" [13.10]. The first two answers have this form, and are therefore perhaps too "standard.") There is delight and spontaneity in his relation to others and this is described not merely through leisurely activity, but at the same time, in terms of the rites. His response to Confucius symbolizes the perfect integration of the rites with one's attitudes. Mention of the Rain Altar by the River Yi is a reference to a certain practice of the rites.[33] It is significant that Zengxi is unselfconsciously playing the lute while the rest respond brashly or stiltedly to Confucius's question. Music and the *Odes* have instilled in him not only knowledge of the rites, but delight in their form, and this is expressed through his harmonious relation with others.

One might naturally be tempted to say that here is an almost Daoist interpretation of the *Analects*.[34] But the passage is consistent with the account of *li* and the harmonization of motivational attitudes discussed above. Zengxi's puzzlement (when he asks Confucius why he smiled at Zilu and did not seem to approve of the others) indicates the unselfconsciousness of one who has harmonized his motivational attitudes and his emotions with *li*, thus expressing his relationship with others in the way of *yi*. He is our ethico-aesthetic character, the noble person who is *wen zhi bin bin*.[35]

Clearly, a concern with character is required to ensure right action. Thus, although Confucius may not be a moral philosopher in the sense of being interested in theoretical questions of ethics or human nature, he is nevertheless an ethical teacher who is highly concerned about the motivational attitudes and character of his disciples. We learn from his concern that knowledge of what is right does not guarantee right action if the correct motivations are not in place. Even this, however, does not quite have the right emphasis. More exactly, it should be said that without the necessary motivations one may be blind to what *is* right action. Thus, an ethico-aesthetic education is required to ensure the correct motivations. But not only this, character is also related to right action in the sense with which an action is carried through and completed. In the absence of this sense or spirit, there is an important ethical sense in which the right thing cannot be said to have been done. Thus, as far as the *Analects* is concerned, *zhi* or the "basic stuff" has more to do with these aspects of character that we have described than with any inborn substrate of goodness.

Conclusion

In this chapter, I have argued that the air of mystery or paradox surrounding the term *zhi* translated as "native stuff" or "native substance" dissolves when we understand *zhi* as related to other concepts such as *li*, *yi*, and *wen*. *Zhi* is the "stuff" that results from an educational process of self-cultivation through the learning and practice of *li* or the rites. The term *yi*, translated as "morality," "right," "righteousness," and so on is better understood as involving an ethical motivational attitude that is part of the wider range of motivational attitudes that are important to ritual practice. Described as *wen*, *li* or the rites is not just an adornment or embellishment of some original "inner substrate" of *zhi*. Instead, it is part of an educational program toward forming a character whose motivational attitudes are in harmony with one's actions. These actions are, ideally, performed in accordance with the spirit of the rites in an aesthetically balanced and elegant way. We have looked at some tendencies to attribute a nascent theory of human nature to the *Analects*. These tendencies to speculate about Confucius's view about human nature give the wrong focus—they direct us away from a proper understanding of Confucius's educational concern with self-cultivation, character development, and the instilling of motivational attitudes central to the individual's ethical life.

The Orientation and Practice of *Ren*

In this chapter, I continue the description of Confucius's character and motivational ethics through an examination of the concept of *ren* 仁. Just as there is a tendency to read *zhi* 質 as referring to some inner substrate of goodness, there has been a similar tendency to read *ren* in the *Analects* as referring to an original source of goodness residing in the heart-mind. As we shall see, this is a result of the strong influence of the *Mengzi* 孟子 or *Mencius*, where *ren* is indeed discussed in the context of a theory of the heart-mind and human nature. Although it is undeniable that a reading of the *Mencius* sometimes throws light on the *Analects*, this is not generally the case for a proper understanding of *ren* in the latter text. The *Mencius* places *ren* in the context of a philosophical theory of *xing* or nature, but it would not do justice to the *Analects* to read *ren* similarly, as some have done. *Ren* is a more elusive concept in the *Analects*. By "elusive" I do not mean the difficulty of tracking the concept as evidenced by the perennial discussions of it. Instead, it has to do with the sense in which self-cultivation is a never-ending task and the attitudes and values that this task involves. In describing these attitudes and values later, I shall talk of an "immediacy of ethical commitment."

The focus here is on *ren* as an ethical orientation and a practice. One advantage of such a reading is that it helps to resolve the paradox in 9.1 where it is stated that Confucius rarely talked about *ren*, despite its numerous occurrences in the text. Another advantage is that focusing on the orientation and practice of *ren* enables us to talk of an internal relation between *ren* and *li* 禮. *Ren* is absent when *li* is performed without the proper spirit, and the rituals of *li*, seen in this light, have an educational function in bringing about the attitudes and values incorporating *ren*. In this regard, some recent writers have tended to say that they are different aspects of the same thing. While acknowledging their insights, I shall conclude with a statement about the orientation of *ren* that differentiates it from *li*. A third advantage is that describing the orientation and practice of *ren* enables us to go beyond the static definitions and translations that have been given of the term, such as "benevolence," "love," "altruism," "kindness," "perfect virtue," "goodness," "human-heartedness," "humanity," and so forth.[1] These definitions may be useful in certain contexts, but they are not wholly satisfactory. I shall leave *ren* untranslated and hope instead to bring out its meaning through an extended discussion of the sense in which it is an ethical orientation and practice. The form of my main thesis has been anticipated by others such as Wing-tsit Chan, for instance, who asserts that certain "apparent contradictions" in the *Analects* "are not difficult to understand if one remembers that Confucius was not interested in abstract concepts. He was not concerned with the reality or nature of *ren*; he was interested primarily in its application."[2] Nonetheless, Chan goes on to say that "generally speaking, however, there can be no doubt that *ren* is love for all."[3] As we shall see, this definition is not unproblematic, and it is just such generalities that I wish to avoid.

I shall begin the discussion of *ren* with *Analects* 1.2. This shall be analyzed in some detail since it brings out a central problem in the interpretation of Confucius's ethical system that runs through Mencius, and the Song dynasty Neo-Confucians Cheng Yi 程頤 and Zhu Xi 朱熹 (I shall sometimes refer to the views of the latter two collectively as Cheng-Zhu). Just in case it is wondered why a discussion of these Neo-Confucians is relevant, it should be stressed that, at least in the context of *ren*, their reading of the *Analects* is filtered through the lens of the *Mencius*, and (as we shall see) this reading has been influential and persists to the present day. Arising from the analysis of *Analects* 1.2, the interpretation of Confucius's concept of *ren* as an orientation and practice that I shall defend will depend on the cogency of my arguments in bringing to bear other passages in the *Analects* in relation to 1.2, and in my evaluations of what Mencius, Cheng-Zhu, and some contemporary commentators have to say about *ren*.

Mencius's Influence

The concept of *ren* in the *Analects* first appears in 1.2:

> Youzi said: He whose character is *xiaoti* 孝弟 (being filial toward parents and re-spectful of elders) yet likes rebelling against superiors—this is rare. He who dislikes rebelling against superiors yet likes creating disorder—this has never been the case. The noble person devotes himself to the root; the root established, *dao* 道 grows. *Xiaoti*—this is the root of (practicing) *ren*, is it not?[4]

Zhu Xi[5] comments that "*ren* is the principle of love (*ai zhi li* 愛之理) and the virtue/power of the heart-mind (*xin zhi de* 心之德)." The last sentence of 1.2 reads, *Xiaoti ye zhe, qi wei ren zhi ben yu* 孝弟也者，其爲人之本與. Zhu Xi takes the *wei* in *wei ren* as a verb, reading the phrase as "practicing *ren*." He adds that in this sense, *xiaoti* is the root of practicing *ren* and quotes Cheng Yi's remark that "*xiaoti* is practiced or effected within the family before *ren-ai* is extended to other things—what is meant by *qin qin er ren min* 親親而仁民 [*Mencius* 7A:45]. Hence, *xiaoti* is the root of the practice of *ren*. [If we] speak of nature (*xing* 性), then *ren* is the root of *xiaoti*."

Zhu Xi goes on to quote a question and answer from Cheng Yi: "Can *ren* be attained from *xiaoti*?" The reply is negative, with a reassertion of the practice of *xiaoti*:

> To talk of practicing *ren* beginning with *xiaoti*, *xiaoti* is [but] one aspect (*shi* 事) of *ren*. It is permissible to speak of it as the root of practicing *ren*, but not to speak of it as the root of *ren*. This is because *ren* is *xing* (nature), whereas *xiaoti* is *yong* (function). Within *xing* there are only the four attributes *ren*, *yi* 義, *li*, *zhi* 智 [*Mencius* 6A:6, 7A:21]—from whence comes *xiaoti*? However, the chief expression (*zhu* 主) of *ren* is *ai*, *ai* is no larger than *ai qin* [love or affection for one's parents]. Therefore it is said, *xiaoti* is the root of practicing *ren*.[6]

Zhu Xi's rendering of *wei ren* as "practicing ren" is debatable. If we take *wei* as attributive, the phrase *wei ren zhi ben* could be read as "to be the root of *ren*." The Qing commentator Liu Baonan, however, cites various passages in the *Analects* to show that "practicing *ren*" is a consistent reading.[7] This does not establish that all the instances of *ren* are those which mention its practice. However, my concern is with the rather muffled distinction between (1) the root of the practice of *ren* and (2) the root of *ren*. What exactly is the difference?[8]

As we have seen, Cheng Yi is quoted as stating that "*xiaoti* is [but] one aspect of *ren*." And *xiaoti* is said to be a practice. This implies that there is more than one aspect to the practice of *ren*. But if *xiaoti* is merely one aspect of *ren*, it cannot be said to be its root, whether it be the root of practicing *ren*, or the root of *ren*. Cheng Yi concludes that "[If we] speak of *xing*, then *ren* is the root of *xiaoti*," by claiming that the Mencian virtues of *ren*, *yi*, *li*, and *zhi* constitute *xing*. Still, some explanation has to be given for the idea that *xiaoti* is "the root of practicing *ren*," and this is found in what it means to *ai qin*, or *qin qin* (see below).

The reference to the root of *practicing ren* brought Cheng-Zhu very close to an explication of *ren* that I shall show lies at the heart of the *Analects*. It would have been possible, for instance, to discuss various other aspects of this practice beside *xiaoti* and love. Instead, they adopted and focused on Mencius's philosophical agenda. This involved the interpretation of *ren* as love in opposition to the Mohists by maintaining its universal extension while at the same time insisting on familial distinctions and the provision of a metaphysical basis for *ren*.[9] Before explaining this, it is necessary to bring out more fully the references made implicitly by Cheng-Zhu above to certain passages in the *Mencius*.[10] Thus, in 6A:6 Mencius asserts that every person possesses the four predispositions of the heart-mind, namely, compassion, shame, respect, and (the ability to distinguish) right and wrong (*ce yin zhi xin* 惻隱之心, *xiu wu* 羞惡 *zhi xin*, *gong jing* 恭敬 *zhi xin*, *shi fei* 是非 *zhi xin*). These are identified respectively with *ren*, *yi*, *li*, and *zhi*. In 7A:21 these are said to be rooted in the heart-mind (*ren yi li zhi gen yü xin* 仁義禮智根於心). In both passages, the context is a discussion of *xing*. It is evident that the Cheng-Zhu emphasis on the root of *ren* as opposed to the root of the practice of *ren* is based on this account, that *ren* has its source in the heart-mind.

Xiaoti as the "root of the practice of *ren*" on the other hand, with its reference to *ai qin* or *qin qin*, is found in 7A:45 which spells out a gradation from intimate affection toward one's parents followed by benevolence toward (other) people and sparingness toward creatures and plants (*qin qin er ren min, ren min er ai wu* 親親而仁民，仁民而愛物).[11] We may say that *qin qin* is the root of practicing *ren*, in the sense that the gradation beginning with *qin qin* is a practical guide. The priority of *qin qin* is illustrated elsewhere. In 4A:19, for instance, it is stated that duty toward one's parents is the highest and the example of Zengzi's filial piety is given. In 5A:3 Wan Zhang cites the case of Emperor Shun's "banishing" his brother Xiang and enfeoffing him instead of punishing him like four others, even though Xiang was the most wicked (*zhi bu ren* 至不仁). Mencius replies:

> A *ren* person never harbors anger or nurses a grudge against a brother. All he does is to love him (*qin ai er yi yi* 親愛而已矣). Because he loves him (*qin zhi*), he wishes him to enjoy rank; because he loves him (*ai zhi*), he wishes him to enjoy wealth. If as Emperor he were to allow his brother to be a nobody, could that be described as loving him (*ke wei qin ai zhi hu* 可謂親愛之乎)?[12]

Clearly, through the influence of Mencius, *xiaoti* is said by Cheng-Zhu to be the root of practicing *ren* in that it gives priority to one's immediate family or loved ones. In 6B:3 and 7A:15 we find the definition *qin qin ren ye*. This practical and particularistic aspect of *ren*, however, gives rise to a problem of how the practical root of *ren* as familial affection and reverence can be extended universally. Wing-tsit Chan has argued that this realistic assumption of love with distinctions does not deny the universality of *ren*. Mencius is said to have dealt with this issue through his concept of righteousness (*yi*), which allows for distinctions in the application of *ren* as love.[13] But it is doubtful that the issue can be resolved so easily. We shall deal with it in a separate chapter (see chapter 4). For now, the key question is whether the metaphysical basis that Mencius gives to *ren* in terms of the theory of the heart-mind is sufficient for universality. As we have seen, in 6A:6 everyone is said to have compassion as one predisposition of the heart-mind, and compassion is identified here with *ren*. Although Mencius may have intended *ren* to be a universal compassion, we should contrast 6A:6 with 2A:6 where the heart-mind of compassion is said to be the beginning or, as mentioned above, the source of *ren*. In this regard, *ren* cannot logically be seen as universal love, but merely its potentiality. In 7A:21, where *ren* is said to be rooted in the heart-mind, it is also possible to read "rooted" as the beginning of compassion or love. Cheng Yi, for instance, would have sanctioned this reading given his statement that:

Since Mencius said that the sense of commiseration is *ren*, scholars have considered love as *ren*. But love is man's feeling, whereas *ren* is man's nature. . . . The sense of commiseration is only the beginning of *ren*. . . . It is incorrect to equate universal love with *ren*.[14]

Chan notes that to Cheng Yi and other Neo-Confucians, "*ren* is a reality while love is a function. In making such a distinction, these philosophers made two contributions at the same time, namely, treating *ren* as a metaphysical reality and distinguishing it from love."[15] This is consistent with my earlier analysis, where as we have seen, Cheng Yi denies that *xiaoti* can be taken as the root of *ren* since it is *yong* or function, in contrast to *xing* or nature.

The terms "reality" and "function" are Chan's translations of *ti* 體 and *yong* 用. The former can also be taken to refer to substance, nature, or principle.[16] As a pair, "reality" and "function" are technical terms in the Neo-Confucian lexicon, which among other things, encapsulates the attempt by Cheng-Zhu and others to give a metaphysical explanation for the simultaneity of universal love and love with distinctions. Their predecessor Zhang Zai 張載 had taken love to be universally applied to all things as well as people, supplying also the theory that "the Principle is one but its function is differentiated into the many (*li yi fen shu* 理一分殊)." This paved the way for Cheng-Zhu to harmonize universal love and love with distinctions.[17]

Note that the word *yong* could ordinarily be taken to mean "practical usage" or, in short, "practice." I am not suggesting, however, that we replace the Neo-Confucian "function" with "practice." Instead, I wish to refocus attention on the *practice* and the orientation of *ren* in the *Analects*. As distinct from "function," the term "practice" is nontechnical. The shift of focus to "practice" holds no metaphysical baggage and shall free us to discuss other important aspects of *ren*. Some contemporary writers too, as we shall see, have tended to explicate *ren* in the *Analects* in both Mencian and Neo-Confucian terms.

Confucius on *Ren*

There are two or three noncommittal occurrences of the term *xing* 性 or nature in the *Analects*.[18] It is clear that *ren* is not discussed in terms of *xing* in the text. We are also told that Confucius hardly talked about *ren*: "The occasions on which the Master talked about profit, Destiny and *ren* were rare (*zi han yan li yu ming yu ren* 子罕言利與命與仁)" (9.1). This has puzzled most commentators. Thus, according to Wing-tsit Chan:

58 of the 499 chapters are devoted to the discussion of *ren*, and the word appears 105 times. No other subject, not even filial piety, engaged so much of the attention of the Master and his disciples. This fact makes the often-quoted passage that "Confucius seldom talked about profit and fate and *ren*" (*Analects* IX.1) most puzzling.[19]

After mentioning some rather contorted explanations, Chan concludes that "unless better evidence is discovered, we had better leave the contradiction unsolved."[20] Similarly, James Legge comments: "With his not speaking of [*ren*] there is a difficulty which I know not how to solve. The fourth Book is nearly all occupied with it, and no doubt it was a prominent topic in Confucius's teachings."[21] I suggest that the puzzle can be resolved if we explicitly recognize that Confucius did not discuss *ren* in the sense that Mencius did, that is, he rarely discoursed on *ren* as a theory of human nature. This is consistent with Zigong's remark in 5.13, "One cannot get to hear of his views on human nature and the Way of Heaven."

This way of looking at the matter will also enable us to resolve another "puzzle." Yü-sheng Lin has claimed that "if *ren* is the loftiest ideal of moral excellence most difficult of attainment, it is puzzling to note that Confucius also said, 'Is *ren* indeed so far away? As soon as we want it, we should find that it is at our very side' (7.29)."[22] According to Lin, the puzzle disappears if we conceive the highest attainment of *ren* as a development of the human being's "distinctive nature." In the beginning of his paper, Lin argues that the *Analects* retains an earlier, formal sense of *ren*, namely, the "distinctive quality" of a noble hunter as described in the *Odes*. Confucius however subtly transformed the substantive meaning of this quality ("manliness" or "daringness") through his constant discussions of *ren* in terms of moral excellence. Lin argues that this explains 4.7, which he translates as follows: "The faults of men are characteristic of the [different] classes to which they belong. By observing [a man's] faults [we shall] then have known his distinctive quality." Lin claims that the term "distinctive quality" here makes the passage more comprehensible than "virtuous" or "Goodness" as rendered by other translators.[23] Nonetheless, we should note that instead of the term "distinctive quality," Lin uses "distinctive nature" in his later discussion. In this way, Lin holds that "Confucius's concept of *ren* entails an implicit notion of innate goodness of man."[24] This slide indicates that Lin reads more into the *Analects* than is warranted. Another evidence of this is his tendency to put Confucius's remarks in the context of germinative terminology which is distinctively Mencian. For instance, in a passage that begins by discussing Confucius, Lin later brings in Mencius and mentions the belief that although human beings have certain animal elements, they also have a distinctive quality because "that which makes man generically different from other animals is the 'seed' of moral growth in him." It is clear that he is applying this germinative terminology to Confucius, especially when in the next sentence he states Confucius's belief "that moral excellence should be a natural growth of what is distinctive in man," and "Man should cultivate and develop it insofar as he wants to keep and sharpen this identity."[25]

No doubt, given Mencius's circumstances in defending (what he saw as) the Confucian faith against opponents like the Mohists, Yangists, and others like Gaozi,[26] it was necessary to develop a philosophical theory about human nature.

But it may not be legitimate to read this philosophy, no matter how nascent, back into the *Analects*. In any case, the puzzle that Lin mentions is spurious if we remember Confucius's role as a teacher who exhorts and admonishes his students toward self-cultivation. He is urging that *ren* is near at hand—if we want to cultivate ourselves, and if we are determined enough, we can do it—it is a matter of not wanting, instead of the lack of ability. For example, in 4.6 Confucius states that he has not come across anyone whose strength is insufficient in devoting himself to *ren* in the space of a single day. We may understand this remark in the context of 6.12, where Ran Qiu says apologetically, "It is not that I am not pleased with your way, but rather that my strength gives out." Confucius replies pointedly, "A person whose strength gives out collapses along the course. In your case you set the limits beforehand."[27]

These remarks should not be taken to mean that self-cultivation is an easy task. Confucius thought poorly of anyone who showed in words or action that they presumed this. Mention was made in the beginning of this chapter, of the "elusiveness" of *ren*. Some of Confucius's disciples recognized this. Thus, in 8.7 Zengzi says: "A scholar (*shi* 士) must be strong and resolute, for his burden is heavy and the road is long. He takes *ren* as his burden. Is that not heavy? Only with death does the road come to an end. Is that not long?" This elusiveness is more directly described by Yan Yuan or Yan Hui in 9.11:

> The more I look up at it the higher it appears. The more I bore into it the harder it becomes. I see it before me. Suddenly it is behind me. The Master is good at leading one on step by step. He broadens me with culture and brings me back to essentials by means of the rites. I cannot give up even if I wanted to, but, having done all I can, it seems to rise sheer above me and I have no way of going after it, however much I may want to.

The "it" of this passage, according to D. C. Lau, refers to the way of Confucius.[28] If we take the practice of *ren* as central to this way, it follows that Yan Hui is talking of the elusiveness of *ren* and its cultivation as an endless task. Seen in this light, it should not be puzzling that Confucius hardly ever conceded that anyone attained *ren*.[29]

Some commentators have emphasized the importance of *shu* 恕 and *zhong* 忠 as the method of practicing *ren*. For instance, Lau says that the method of *shu* "consists in taking oneself—'what is near at hand'—as an analogy and asking oneself what one would like or dislike were one in the position of the person at the receiving end." This is complemented by *zhong* which is "the doing of one's best and it is through *zhong* that one puts into effect what one had found out by the method of *shu*." Lau argues that *shu* "cannot be the whole of benevolence [*ren*] as it is only its method."[30] While agreeing that *shu* cannot be the whole of benevolence, I would say instead that it is better to see *shu* and *zhong* as general ethical attitudes instead of an ethical method or principle, despite assertions of there being "one thread" to Confucius's teachings.[31] The different personalities of his disciples call for different corrective "stratagems" rather than a method or principle, as attested by the different answers he gives to their queries about *ren* and other concepts. And no doubt Confucius was well aware that there is no formula that could, in itself, do the trick of ethical commitment.

But more fundamentally, it is not Confucius's concern to arrive at any philosophical position regarding *ren* as a principle or a universal principle as some have claimed. For example, Xinzhong Yao argues that *ren* is not only the ethical commitment of *shu* and *zhong*, but in addition, "the universal principle that aims at integrating all beings and all people." It is clear that he includes Confucius as holding this principle when he immediately adds:

> The greatest contribution that Confucius made to the understanding of *ren* is not his explanation of *ren* as virtue, or even his promotion of *ren* as the highest virtue . . . but his redefinition of *ren* as love and his refinement of such love as ethical commitment and metaphysical principle. In this love Confucian secularism and transcendentalism are integrated.[32]

I have already said that Confucius's concern is the practice of *ren*. This may seem a bit too mundane. But it is precisely this that irritates Confucius—the thought that his admonishments and answers are too mundane. He says in 1.3 that "It is rare, indeed, for someone with cunning words and an ingratiating face to be *ren*." Opposed to these are the trustworthiness and earnestness mentioned in 1.4 and elsewhere. Of central importance here is the nature of speech. In 12.3 Sima Niu asks about *ren* and is given the answer, that the person who is *ren* is "cautious and slow in speech." There is a tone of dissatisfaction with this answer when Sima Niu persists in asking whether this is (really) what is meant by *ren*. Confucius replies, "When a person feels the difficulty of doing, can he be other than cautious and slow in speaking?" In the very next passage Sima Niu gets a reply to his question about the noble person, that he has "neither anxiety nor fear." He reacts with some skepticism whether this could be all there is to *ren*, to which Confucius simply replies, "When internal examination discovers nothing wrong, what is there to be anxious about, what is there to fear?"[33]

Sima Niu's incredulity indicates a tendency to expect something more philosophically substantive from Confucius about *ren* and other related concepts. This incredulity is shared, for instance, by Zilu when he asks in 13.3 about "the first thing to be done" in administering the government. To the answer that it is to "rectify names," Zilu answers: "So, indeed! You are wide of the mark! Why must there be such rectification?" Confucius replies angrily: "How uncultivated you are, You (由 or Zilu)! A noble person, in regard to what he does not know, shows a cautious reserve. If names be not correct, language is not in accordance with the truth of things."[34]

Evidently, even before the influence of Mencius, some of Confucius's disciples had already expected theoretically substantive answers from their master. This may give an explanatory context to the remark in 9.1 that Confucius rarely spoke about *ren*.[35] But the expectations of these disciples are misconceived. For Confucius, the immediacy of ethical commitment is missed if one expects any theory from him. We may speculate that this is precisely why Yan Hui is regarded by Confucius as the disciple who is nearest to the attainment of *ren*—because he did not speculate about *ren* but lived or practiced what he had been taught. Thus, Confucius says of him:

> I can speak to Hui all day without his disagreeing with me in any way. Thus he would seem to be stupid. However, when I take a closer look at what he does in private after he has withdrawn from my presence, I discover that it does, in fact, throw light on what I said. Hui is not stupid after all. (2.9)

The immediacy of ethical commitment involves attitudes and values central to *ren*, such as affection and reverence for elders, earnestness, sincerity, the lack of pretentiousness, not being glib or specious, and so forth. But what binds them together and makes them "immediate" is the requirement of congruence between attitude and action. This is not a requirement in the sense that it is merely prescribed. Instead, its appeal lies in a straightforwardness which enables one to have a state of mind described in 4.2 as being "at home" or "at rest." At the same time, any incongruence would very likely show itself—any unease, hypocrisy, pretentiousness, evil, and so on, is either directly or indirectly revealed in or through the character and action of the individual. The force of this lies in the exposure of a fact about oneself, that this *is* what one is.

A good example of this is Confucius's treatment of Zai Wo when the latter questions the need for a three-year mourning period, adducing the neglect of other rites and music as a result of such a prolonged practice (17.21). Confucius is scathing in his reply: if he (Zai Wo) feels at ease with wearing finery, eating fine food, and so on (a biting way of referring to a shorter mourning period), he may proceed. Later, Confucius refers to Zai Wo as "unfeeling (*bu ren* 不仁, literally, not *ren*)." Qian Mu has commented that Zai Wo intended to discuss the system of rites and there is no evidence to show that the three-year mourning period was generally practiced. Qian Mu states that he fails to understand why Confucius treats Zai Wo harshly here, just as he does in another instance (5.10).[36] But Qian Mu is taking Zai Wo's question at face value, as a serious and legitimate question about a particular rite that perhaps requires to be changed. However, we learn something about Zai Wo's character in 5.10. He seems to have been in the habit of sleeping during the day—he is lazy and does not put in any effort toward learning. Confucius likens him to a piece of "rotten wood that cannot be carved," and "dried dung that cannot be trowelled," adding: "I used to take on trust someone's deeds after having listened to his words.

Now having listened to someone's words I go on to observe his deeds. It was on account of [Zai Wo] that I have changed in this respect." Thus, Confucius must have distrusted Zai Wo's motives in questioning the three-year period of mourning. A corollary of this is to see where *he* is coming from, that is, to question his whole orientation. In Confucius's view, Zai Wo's rotten behavior gives him no credentials, so to speak, with which to raise doubts about the period of mourning.

Of course, it is possible for someone to be perfectly congruent in having both evil attitudes and actions. Confucius does not seem to have discussed this, and seems to have believed that people with less than perfect motives will tend to hide, implying a state of unease. Another reason for not discussing the possibility of perfect evil is that Confucius constantly stressed the need for self-cultivation and the attainment of *ren*. Some may point to this as evidence that Confucius believed in the goodness of human nature. While this is a possibility, I have already argued in this and the last chapter that the textual evidence of the *Analects* does not support this. Further, a belief in the perfectibility of character does not imply any definite belief, one way or another, about human nature. In this regard, it is interesting to note that although Mencius shares Confucius's concern with character, he was not always concerned with this alone. In *Analects* 2.10 Confucius says:

> Look at the means someone employs, observe the path he takes and examine where he feels at home. In what way is a person's true character hidden from view? In what way is a person's true character hidden from view (*Ren yan sou zai, ren yan sou zai* 人焉廋哉)?"

In 4A:15 of the *Mencius*, after stating that the pupils of a person's eyes may reveal his character, Mencius exclaims, "How can a person conceal his true character if you listen to his words and observe the pupils of his eyes?" The words used here, *ren yan sou zai*, exactly repeat Confucius's. But we should be careful about any general comparison. Elsewhere, while Confucius is talking directly about attitudes and other aspects of self-cultivation, Mencius, on the other hand, is providing evidence for the heart-mind and its contents. For instance in 3A:5, Mencius responds indirectly to the Mohist, Yizi, by referring to people in earlier times who threw the bodies of their deceased parents into the gullies. Later observing that the bodies were eaten by creatures and flies, they broke into a sweat. Mencius comments, "The sweating was not put on for others to see. It was an expression of their innermost heart." Quite clearly, this is cited as evidence of the existence of the incipient moral qualities in the heart-mind. Contrast this with *Analects* 4.7 where Confucius says, "In his errors a person is true to type. Observe the errors and you will know the person."[37] The focus here is very immediate or direct—it is on knowing the individual person.

In 12.20, Zizhang asks about what is meant by "getting through (*da* 達)." When asked what he means, he talks about "being known (*wen* 聞)." Confucius makes a distinction between the two by saying that the former "describes someone who is straight by nature and fond of what is right, sensitive to other people's words and observant of the expression on their faces, and always mindful of being modest." The latter "describes someone who has no misgivings about his own claim to *ren* when all he is doing is putting up a façade of *ren* which is belied by his deeds." Again, we have a direct and very pointed reference to character as Confucius concludes, "Such a person is sure to be known." Clearly, the immediacy of ethical commitment has to do with the straightforward expression of certain attitudes, not with being known to have these attitudes, or for that matter, taking them as evidence for the goodness of human nature.

To conclude this section, we should spell out some of the attitudes and values already referred to. Take, for example, the aspect of *ren* with which we began, being *xiaoti*. It is reported in 1.2 that Youzi regarded the basis of non-rebelliousness as the affection and reverence one has for one's immediate family and elders. Through an educational and cultural process, this feeling is extended outwards hierarchically to others. It is in this respect that the statement is made, "He who dislikes rebelling against superiors yet likes creating disorder—this has never been the case." This is an emphatic statement of an ethical norm, about the internalized familial basis for social order. The firmness of the order is believed to be held in place by an attitude of love and reverence. Confucius's concern (if we take him to condone Youzi's remarks) is not that of deducing or speculating how familial love and reverence could be extended outwards, but it is that of maintaining a hierarchical order through the educational process of internalizing the attitudes of love, reverence, and respect for one's elders.

Another group of attitudes and values is revealed through the insistence on the various aspects of speech (*yan* 言), that it should be cautious, be consistent with action and not glib. These bring out the importance of trustworthiness, sincerity, earnestness, doing one's best, and a regard for truth. As we have seen, Confucius was extremely annoyed with Zilu for slighting the significance of the rectification of names. On the negative side, Confucius disapproved of specious and clever talk, pretentiousness, and insinuating appearance. To him, such dissemblance could have implied a state of disharmony and unease in contrast to the *ren* person: "One who is not *ren* cannot remain long in straitened circumstances, nor can he remain long in easy circumstances. The *ren* person is attracted to *ren* because he feels at home in it. The wise person is attracted to *ren* because he finds it to his advantage" (4.2). Elsewhere, the following terms are used—"rely on *ren*" (7.6), and "dwell in *ren*" (4.1, 4.2). Perhaps this is also the reason for the metaphors concerning the *ren* person, that he delights in the mountains and is still and long-lived (6.23). It is also stated that "the wise are free from perplexities; the virtuous from anxiety; and the bold from fear" (Legge, 9.28, 14.30; Lau, 9.29, 14.28). Here we seem to have tautologous statements.[38] They suggest that just as wisdom and freedom from perplexity, courage, and lack of fear are synonymous, so is *ren* and freedom from anxiety. Together with the statement about being at home, this seems to refer to the possession of *ren* as being in a state of equanimity.

Ren and *Li*

The preceding discussion on the congruence between attitudes and actions allows for a way of looking at the relation between *ren* and *li* as an internal one. The relation between the two concepts has been controversial, especially since Herbert Fingarette's interpretation that the core of the *Analects* is its presentation of *li* as sacred ceremony that effects action. It is the power of ceremony and not an inner mental act that characterizes Confucius's ethical thinking. In this regard, *ren* is but the personal aspect of *li*. The *ren* person is perfected in *li*. Fingarette thus regards the statement in 12.1 that "he who can submit himself to *li* is *ren*," to be among the "most specific and helpful" comments about *ren*.[39]

The controversy surrounding Fingarette's emphasis on *li* may have been partly caused by misunderstandings of the method that he uses to highlight the "sacred" aspect of *li*. This is the criterial analysis of mid-twentieth century "linguistic" philosophers who were concerned, for various reasons, to exorcise the ghost of Descartes from modern philosophy. The following statement of Fingarette's succinctly sums up an important aspect of this whole movement:

> The ceremonial act is the primary, irreducible event; language cannot be understood in isolation from the conventional practice in which it is rooted; conventional practice cannot be understood in isolation from the language that defines and is part of it. No purely physical motion is a promise; no word alone, independent of ceremonial context, circumstances and roles can be a promise. Word and motion are only abstractions from the concrete ceremonial act.[40]

The emphasis on public criteria of "inner" attitudes and mental events can sometimes be taken to deny the existence of such attitudes and events. This was certainly not Fingarette's intention, even though his statement that "the ceremonial act is the primary, irreducible event" seems to endorse the view that the exertion of will, the cultivation of the proper emotions and attitudes, and so forth, are either not significant or less significant than the return to ceremony. As a result, some of Fingarette's critics have sought to redress what they see as an imbalance through an emphasis on the existence of certain sustained attitudes and an inner life, in relation to *ren*. However, this perspective assumes a dichotomy between something "inner" and something "outer," which is precisely what Fingarette is concerned to deny. To reassert the importance of *ren* as something inner, as opposed to *li* as outer, does not help very much to advance the understanding of both concepts.[41]

Fingarette himself has stated that *ren* and *li* are "two aspects of the same thing."[42] Mary Bockover states that both are "inseparable concepts." Elaborating on Fingarette's views on this matter, she mentions their "essential relation," which is that "*li* are forms of conduct done with the right spirit, and *ren* tells us what that spirit is: to approach others empathetically and to treat them with the dignity they deserve."[43] Bockover is right in stating that *ren* tells us something about the spirit of *li*, although I would not describe that spirit as she does.[44] Besides the understanding of *ren* as supplying the spirit of *li*, there has also been a recognition that, as Benjamin Schwartz says, "Without the structuring and educating effects of *li*, *ren* as the highest ideal of personal excellence cannot be attained."[45]

There are two insights here about the relation between *ren* and *li*, each asserting a different necessary relation. The first is a spiritual one, the other institutional or structural. What I call an "internal relation" between the two would incorporate both kinds of necessary relation. To describe this in more detail it is convenient to first discuss Kwong-loi Shun's description of two seemingly opposed views of the relation between the two concepts which he calls "instrumentalist" and "definitionalist."[46] While the instrumentalist sees the observance of *li* as a means to cultivating and expressing *ren*, the definitionalist regards observing *li* as definitive of *ren*. Further, while the instrumentalist sees room for revising the rules of *li*, the definitionalist sees the attitude toward existing *li* practices as conservative. The most prominent passage for the instrumentalist is 9.3, where Confucius approved the majority's use of ceremonial caps made of black silk instead of the linen prescribed by *li* because it was more frugal. This seems to justify departure from an existing rule of *li* so long as the cultivation and expression of *ren* are unaffected. What is relevant here is the expression of reverence. On the other hand, the definitionalist cites 12.1, where Confucius says, "To return to the observance of the rites through overcoming the self constitutes *ren* (*ke ji fu li wei ren* 克己復禮為仁)." Responding to Yan Hui's request to be more specific, Confucius replies that one should not look, listen, speak or move unless it is in accordance with the rites (*fei li wu shi* 非禮勿視, *fei li wu ting* 聽, *fei li wu yan* 言, *fei li wu dong* 動). This seems to justify the argument that the observance of *li* is definitive of *ren*, that is, the very observance of the rules of *li* constitutes *ren*.

Shun's solution to this seeming impasse is to argue that although performances of the *li* rituals are necessary and sufficient for expressing certain attitudes like indebtedness (toward ancestors and parents) and reverence, these attitudes transcend the particular rituals. As such, the rituals could be said to be means of cultivating and expressing the attitudes. But at the same time, this transcendence may provide "a perspective from which revision of the existing ritual practices can be assessed."[47] Nonetheless, a general conservativeness is maintained since it is the whole corpus of ritual practice that gives stability and expression to the feelings and attitudes.

Shun calls his interpretation a "constitutive relation" between *ren* and *li*. He sometimes explains the definitionalist view in terms of the practices of *li* being "constitutive" of *ren*, and it is easy to confuse his sense of "constitutive relation" with the definitionalist's.[48] But what is interesting about Shun's analysis is his conclusion that *ren* comprises a "cluster of emotional dispositions and attitudes" that have a certain relation to the norms of *li*.[49] We should note that earlier, while describing the sacrifices to ancestors as being necessary and sufficient for having the attitude of indebtedness and reverence toward them, Shun had to qualify that these have to be performed with the proper spirit. As he says, "general participation in sacrificial rites (with the proper spirit) is both necessary and sufficient for one's having an attitude of indebtedness and reverence toward ancestors."[50] This qualification is perhaps necessary to avoid the objection that Confucius despaired of the mechanical performance of the rites, and any mechanical performance cannot be said as such to constitute both a necessary and sufficient condition of having the relevant attitude. Nonetheless, Shun's insight is that performing the ceremonies of *li* constitutes *ren* insofar as the right spirit is present, and there need be no conflict as to which has evaluative priority over the other. In other words, the relation between *ren* and *li* is internal, not external.

To establish this, we need to remind ourselves of the spirit of *li*, something I discussed in chapter 1. For example, remember Confucius's exclamation: "What can a person do with *li* who is not *ren*? What can a person do with music who is not *ren*?" (3.3). If Shun is right about *ren* comprising a "cluster of emotional dispositions and attitudes" that are formed through the cultivation and expression of the traditional norms of *li*, we should know in more detail what the contents of this cluster are. He has mentioned reverence and indebtedness toward one's ancestors as one attitude, and respect for elders as another. It is important that we do not stop here, if we are to take seriously his idea that the attitudes comprising *ren* can serve to evaluate the practice of traditional norms.[51]

My description of the spirit of *li* in the previous chapter shows that we need not restrict ourselves to emotions and attitudes in this context, but also talk about the expression of certain values such as sincerity, earnestness, frugality, genuineness of feeling, aesthetic sensitivity, harmony and balance, dignity, and having a sense of order. In addition, one should guard against arrogance, presumptuousness, hubris, and extravagance (in the sense of mere display). If all these are constitutive of *ren*, they are at the same time crucial to the very meaning of the rites, not external to them.

My earlier analysis of *ren* in this chapter gives credence to the formation of this cluster of emotions, attitudes, and values in terms of the educational and cultural processes of *li*. We may be said to have arrived at the same place from two different directions. From *ren* we derived attitudes and values such as affection and reverence for elders, earnestness, sincerity, unpretentiousness, cautiousness in speech, and equanimity. From *li*, we derived similar attitudes and values of love and reverence, sincerity, earnestness, genuineness of feeling, and others such as dignity and frugality. In addition, we noted the importance of music to the spirit of *li*, including the cultivation of aesthetic sensitivity, and achieving a sense of balance and harmony. This last category of aesthetic qualities is especially interesting because it brings out the role of an aesthetic education in shaping character and in motivating one to desire, to feel and act in the right ethical spirit.

This illustration of the internal relation between *ren* and *li* should not lead us to conclude, however, that they are the *same* thing. Yan Hui's statement in 9.11 can be enlisted once more to help us see this. Besides talking metaphorically about the elusiveness of Confucius's way, he also says: "The Master is good at leading one on step by step. He broadens me with culture and brings me back to essentials by means of the rites." Suppose we ask: Why is Yan Hui unable to describe the "it" (*zhi* 之) that eludes him? A skeptic might reply that if Yan Hui cannot describe what he is after, then he is pursuing a red herring. Beyond the culture and the rites that Yan Hui refers to in his remarks, there is nothing else. But the skeptic's answer brings out the fact that there is a particular orientation that shows itself through what Yan Hui says, and if we could observe him as Confucius did, how he says it and what he does. This, we might say, is the orientation of *ren*. Doubtless, the attitudes and values that make up the content of *ren* cannot be described independently of the structures of *li* and the spirit in which *li* should be performed. But in describing these contents, we are only doing so from a third-person perspective. To have *ren*, however, is not to describe *ren* — it is to express *ren* in one's life, which is why I have talked of the "immediacy of ethical commitment." No one can guarantee that he or she expresses *ren*, or is in a state of *ren*. This is partly because no one can possess all the attitudes and values mentioned at one time. But more importantly, these are not things that one can be said to have, in the sense of storing them and producing them when required. Rather, the attitude of *ren* is an ethical orientation or perspective *from* which the person speaks or acts, it does not consist of particular qualities that one might enumerate and claim to possess.[52] One way of putting this is that you have not arrived if you think you have. As such, it is an orientation that can easily elude one, as Yan Hui saw.

Conclusion

There have been various tendencies to read *ren* in the light of Mencius's theory of human nature. I have argued that this distracts from seeing what is significant about *ren* in the context of Confucius's ethics. That is, *ren* is an ethical orientation of the person. Although the orientation is effort-driven, there is no end point, because the very idea that one has achieved a state of *ren* is a denial of that very orientation. This, one could say, explains why Confucius hardly ever says that anyone has achieved *ren*. Confucius does not speculate about human nature, but is more concerned with what I have referred to as the "immediacy of ethical commitment." This is a concern with whether one's words and deeds cohere or not, and at the same time, with the kind of person that one is, as expressed through one's words and behavior. We described some examples where Confucius judges that this orientation is lacking. For instance, Ran Qiu who says that it is not that he is not pleased with Confucius's teaching, but that he lacks the strength to practice it (6.12); and Zai Wo's questionable motives in wanting to discuss shortening the three-year mourning period.

Coming back to the discussion with which I began, we may say that although Cheng Yi was right that *xiaoti* is but one aspect of *ren*, he and Zhu Xi were swayed by Mencius and did not go far enough to see that it encompasses a much wider confluence of emotions, attitudes, values, and ultimately, a particular ethical orientation that in the final analysis would bring about social order. This is of course an ideal, one that is shared to some extent by Mencius, although he was forced to defend (what he saw as) the Confucian faith and hence put *ren* in the philosophical context of *xing* or (human) nature. We shall, in the next chapter, discuss Mencius's project in greater detail.

Debating Human Nature:
Mencius and Gaozi

3

In the earlier chapters, we have referred at certain points to a tendency to read the *Analects* in terms of the theory of *xing* 性 or (human) nature found in the *Mencius*. This theory is described in this chapter through a discussion of the debate between Mencius and Gaozi 告子, in Book 6 of the *Mencius*.[1] Mencius's theory was developed against some intellectual challenges,[2] one of these coming from Gaozi.[3] As we shall see, Mencius regarded his views on *xing* to be morally subversive. However, there has been controversy over the logical status of the individual moves made by Mencius and Gaozi in the debate. Thus, Arthur Waley has stated, "As a controversialist he [Mencius] is nugatory. The whole discussion (Book VI) about whether Goodness and Duty are internal or external is a mass of irrelevant analogies, most of which could equally well be used to disprove what they are intended to prove."[4] D. C. Lau, on the other hand, has argued that it is wrong to think that "Mencius . . . could have indulged consistently in what appears to be pointless argument or that his opponents were always effectively silenced by *non sequiturs*."[5] But, according to Chad Hansen, it is precisely this that Mencius is guilty of.[6] A. C. Graham, however, credits Lau with converting him from sharing Waley's point of view.[7]

Given these disagreements, there is a need to reexamine the debate. A major feature of it is the use of analogies by both Mencius and Gaozi. I shall draw out certain assumptions and implications of these analogies that have not been sufficiently clarified. As we shall see, Mencius fails to refute Gaozi in 6A:1–3. But the real issue emerges in 6A:4 and 6A:5 where the terms *nei* 內 and *wai* 外 or "internal" and "external" are prominent. Some writers have noted that this is one crux of the debate, and some also share my belief that Gaozi deserves better credit for his arguments than has generally been acknowledged.[8] However, I think there is a certain logical move that Mencius and his disciple Gongduzi make in 6A:4 and 6A:5 that has not been sufficiently appreciated.

Later on, I shall spell out this logical move schematically. But in general terms, we can put it in the following way first. It is crucial to note that, in the debate, the terms "internal" and "external" are introduced by Gaozi and questioned by Mencius. Through the analogies of food and drink in 6A:4 and 6A:5, Mencius (and also Gongduzi) exposes the sensory and appetitive assumptions behind Gaozi's use of these terms. I use the terms "sensory and appetitive" to refer to two broad phenomena of desires. One, those stimulated by the sensations of taste, sight, sound, and so on (as mentioned for example in 6A:7). Two, the appetite for food and sex, as mentioned for example by Gaozi to be definitive of *xing* in 6A:4. Mencius throws doubt on whether "internal" and "external," as understood by Gaozi, can be applied to show that *ren* 仁 is internal and *yi* 義 is external. This interpretation goes against the usual view: that Mencius agrees with Gaozi that *ren* is internal, but disagrees that *yi* is external. On my interpretation, however, Mencius is questioning Gaozi's application of "internal" and "external" to both *ren* and *yi*, and showing that it has absurd consequences for his use of both terms.

I shall not reproduce the passages in full. Instead, there is a progression of argument best displayed in terms of paraphrase. Although reference shall be made to Lau's paper because of its centrality in the controversy, my aim is to analyze the arguments between Gaozi and Mencius so as to reveal their philosophical underpinnings. Thus, it is essential to Mencius's rebuttal of Gaozi that we understand his own application of "internal" and "external." But as an important preliminary to this, we need to see that Mencius provides a moral psychology of the *xin* 心 or the heart-mind which describes the possibilities of relationships and attitudes based on responses other than desire. A detailed account of this moral psychology will be provided after a discussion of the debate. In contrast to Mencius, Gaozi emphasizes the biological processes of life or *sheng* 生 and this limits him to a psychology of desire. Ultimately, as we shall see, it is Mencius's description of what it is to be human that allows him a conception of both *xin* and *xing*.

The Willow Analogy (6A:1)

In 6A:1, Gaozi draws an analogy between *xing* and the *qi* willow (*qi liu* 杞柳): to make *ren yi* 仁義 or morality[9] out of the *xing* of human beings is like making cups and bowls out of the willow. Some commentators have taken Gaozi to imply that *xing* is bad. For instance, Zhu Xi has commented that according to Gaozi, human *xing* originally has no *ren yi*. It must be worked upon before *ren yi* can be established, and that this is similar to Xunzi's 荀子 saying that *xing* is originally bad.[10] But contrary to Zhu Xi, this last comparison does not follow, for two reasons. First, the belief that *ren yi* is constructed need not imply that human *xing* is originally bad. Nothing is implied one way or another, about the original state of human *xing*. Second, as recent scholarship has shown, the sense in which Xunzi says that human *xing* is bad may have nothing to do with any original nature. Instead, badness or evil is a result of the nonregulation of desires in human interaction and given the limitedness of material resources.[11]

In response, Mencius poses two questions. First, would making cups and bowls out of the willow not involve doing violence to it? Second, on this analogy, would it not mean doing violence to human beings to make them *ren yi*?

To be consistent with Gaozi's analogy, Mencius should talk of doing violence to the *xing* of human beings, and not human beings *per se*. Perhaps it would be fair to say that this is what he has in mind, as he had prefaced the above questions by asking whether one could follow the *xing* of the willow in making cups and bowls. As Kwong-loi Shun has shown, while Gaozi compares *xing* to the willow, emphasizing that human *xing* is pliable and can be molded in a good or bad direction, Mencius, on the other hand, compares human *xing* to the *xing* of the willow: since making the willow into cups and bowls involves going against its nature (to grow into a full-grown plant), Mencius argues that Gaozi's analogy commits him to saying that making humans moral also involves going against their *xing*.[12]

But in any case, there is so far no real argument between Gaozi and Mencius. All we have is an analogy and its construal. There is no telling whether Gaozi accepts this construal. If he accepts it, no contradiction need arise vis-à-vis his analogy. It may be that making *ren yi* out of the *xing* of human beings would involve force or violence. However, the extent of "violence" depends on how pliable the *xing* of the willow is. Similarly, the extent of "violence" to human *xing* depends on its pliability. In this sense, violence need not imply a "violation" of anything.

There are two possible replies here, in support of Mencius. One is that in order to make cups and bowls out of the willow, one would have to kill the tree first.[13] Another is that "pliability" does not imply nonsuffering—a "pliant" person can be made to suffer terribly, in which case violence may increase with pliability. Perhaps it is possible objections like these that lead Gaozi to his next analogy of water, where no damage is done no matter how one forces it.

Mencius's comment on Gaozi's willow analogy is, "Surely, it will be your *yan* 言 (words, teachings) which lead people of the world to *huo* 禍 (bring disaster upon, regard as a disaster) *ren yi*." But this is a consequence that Gaozi could accept. After all, there is no saying that Gaozi wishes to uphold *ren yi*. On the other hand, Gaozi may want to uphold *ren yi*. Still, he could dispute the consequence.

However, Lau has developed two arguments for Mencius.[14] First, by implying that it is necessary to do violence to human nature in making people moral, one is saying that it is bad to do so—that it is unnatural and artificial to make humans moral. But, according to Lau, these *are* moral judgments. Gaozi cannot escape making moral judgments and this shows that they cannot be artificial and unnatural. Second, Gaozi's position implies that it would be just as much a violation of human nature if people were to be made immoral. But it would be easy for anyone "hostile to morality" to argue that "since it is unnatural for man to be moral it must be natural for him to be immoral." It is in this sense that Gaozi's saying would be disastrous for morality.[15]

In Gaozi's defense, we may deny that he is making any moral judgment about the badness of making humans moral or that he is committed to any such judgment. Another sense of "inescapably" making moral judgments would be that Gaozi has to make such judgments in his everyday life. Nonetheless, we may invoke the distinction between first-order and second-order levels of discourse here. Thus, the fact that Gaozi inescapably makes moral judgments is logically distinct from how he views the nature of such discourse, that is, at the second-order level. Gaozi is proposing the theory that *ren yi* is established through the process of working upon *xing*. This is consistent with either upholding or not upholding *ren yi*, at the first-order level of moral discourse. This distinction also enables us to look at Lau's second argument as simply a reiteration of the moral anxiety felt by Mencius, at the first-order level, reflective of Mencius's earnest moral faith. Interestingly, Lau himself does not say that Gaozi is hostile to morality. Instead, he thinks that Gaozi may be "misrepresented," since it is easy for anyone hostile to morality to argue that it would be natural to be immoral.[16]

The Water Analogy (6A:2)

In 6A:2, perhaps sensing a misunderstanding on Mencius's part, or wishing to circumvent Mencius's objections to his willow analogy, Gaozi resorts to an analogy with water. Human *xing* is, like whirling water, directionless until it is channeled. The fluidity of water allows Gaozi to bypass the earlier objection that to make *ren yi* out of human *xing* would involve a violation. Water being fluid, no violence is done to it when channeled. It could be said that human *xing*, like water, does not have any inherent direction.

Mencius replies that although water may be indifferent to east or west, it cannot be indifferent to up or down. He asserts that the goodness of human *xing* is like the tendency of water to flow downward—there is no human being who is not-good (*bu shan* 不善), just as it can never be the case that water does not tend to flow downward. Further, just as water may be forced upward by splashing and damming, human beings may be made to be not-good. But this state of affairs may not be said to constitute the *xing* of water or humans.

Although some have thought that Mencius wins the argument here,[17] the comparison between the tendency of water to flow downward and the tendency of human nature to be good does no logical work. In other words, there is no logical connection whatsoever between the former and the latter tendencies. What is happening here is that a *belief* is being stressed, that human nature *must* be good, just as water must, ordinarily, flow downwards. But this belief does not constitute an *argument*.

We should note the aptness of Gaozi's water analogy, as a response to Mencius's earlier objections to the willow analogy. There is a dynamism to water that makes it hard to accept that any damage is done to it in the process of splashing and damming. We saw earlier that Gaozi could accept Mencius's construal of his willow analogy. The notion of violence being done to the willow need not imply a "violation" of anything, because the suitability of the willow for making cups and bowls depends on its pliability. The water analogy extends this point, because the dynamic fluidity of water enables it to be shaped and channeled in any direction whatsoever.[18] Again, there need be no connotation that human beings are naturally and originally bad. The emphasis is still on *ren yi* being a construction.

Xing as *Sheng:* Mencius's *Reductio* (6A:3)

Gaozi next gives a definition of *xing*: *sheng zhi wei xing* 生之謂性 ("The life process is what meant by 'nature'"). Mencius's interrogations about the tautologous nature of whiteness as applied to various things (for example, "Is the whiteness of white feathers the same as the whiteness of white snow?") show that *sheng* and *xing* are taken by Gaozi tautologously. Mencius further asks whether, in this regard, there is any difference between the *xing* of a hound and an ox, on the one hand, and the *xing* of an ox and a human being, on the other. This is meant as a *reductio ad absurdum* of Gaozi's assertion that there is nothing more to human *xing* than *sheng*, the life process, or the related biological processes of food and sex, as given in Gaozi's statement in 6A:4, *shi se xing ye* 食色性也 ("The appetite for food and sex is 'nature'").

Although there is no indication in the text that Gaozi is floored by this attempted *reductio*, commentators like Lau and Graham take this as the clincher, thinking that Gaozi himself has no choice but to accept the argument.[19] But there is no reason why Gaozi cannot accept the conclusion that human *xing* is the same as that of animals. To make this more reasonable, we need to look more closely at Gaozi's overall position. His belief that *xing* is without inherent direction is spelled out more explicitly in 6A:6 by Mencius's disciple, Gongduzi, as *xing wu shan wu pu shan* 性無善無不善. This should not be rendered simply as "*Xing* is neither good nor bad," but instead as, "*Xing* is without good, and without not-good." In other words, the category of *shan* or goodness is wholly inapplicable to *xing*. The assertion that *xing* and *sheng* are tautologous reinforces this decategorization, bringing into focus instead the animal and biological instincts of human beings.

The reason why Mencius's *reductio* fails is that it simply reiterates Gaozi's view, that human nature is to be seen in terms of the necessary animal and biological processes of life. To say that human *xing* is the same as the animal and biological processes of life seems to imply that there is no difference between human being and animal. This is shocking. However, this merely begs the question. Neither does it follow that Gaozi believes there is no difference between human being and animal.[20] The assertion that *xing* and *sheng* are equivalent is still consistent with the view that *ren yi* is constructed out of *xing*. For even if *xing* consists of the sensory and appetitive desires, it may still be shaped, constructed, or enculturated into *ren yi*, and this is what differentiates human being from animal. Later, we shall see how Mencius provides an argument for the difference between human being and animal in terms of the possibilities of human relationships and reflective thought, but that argument does not belong here.

Gaozi on Internal and External (6A:4, 6A:5)

In 6A:4, Gaozi says: "Appetite for food and sex is nature (*shi se xing ye*). *Ren* is internal, not external; *yi* is external, not internal." He is asked by Mencius to clarify the latter of the two statements. Evidently, *ren* is thought to be internal in some sense similar to the sensory and appetitive desires. An example of *ren* is given further in the passage, in terms of love or affection for one's brother, as against the brother of a person from Qin whom one would not love. The word *yue* 悦 is used here, indicating that in loving my brother and not another's, I am doing what "pleases" me.[21] This, together with the examples of food, sex, and affection, shows that by "internal" Gaozi is referring to the motivational basis for action, as arising from the sensory and appetitive desires.

This is reinforced by the contrast with *yi*. Gaozi describes the externality of *yi* in terms of the concepts of elderliness and respect for elders. An analogy is made with whiteness. Elderliness is said to be an external quality in the same way as whiteness. Just as it is on account of something's being white that I regard it as white (*bai zhi* 白之), Gaozi states that it is on account of someone's elderliness that he respects him (*bi zhang er wo zhang zhi* 彼長而我長之). Respect, in other words, is due to someone in relation to his position. One is fulfilling *yi* if one pays attention to the circumstances under which it is due, and shows respect accordingly. *Yi*, in this sense, is a social construct and hence, external.

Mencius replies that (admittedly) there is no difference between the "whiteness" of a white horse and of a white person, but is there no difference between the two "*zhang*" in *zhang ma* 長馬 (old horse) and *zhang ren* 長人 (old or elderly person)? The ambiguity of *zhang* either as adjectival (attributing oldness) or as verbal (to treat with respect) is brought out in his next question: Whether we say that it is the object of respect—that is, the elderly person (*zhang zhe* 長者)—or the person evincing respect (*zhang zhi zhe* 長之者), who is *yi*?

Mencius is drawing attention to the fact that the *yi* that is shown in respecting the elderly comes from the person who shows respect, not the object of respect. Gaozi's reply is that since there is no difference between respecting an elder from Chu and my own elder, this is due to the quality of being elderly and hence it is called external. Presumably, in the case of one's own elder, there is affection as well as respect. But because the respect shown is identical in both cases, this is *yi* and it is an external source that identifies whether respect is due.

Replying to this, Mencius poses the following question: Although there is no difference between enjoying the roast of a person from Qin, and enjoying my own roast, does it follow that there is externality in my enjoying a roast?

In 6A:5, Mengjizi (presumably a follower of Gaozi's) has a dialogue with Gongduzi (Mencius's disciple). Mengjizi claims that since *jing* 敬 or respect varies with the circumstances, this shows that respect (as an expression of *yi*) is external. The example cited is that although normally priority of respect is accorded my eldest brother over a more elderly villager, in a village gathering however, I would accord priority to the villager (by pouring wine for the villager first). Gongduzi is stumped by this, and informs Mencius of what has transpired. Mencius provides the example of the respect shown for one's younger brother having priority over one's uncle when the former is involved in a sacrifice where he is impersonating an ancestor.[22] Gongduzi relays this to Mengjizi, who replies, "It is the same respect whether I am respecting my uncle or my younger brother. It is, as I have said, external and does not come from within." To which Gongduzi replies: "In winter, one drinks hot water, in summer cold. Does that mean that even (the sensation of) drinking and eating can be a matter of what is external?"

There are various explanations about what is going on with regard to the roast and drink analogies in 6A:4 and 6A:5. I shall discuss some of these before presenting my own explanation.

The Roast and Drink Analogies

Kwong-loi Shun's explanation of the roast analogy is as follows:

> We like a roast whether it belongs to us or to someone else, but we do not do so because we recognize it as proper to like a roast by virtue of its quality of being a roast, which is independent of us. This idea Mencius puts by saying that there is no externality in liking a roast. . . . Rather, as Kao Tzu (Gaozi) would presumably agree, it is explained by the fact that we have a taste for roast in general, without regard to whether it belongs to us or to another. Likewise, in the case of treating old people as old, we recognize that it is improper not to extend the same respectful treatment to all old people because we are already inclined to treat old people in general with respect, whether they belong to our own family or not.[23]

In this explanation, the stress is on the fact that there is a shared taste, and on a shared inclination for respect and hence *yi*, irrespective of the object of taste or respect. Shun refers to 6A:7, for instance, where the point is made that there are certain predispositions of the heart-mind shared by all, just as there are shared tastes.[24] The same emphasis is made in Shun's explanation of the drink analogy:

> According to [Gongduzi], we just prefer to drink hot water in winter and cold water in summer; although our preferences vary with external circumstances, they are a matter of taste and not preferences we regard as proper to have by virtue of external

circumstances. . . . Kung-tu Tzu (Gongduzi) took the example to illustrate the point that although the objects of our greater respect may vary with external circumstances, it does not follow that our greater respect is something we regard as proper to have by virtue of such circumstances. Rather, the variation may be a result of the way we ourselves are constituted, and hence Meng Chi-tzu's (Mengjizi's) argument does not show that propriety lies on the outside.[25]

However, the same stress on taste has been taken as irrelevant by Whalen Lai. After clarifying that for Gaozi, nature is what is inborn, and that the desire for food and sex that is central to this nature is morally neutral just as water can be channeled in different directions, Lai says: "Mencius and a disciple on two occasions used 'the love of roast meat independent of location' (6A:4) and 'the instinct to drink cold water in summer and hot beverages in winter' (6A:5) to disprove Kao Tzu's (Gaozi's) use of the 'inner/outer' distinction. By our clarification . . . both meat and drink come under 'food and sex' and should therefore be ruled not applicable to an analysis of moral attitude."[26] It is clear that Lai is saying that the analogies do not work, since these remarks are prefaced by the statement that "Kao Tzu (Gaozi) can withstand some of the Mencian charges against him."[27]

Curiously, what Lai says about the inapplicability of food and sex to an analysis of moral attitude can be taken as supportive of what Mencius wants to say. In other words, Mencius *is* denying the applicability of the sensory and appetitive desires to a proper description of moral concepts, when he claims that both *ren* and *yi* are internal. We shall see this in more detail later. Here, I want to offer an alternative explanation of the roast and drink analogies that brings out a strong logical move that I think both Mencius and Gongduzi are making. But first, we need to see the overall point of the analogies. In this regard, a clue is given by the following remarks of Lau's in reference to 6A:4 and 6A:5:

> The arguments are obviously not conclusive, but this is in part due to Mencius' limited purpose. All he set out to do, in both cases, was to show that his opponents failed to establish the externality of *yi*. He did not attempt to go beyond this and to establish positively that *yi* was internal.[28]

This is an important observation. Mencius is seeking a clarification of the terms, "internal" and "external," extending the question he had posed earlier in 6A:4, "Why do you say that *ren* is internal and *yi* is external?" Mencius is pointing to a difficulty with "internal" and "external," because the evincing of respect is not just an external quality like whiteness or being elderly (whether it be an old horse or an old man). The roast and drink analogies bring out further, logical, difficulties.

The roast analogy in 6A:4 parallels Gaozi's argument that since the respect shown for both a family and nonfamily member is the same, this shows that respect for the elderly must be external. Mencius points out that by the same token, since there is no difference between enjoying my own roast or another's, my enjoyment would be deemed external. This is of course absurd, for enjoyment of a roast must be internal in the sensory and appetitive sense. The argument can be presented schematically, to show the logical parallels. Taking X to be "my" and Y to be "another":

Gaozi argues

(1)		愛 X 之弟	Love my brother
	But Not:	愛 Y 之弟	Love another's brother
	Therefore:	*Ren* (love) is internal	
(2)		長 X 之長	Respect (literally, "to elder") my elder
	Similarly:	長 Y 之長	Respect another's elder
	Therefore:	*Yi* (respect) is external	

Mencius shows

(3)		嗜 X 之炙	Relish my own roast
	Similarly:	嗜 Y 之炙	Relish another's roast
	Therefore:	Relish is external	

As we can see schematically, (3) has the same logical form as (2). However, its conclusion is absurd. This is what logicians refer to as a *reductio ad absurdum* (or a *reductio*, in short): a refutation of an argument by displaying its absurd consequences, where these consequences follow as a matter of logical necessity.

The same absurdity is illustrated in the drink analogy of 6A:5. Schematically, with "X" for "uncle" and "Y" for "younger brother impersonating an ancestor in a sacrifice":

Mengjizi responds to Mencius's example of the younger brother impersonating an ancestor at a sacrifice:

(4)	*Jing X ze jing*	敬 X 則敬	Respect for X then (makes up) respect
	Jing Y ze jing	敬 Y 則敬	Respect for Y then (makes up) respect
	Guo zai wai	果在外	Therefore, (respect is) external

Gongduzi replies:

(5)	*Dong ze yin tang*	冬則飲湯	Winter then drink hot water
	Xia ze yin shui	夏則飲水	Summer then drink cold water
	Ran ze yin shi zai wai ye?	然則飲食在外也?	Therefore, (the sensation of) drinking/eating is external?

The *ze* 則 in (4) is not just one of implication, but also connotes the fact that the respect accorded is a result of the practice of respect itself. That is, the respect is constituted or made up by the very performance of respect. Thus, there could be various such acts, under varying circumstances. The drink analogy parallels Mengjizi's argument that respect is external because the variation in circumstances calls for different objects of respect.

As can be seen in the above schematic presentations, the analogies of roast and drink are, in each case, consistent with the form of the arguments given by Gaozi and Mengjizi, respectively, in 6A:4 and in 6A:5. Just as the roast analogy parallels Gaozi's argument that respect (and hence *yi*) is external because there is no difference in the respect shown to my elder brother and an elder person unrelated to me, similarly, the drink analogy parallels Mengjizi's argument that *yi* is external because of the varying circumstances. In each case, an absurd consequence follows: (1) Since there is no difference in the relish of my roast or someone else's, it follows that relish is external, and (2) Since different seasons (that is, varying circumstances) call for drinks of different temperature, it follows that the sensation of drinking/eating is external.

Mencius's and Gongduzi's use of these "absurd" analogies was deliberate. The parallel formal resemblance to Gaozi's and Mengjizi's arguments show that, logically speaking, similarity of respect and variation of circumstances have nothing to do with whether something is to be regarded as internal or external. Gaozi's claim that *yi* is external is therefore invalidated.

At the same time, we are made aware that this does not mean that *yi* is internal either, *in the sense that taste and sensation are internal*. The same holds for *ren*. Most commentators have assumed that since Gaozi holds that *ren* is internal, Mencius does not question this, but instead questions only the assertion that *yi* is external.[29] However, Mencius is not counter-asserting that *yi* is internal, as most readers believe. Remember Lau's statement above: "All he (Mencius) set out to do, in both cases, was to show that his opponents failed to establish the externality of *yi*. He did not attempt to go beyond this and to establish positively that *yi* was internal."

Lau's last remark should be understood as saying that Mencius did not try to establish that *yi* was internal, *in* the arguments of 6A:4 and 6A:5. If the reader has followed the argument so far, Lau is *not* (and neither am I) denying that Mencius himself holds *yi* (and *ren*) to be internal! We shall go on to see the sense in which he does hold *yi* to be internal. Having shown up the absurdity of Gaozi's position, the onus is on Mencius to provide his own understanding of "internal" and "external." Although this is not a stated task in the context of the debate with Gaozi, it is necessary to complete the argument, one that may be seen as lying in the background. Thus, another way of looking at the debate with Gaozi is to see it as preparing the way for an account of Mencius's own understanding of "internal" and "external." Before discussing this, it is necessary to analyze his concept of *xin* first.

Xin—The Heart-Mind

In 6A:6 Mencius is asked by Gongduzi to elaborate on his position that *xing* is good (*xing shan* 性善). According to Mencius, it is not the fault of a person's native endowment (*cai* 才) if he does not do good. Everyone has the *xin* or heart-mind of compassion, shame, respect, right and wrong (*ce yin zhi xin, xiu wu zhi xin, gong jing zhi xin, shi fei zhi xin* 惻隱之心，羞惡之心，恭敬之心，是非之心). It is clear from 2A:6 that these are *duan* 端, sprouts or beginnings. Mencius says in 6A:6 that these four sprouts "do not give me a lustre from the outside, they are in me originally. It is only that I have not reflected (*si* 思) upon this."[30] Mencius's denial of a luster can be taken as a direct rebuttal of Gaozi's emphasis on *ren yi* as having an external source. He is disagreeing with Gaozi that *ren yi* is a social construct, and internality for him has to do with a potential goodness. This consists of the four sprouts. These sprouts require reflective thought and nurturance or nourishment (*yang* 養) to develop into the virtues of *ren*, *yi*, *li*, and *zhi* 仁，義，禮，智 (Lau: benevolence, dutifulness, observance of the rites, and wisdom).

The example of the child about to fall into a well (2A:6) has been regarded by most commentators as evidence for the existence of the heart of compassion. It has to be said that as evidence, this is rather thin. The sudden feeling one has may be of alarm, not amounting to compassion.[31] Instead, it would be better to regard this and other examples as providing a moral psychology that, when expanded upon (as we shall see), is more sophisticated than Gaozi's.

Mencius is especially careful to differentiate the feeling of compassion from wishing to please the child's parents, winning the praise of others, or even disliking the cry of the child. In other words, the compassion is a direct concern *for* the child. It is not indirect or secondary, as a means to pleasing the parents. Neither is it for the anticipated pleasure of winning the praise of others. And lastly, it is not a deflection of an unpleasant sensory state. Note that these are various modes of desire. Suppose one describes the compassion as a desire for the welfare of the child. Even so, it is clear that it is not like the desire for a pleasurable state or for deflecting an unpleasurable state. In the latter cases, the focus is on consummating a desire-state. Compassion, on the other hand, is outward-directed. The difference can be accentuated by considering that an unfulfilled sensory state may yet be fulfilled by "transferring" one's desire elsewhere. For example, frustrated in my attempt to buy a piece of property, I can look for another with similar characteristics. On the other hand, what would it mean to recommend that I "transfer" my compassion for the child elsewhere?

Consider the following example. In George Eliot's *Middlemarch*, Dorothea is disappointed to find that the villagers in her parish are not so poor as to require her charitable work. We might recommend that she should transfer her "compassion" elsewhere. This contrasts with the "nontransferability" of compassion, the point being that the phenomenological description of (genuine) compassion precludes such transference; that is, my compassion is for *you*, not some substitute, and this is precisely what Mencius is getting at in his contrast of the compassion for the child with other motives.[32]

Mencius can also be construed as describing the relations that can obtain between oneself and others or certain states of affairs, on the basis of certain primitive responses. Again, these are not relations of desire. In 2A:6, Mencius associates having the four sprouts with having the four limbs. A lack of any of these would cripple one. In other words, the capacity to uphold oneself and to relate to others in certain ways would be absent. As Mencius says:

> For someone possessing these four sprouts to deny his own potentialities is for him to cripple himself; for him to deny the potentialities of his prince is for him to cripple his prince. If a person is able to develop all these four sprouts that he possesses, it will be like a fire starting up or a spring coming through. When these are fully developed, he can tend the whole realm within the Four Seas, but if he fails to develop them, he will not be able even to serve his parents.

Earlier in the same passage, Mencius says that anyone who lacks any of the four sprouts would not be a human being. Clearly, the sprouts are said to define the human being in terms of enabling one to relate to others in certain ways, which, if developed, would be the virtues of *ren*, *yi*, *li*, and *zhi*. Although not mentioned in this passage, there is also the upholding of oneself in relation to certain things.

Two examples are given in 6A:10 of this last relation. Referring to the fact that the heart-mind loathes (*wu* 惡) certain things more than death, Mencius states that this is not an attitude confined to the virtuous person, but common to all men. It is simply that the virtuous person (*xian zhe* 賢者) never loses this heart. Given that it would not only be loathsome but also shameful (*xiu* 羞) to do something that is worse than death, one develops the virtue of *yi* by maintaining this sense of shame and loathing (*xiu wu*). The second example makes the same point. When getting food means life instead of death, even a beggar would not accept food that is first trampled upon (in other words, given in a thoroughly insulting manner). Mencius goes on to say, however, that some people seem to forget the proprieties of *li yi* 禮義 when they accept certain things improperly, such as beautiful houses, concubines, and the gratitude of others, although like the beggar, they believe that they would rather die than accept food that has been given in the manner described earlier. Mencius concludes by saying, "This way of thinking is known as losing one's original heart (*ben xin* 本心)."

Environmental factors play a role in the failure to nourish, nurture, and sustain one's heart-mind. This is described, for example, in 6A:8 in terms of the Ox Mountain where it is argued that it would be mistaken to think that its denuded state constitutes its original nature (see also 6A:9). But the failure is also attributed to the failure to reflect (*si*), in several places (6A:6, 6A:13, 6A:15, 6A:17).

In 6A:7 Mencius says that there is something possessed in common by all hearts (heart-mind):

> all palates have the same preference in taste; all ears in sound; all eyes in beauty. Should hearts prove to be an exception by possessing nothing in common (*du wu suo tong ran hu* 獨無所同然乎)? What is it, then, that is common to all hearts? Reason and rightness (*wei li ye yi ye* 謂理也義也). Thus reason and rightness please my heart (*yue wo xin* 悦我心) in the same way as meat pleases my palate (*yue wo kou* 悦我口).

Our earlier analysis has shown that it would be wrong to construe Mencius as suggesting that the heart-mind is a sensory organ in the way that the palate is. Instead, he is making a naturalistic assumption that just as there is something that pleases my palate, there is also something that pleases my heart-mind. It is clear, however, that it is *li* 理 and *yi* that please the heart-mind, not the sensation of taste. Lau translates *li* as "reason." Together with his translation of *tong ran* 同然 as "common," this may suggest that reason and rightness are distinctive of the heart-mind, to the extent that they bind the four sprouts together. But, alternative translations of *tong ran* are "agreed upon," or "agree in approving of."[33] And *li*, which occurs only in three passages in the *Mencius*, seems more appropriately translated as "pattern" or "principle."[34] In 5B:1, it occurs as order or *tiaoli* 條理 in the context of the orderly progression of music from beginning to end, and analogously, the beginning and end of wisdom and sageness.[35]

In the light of these other translations, we may read Mencius as saying that the contents of the heart-mind, that is, the four sprouts, are such that they affirm and are pleased with pattern, order or principle, and rightness. In other words, they are able to distinguish and judge what is right. We may say that Mencius is asserting the ability of the four sprouts to register certain modes of awareness, that is, both cognitively and affectively at once.[36]

Thus, the perception of the child about to fall into a well is not a mere cognition. Rather, it registers a moral awareness of an alarming situation. The compassion or feeling of concern for the child is not a concomitant part of the cognition but constitutes the mode in which the situation is registered. This applies also to the other examples discussed in 6A:10. The perception that something is both loathsome and shameful is a direct mode of awareness, not something added on to a pure cognition. In 3A:5, Mencius gives the example of people in earlier times who threw the bodies of their deceased parents into the gullies. Later observing that the bodies were being eaten by creatures and flies, they broke into a sweat and returned home for baskets and spades to bury them. Mencius comments, "The sweating was not put on for others to see. It was an expression of their innermost heart (*zhong xin da yu mian mu* 中心達於面目)." Again, we have a mode of cognition that brings about a particular form of action. This is not confined to a single case, but as Mencius says, "(If in this case) burying them is the thing to do (*yan zhi cheng shi ye* 掩之誠是也), then the burying of their own parents by filial sons and *ren* persons also must have (a) *dao* (*ze xiao zi ren ren zhi yan qi qin yi bi you dao* 則孝子仁人之掩其親亦必有道)."[37] The perception of the thing to do here is not a function of reason but of what all heart-minds *tong ran*, that is, what they would all affirm.

Through his usage of organic and developmental terms in his description of the heart-mind, Mencius would be hard put to explain why it is that some people fail to nourish their heart-mind.[38] As we have seen, he has referred to environmental interference and he also mentions the failure of people to reflect, both cognitively and affectively, on their priorities. This last is not an explanation, but nonetheless, a realistic psychological observation. Time and again, Mencius laments the fact that many people are imprudent, neglecting the 'greater' part of themselves for the 'smaller'. Comments are made about the person knowing how to tend to various things, such as a tree, one's livestock, one's body or parts of the body such as the mouth and belly, but neglecting the greatest or most precious part of oneself, the heart-mind (6A:11, 6A:12, 6A:14).[39]

Mencius on Internal and External

With this picture of Mencius's (account of) moral psychology, we are now in a position to appreciate his understanding of "internal" and "external." As we have seen, the sprouts of compassion, shame and loathing, respect, right and wrong are not sensory and appetitive desires. The latter are transferable, and their objects substitutable and negotiable. To use Mencius's example in 6A:10, if he cannot get both delicacies of fish and bear's palm, then he would settle for bear's palm. Similarly, the desire to remain alive could be such that someone may resort to any means to keep alive. But Mencius goes on to say:

> Yet there are ways of remaining alive and ways of avoiding death to which a person will not resort. In other words, there are things he wants more than life and there are also things he loathes more than death. This is an attitude not confined to the virtuous person but common to all. The virtuous person simply never loses it.

The want or desire (*yu* 欲) in this case must surely be different from an appetitive desire. Rather than being of a piece with any desire that one will go to any length to satisfy, the want of not avoiding death at any cost puts a stop to certain desires. In other words, it judges the desires. We now see why Gaozi's definition of *xing* as *sheng* (the biological processes of life), and his insistence that the appetite for food and sex is *xing*, are unacceptable to Mencius. The sensory organs, which are attracted to external objects, function differently from the four sprouts and their corresponding virtues. In 6A:15, Mencius says:

> The organs of hearing and sight are unable to reflect (*bu si* 不思) and can be misled by external things. When one thing acts on another, all it does is to attract it. The organ of the heart-mind can reflect. But it will find the answer only if it does reflect; otherwise, it will not find the answer. This is what Heaven has given me. If one makes one's stand on what is of greater importance in the first instance, what is of smaller importance cannot displace it. In this way, one cannot but be a great person.

The sensory organs are part of *xing*, but their nature is such that they are simply attracted or drawn toward external objects. The heart-mind, given its ability to reflect, is able to prioritize and as such can judge the suitability of external objects and not be drawn by them. *Ren* and *yi*, insofar as they are developed from the sprouts of the heart-mind, are internal, in a deeper moral sense. This sense is heightened by the contrast between humans and the brutes. Mencius is giving us a definition of what it means to be human. There are two passages in particular that spell this out, 4B:19 and 7B:24.

In 4B:19, Mencius says:

> Slight is the difference between humans and the brutes. The common person loses this distinguishing feature, while the noble person retains it. Shun understood the way of things and had a keen insight into human relationships. He followed the path of morality. He did not just put morality into practice (*you ren yi xing fei xing ren yi ye* 由仁義行非行仁義也).

Certain remarks in 2A:6 referred to earlier may help us understand what Shun is said to have known. Shun's understanding about things in general and his insight into human relationships amount to understanding the basic constituents of the heart-mind and their nurturance. As we have seen, the person who denies the four sprouts is incapacitated for human relationships. Shun's understanding of this allowed him to flow from *ren yi*. In other words, he acted and moved naturally from within the basic contents of the heart-mind, instead of instituting or imposing principles of conduct. Gaozi's emphasis on the sensory and appetitive desires made him insist that *ren yi* could only be an enforced social construct, and as such, an imposition on natural desires. Mencius is asserting that *ren yi* is a natural mode of conduct, albeit one that arises from principles of the human psyche different from the principle of desire.

In 7B:24, Mencius says:

> The way the mouth is disposed towards tastes, the eye towards colours, the ear towards sounds, the nose towards smell, and the four limbs towards ease is human nature, yet therein also lies the Decree (*ming* 命). That is why the noble person does

not describe it as nature. The way filial love (*ren*) pertains to the relation between father and son, duty (*yi*) to the relation between prince and subject, the rites (*li*) to the relation between guest and host, wisdom (*zhi*) to the good and wise man, sageness (*sheng* 聖)[40] to the way of Heaven, is the Decree, but therein also lies human nature. That is why the noble person does not describe it as Decree.

This describes the attitude of the noble person. Again, Mencius does not deny that the sensory organs and their objects are part of nature. His statement that therein lies *ming* is the idea that the external objects toward which the sensory organs are drawn are contingent. This reading takes *ming* in a descriptive sense,[41] pertaining to the contingency of events. It is consistent with the above analysis of the externality of objects of desire. When Mencius describes the relations of *ren*, *yi*, *li*, *zhi*, and *sheng* (in 7B:24), on the other hand, it is difficult to read *ming* as a contingency, given that he sees them as arising out of the sprouts of the heart-mind. As we have seen, Mencius has argued against Gaozi that, as human beings, we have the potentiality for relations other than the relation of desire. These are relations that may instead judge the objects of desire, and "That is why the noble person does not describe it as Decree." But if we are to be consistent in the use of *ming* in the same passage, Mencius does seem to be saying that nonetheless, there is contingency in human relations too. Despite our efforts in maintaining the forms of relationships, things may go awry.

This is as it should be. Mencius does speak of Heaven as the source of *xin* (6A:15). Fully realizing *xin*, one knows *xing*, and through this, one knows and serves Heaven (7A:1). In this sense, Heaven not only endows one with some potentialities, but there is also a proper destiny, *zhengming* 正命. This is a normative sense of *ming*, which enables one to take a steadfast attitude toward death and to cultivate one's character (7A:1). Both *ming* and *zhengming* seem to be described in 7A:2—understanding that there is nothing that is not *ming*, one does not stand under a wall on the verge of collapse. This implies a cautious attitude to the contingency of events. But if one dies "after having done his best in following the Way," he would have followed *zhengming*.

This difference between *zhengming* and *ming* reiterates and heightens our understanding of "internal" and "external" as Mencius sees it. The four sprouts enable us to relate to others and to act in ways that are proper, ultimately defining us as human beings who can stand to others and to things in terms of the virtues of *ren*, *yi*, *li*, and *zhi*. This is to follow what is internal both literally and normatively, that is, the heart-mind. In doing so, one is obeying what has been decreed by Heaven, *zhengming*. The internality here may also be described in terms of the relation between seeking and getting. Thus, in 7A:3, Mencius says: "Seek and you will get it; let go and you will lose it. If this is the case, then seeking is of use to getting and what is sought is within yourself." We may add that the seeking is a constitutive part of the getting.[42] In other words, the effort to cultivate oneself involves modes of awareness described earlier. These modes of awareness are not means to an end that one may discard after the getting but are an important part of what it means to be a human being. There cannot be a stronger sense of "internal" than this, because it goes right to the heart of one's identity as a human being. The relation between seeking and getting, we may say, is essential. By contrast, the external objects that one seeks even if arrived at properly may elude one, depending on *ming*. In this sense, there is no essential relation between seeking and getting. As Mencius says in the same passage, "then seeking is of no use to getting and what is sought lies outside yourself."

Conclusion

Mencius fails to rebut Gaozi's assertion that morality is a construction in 6A:1–3. Mention was made of how Gaozi could escape the charge of inviting disaster to morality (*ren yi*), given his belief that it is constructed. That is, Gaozi could make a distinction between the second- and first-order levels of discourse. His theorizing at the second-order level need not imply that he cannot engage in first-order moral discourse like anyone else.

It is only when Gaozi mentions that *ren* is internal whereas *yi* is external that Mencius manages to pin him down, given the incoherence of the sensory and appetitive sense of "internal" and "external" when applied to the virtues. The development of Mencius's account of moral psychology enables us to see why the distinction we have made for Gaozi between first- and second-order levels of discourse cannot be maintained for morality, or *ren yi*. For Mencius, denial of the heart-mind and its contents would mean denying the basis on which human relationships are built. You can maintain *ren yi* only if you have a deep faith in it as arising out of your deeper self, not as something artificially imposed.

The debate with Gaozi enables us to appreciate more fully Mencius's philosophy of the human being. We see its basis in a sophisticated moral psychology, which goes beyond the psychology of desire as emphasized by Gaozi. In the final analysis, for Mencius, *xing* or nature rests on *xin* or the heart-mind. And *xin*, as Mencius states in 6A:6 is a potentiality for the virtues of *ren*, *yi*, *li*, and *zhi*. My analysis has shown that Mencius is in fact stressing the potential for relating to others and to things in terms of certain modes of moral awareness when he talks of *xin*. This stands in contrast to the psychology of desire as advocated by Gaozi, where the emphasis is on consummating a desire-state. In other words, it is definitive of human beings that they do not stand in relation to others as consumers, and neither are they objects that are helplessly drawn toward other objects.

My analysis has shown that we can interpret Mencius to be stressing the potential for relationships which are not relations of desire but of compassion, shame, respect, and (a sense of) right and wrong. These are different modes of moral awareness. Mencius is reminding us that it is within the human capacity to have these modes of awareness. We should not forget, however, that these are only potentialities. It is their development into the virtues that give them their worth. There is a feedback effect here. The manifestation of the virtues enable us to talk of potential capacities and their cultivation. Mencius sometimes talks as if what prevents moral growth is the lack of appropriate environmental conditions. Thus, it could be said that one cultivates the seeds of the virtues by providing the conditions for moral growth. But there is another sense of "cultivation" that is nonvegetative and that he emphasizes. This involves thought and reflection of what it is to be human. In this sense, nothing is given and talk of what is potential is worthless if nothing is achieved.[43] The debate with Gaozi enables us to take a particular view of what Mencius is doing when he describes examples to illustrate *xin*—namely, he has provided us with a moral psychology of the possibilities of human relationships. One advantage of this reading is that it alleviates the problem mentioned earlier, that Mencius would find it difficult to explain why some people fail to nourish their *xin*. If we see *xin* from within the framework of what it is to be human and the possibility of human relations, then it becomes an existential possibility, one that some individuals may fail to live up to.

Mencius on *Ren* and the Problem of "Extending"

In this chapter I do for the *Mencius* what was done in chapter 2 for the *Analects*: I discuss the treatment of the concept of *ren* in the work. We have seen how Mencius views *ren* as one of the virtues developed out of the four sprouts of the heart-mind. However, we have not analyzed what *ren* actually means for him in practical terms. This is the task of the present chapter. Contrary to the common impression, *ren* is not a unitary term for Mencius. This will be clear if we situate the discussion of it within a problem for Mencius and the early Confucians—or indeed, for any moral theory, past or contemporary.[1] This is the problem of how one is supposed to extend the love or particular regard that one feels for family members toward others. Sometimes, this may involve a conflict between family commitments and public duty. How, in such cases, should one act? What moral resources does one have to deal with such cases and how may they be resolved?

Before proceeding with my discussion, it should be noted that my discussion is not focused on *Mencius* 1A:7, where Mencius tries to bring King Xuan to see that he can "extend" his compassion for an ox, toward his own people. There has been a debate on this about the nature of the reasons that can apply to this case, whether, for example, Mencius is pointing to a matter of consistency, or whether the reasons for extending compassion are more a matter of "analogical" reasoning pertaining to relevant features of particular cases.[2] Although I shall have some comments on this example later, my discussion focuses instead on how filial love can be extended. This is how the problem of "extending" has traditionally been posed for Mencius and the Confucians generally, and that pits them against the Mohists. As we shall see, there are different motivational sources and principles at work in the *Mencius*[3] that can help to address this problem. I shall also make a distinction later between "conceptual" and "empirical" issues related to the problem of extending a motivational source. There is a conceptual difficulty of extending, if it is a matter of moving from one kind of motivation to another. On the other hand, we should note that very often, the difficulty is not conceptual but empirical, as a matter of the kind of educational circumstances and training that would enable an individual to extend filial love or a particular regard to a wider social concern.

The issue of the extension of particular regard is one that the Confucians— both early and late—and their critics (for example, the Mohists and later, the

Legalists) were fully aware of. The issue can be seen to arise in *Analects* 1.2 (quoted in chapter 2). In this passage, it is held that those expressing filial love[4] would rarely transgress against superiors, and would also be unlikely to create (social) disorder. In addition, filial love is said to be the basis of (practicing) *ren*. This created a difficulty for the Neo-Confucians like Cheng Yi and Zhu Xi, who saw this as a statement of the ethical priority of filial love over *ren*. For Cheng and Zhu, this cannot, philosophically speaking, be the case. According to Zhu Xi, filial love is but one part or aspect of *ren*: one can speak of the former as the beginning of practicing the latter, but not as its root or basis.[5] Zhu Xi can be construed to be saying that although filial love may, in practical terms, come first in the development of *ren*, this does not mean that it forms the ethical basis of *ren*. In other words, filial love may have *developmental*, but not *ethical*, priority. Filial love may be developmentally prior in the sense that it is within the family context that one first has relations of love, and thereby come gradually to learn to have a regard for others in general. *Ren* is ethically prior in that it is the fundamental term of the ethical system for Zhu Xi, such that all other terms and concepts must ultimately be instantiations of it, or explained and justified in terms of it. Irene Bloom has concisely described Zhu Xi's metaphysical project, as found in his *Ren Shuo* 仁説 or *Discussion of Ren*:

> By invoking "the mind of Heaven and Earth" (*tian-di zhi xin*), he places the discussion of *ren* in a universal or cosmic context; in introducing the idea of "the character of the mind" (*xin zhi de*), he designates a metaphysical source for the "four sprouts"; by asserting that *ren* embraces all the four moral qualities, he establishes it as the all-pervasive moral quality; and by analyzing the moral qualities in terms of substance and function (*ti/yong*), he strengthens the notion of a substantial endowment prior to and more reliable than the emotional functions or expressions to which it gives rise.[6]

In effect, as an all-pervasive metaphysical source, *ren* becomes a monistic principle that circumscribes and gives rise to all other moral qualities. Put alternatively, all moral qualities can ultimately be reduced to or can ultimately be seen as, instances of *ren*. But just as Zhu Xi's reading of *ren* as a metaphysical monism fails to bring out the different ways in which *ren* constitutes an ethical *practice* in the *Analects* (as discussed in chapter 2), it similarly glosses over the dynamic tension that can arise among the different motivational reasons in the *Mencius*. This is because, instead of being a monistic principle, *ren* refers to at least three kinds of motivations in the *Mencius*, none of which can be said to be an instantiation of the other—or so I will argue. As such, there is also no one explanatory and justificatory base that would allow for a resolution of conflicts of duty. In fact, Mencius criticized the Mohists and the Yangists for holding on to one overriding principle. Referring to them, he says: "The reason for disliking those who hold to one extreme is that they cripple the Way. One thing is singled out to the neglect of a hundred others." (*Mencius* 7A: 26). These words of Mencius reveal a certain critical spirit of analysis. An investigation of *ren* undertaken in this critical spirit would do more justice to Mencius.

In the next section, I shall describe the three motivational references of *ren* for Mencius. This is followed by an analysis of the concept of "extending," and how it is supposed to work. It should be added that by the problem of "extending," I am not referring to the problem brought about by the phenomenon that although an individual knows that she ought to perform an action (acknowledged to be morally right), she nevertheless fails to perform it. This is not something that I shall discuss, namely, the problem of *akrasia* or the weakness of will that has been characterized by Western philosophers as a paradox and logical conundrum.[7] Instead, as already mentioned, the problem we shall be discussing arises in the context of filial love and how this may be extended. Since this is a philosophical discussion, I shall not restrict myself to examples from the *Mencius*, in order to bring out philosophical points more effectively. If the Mencian account of motivational sources and principles is to have any value, it should be tested against examples from elsewhere. Thus, we shall refer to a critique of the motivational basis of the Confucian school in the *Han Feizi* 韓非子, an example of Mohist reason for action from the *Lü shi chunqiu* 呂氏春秋, and an illustration of compassion in the *Gongyang Zhuan* 公羊傳.

Ren: Three Motivational Sources

As we have seen, Mencius situated *ren* within a theory of human nature, as a virtue that is developed out of the "sprout" (*duan* 端) of compassion, said to be an inherent predisposition of the heart-mind of any human being. Mencius goes so far as to identify *ren* with the heart-mind of the individual and those who do not manifest it are said to have abandoned their heart-mind: "*Ren* is the heart-mind of the human being (*ren, ren xin ye* 仁，人心也), and rightness the path to be followed by the human being (*yi, ren lu ye* 義，人路也). For someone to give up the path instead of following it and to abandon the heart-mind instead of seeking it, this is sad indeed!" (6A:11). However, in the text *ren* can be seen to refer to at least three motivational sources.

(1) Compassion

First, compassion (the inability to bear the suffering of others *bu ren ren zhi xin* 不忍人之心 2A:6) or commiseration (*ce yin zhi xin* 側隱之心 2A:6) is either said to be the sprout of *ren* (2A:6) or more directly referred to as *ren* (*ce yin zhi xin, ren ye* 側隱之心, 仁也 6A:6). In the 2A:6 example of the child about to fall into a well, Mencius holds that anyone witnessing this all of a sudden would have a spontaneous feeling of compassion or commiseration.

(2) Social Concern

Second, the *ren* person is said to love and to have concern for others in general. For instance, "The *ren* person loves others" (*ren zhe ai ren* 仁者愛人 4B:28), and "A *ren* person loves everyone" (*ren zhe wu bu ai ye* 仁者無不愛也 7A:46). Of course, the concept of *ren* itself in this context does not necessarily refer to actually "loving others." Instead, what is stated here is that the *ren* person *would* love others. But this assertion of what the *ren* person would do is strongly contrasted with the next description of *ren*.

(3) Affectionate Attachment

Thirdly, *ren* is also described as the particular love that one has for one's parents: "There are no young children who do not know loving their parents, and none of them when they grow up will not know respecting their elder brothers" (*hai ti zhi tong wu bu zhi ai qi qin zhe, ji qi zhang ye, wu bu zhi jing qi xiong ye* 孩提之童無不知愛其親者，及其長也，無不知敬其兄也). "Loving one's parents is *ren*; respecting one's elders is *yi*. What is left to be done is simply the extension of these to the whole Empire" (*qin qin, ren ye; jing zhang, yi ye; wu ta, da zhi tian xia ye* 親親，仁也：敬長，義也：無他，達之天下也 7A:15).

Mencius emphasizes the special bond between parent and child, and differentiates love of parents from the love for others. The former he calls *qin qin* (親親) which connotes affectionate attachment, and the latter is referred to as *ren min* (仁民) or a concern for the common people. As indicated by the above headings, I shall refer to these as "affectionate attachment" and "social concern," respectively. Both are distinguished from the *ai* (愛) or love for things in general *wu* (物), including animals. In the last case, *ai wu* could mean an attitude toward things or creatures such that one uses them sparingly. Mencius says:

> A noble person is sparing with living creatures but shows no *ren* towards them (*junzi zhi yu wu ye, ai zhi er fu ren* 君子之於物也，愛之而弗仁); he shows *ren* towards the common people but is not attached to them (*yu min ye, ren zhi er fu qin* 於民也，仁之而弗親). He is attached to his parents but is merely *ren* towards the common people (*qin qin er ren min* 親親而仁民); he is *ren* towards the common people but is merely sparing with living creatures (*ren min er ai wu* 仁民而愛物). (7A:45)[8]

Leaving aside the love for things and animals, I have identified three motivational sources referred to by *ren*: compassion, social concern, and affectionate attachment. The above passage spells out the principle that affectionate attachment is held to be lexically prior[9] to social concern and love for things (and animals) in general. It is implied too that there are qualitative differences among them. I use the term "lexical priority" instead of "ethical priority" to distinguish the prior ordering of certain ethical actions from the assumption of a monistic and fundamental concept in terms of which all others are to be understood, as in the case of Zhu Xi. The lexical priority of affectionate attachment over social concern is, however, only a prima facie one. Thus, it does not mean that where there is a conflict of duty between affectionate attachment and social concern, Mencius would simply abandon social concern because it is held to be less important than affectionate attachment. Rather, given a particular case, one would have to weigh the relative principles and consequences of each course of action based on the different motivations. In the process, a dynamic tension can arise between the different motivational reasons that make it difficult to say that one set of reasons and action is more important than, or overwhelmingly overrides, the other set. Another complication is to say where compassion stands in relation to the other two motives. Given the nature of compassion as an expansive motivational source I would argue that it can, on occasion, override the other two. But the mode in which compassion operates is not from the extension of a particularistic concern to a public one. Rather, compassion is a motivational force that cuts across or erases all boundaries. This will be explained in detail.

Textual Reading of "Extending"

Mencius several times describes the possession of *ren* as involving the ability to "extend" the love and concern that is manifested on one occasion to other people. The terms that are used in this regard are *ji* 及, *da* 達, and *tui* 推.

The term *ji* occurs, for instance, in the context of extending the love that one has for members of one's family toward others: "Treat the aged of your own family in a manner befitting their venerable age and extend this treatment to the aged of other families; treat your own young in a manner befitting their tender age and extend this to the young of other families" (*lao wu lao , yi ji ren zhi lao; you wu you, yi ji ren zhi you* 老吾老，以及人之老：幼吾幼，以及人之幼 1A:7). In another instance, we have: "A *ren* person extends his love from those he loves to those he does not love" (*ren zhe yi qi suo ai ji qi suo bu ai* 仁者以其所愛及其所不愛 7B:1). In this last instance, however, it is not necessarily just love for members of one's family that is being extended.

The term *tui* occurs in the following instance: "Hence one who extends his bounty can tend those within the Four Seas; one who does not cannot tend even his own family. There is just one thing in which the ancients greatly surpassed others, and that is the way they extended what they did" (*Gu tui en zu yi bao si hai, bu tui en wu yi bao qi zi. Gu zi ren suo yi da guo ren zhe, wu ta yan, shan tui qi suo wei er yi yi* 故推恩足以保四海，不推恩無以保妻子。古之人所以大過人者，無他焉，善推其所為而已矣 1A:7).

The term *da* occurs in the following: "For every person there are things he cannot bear. To extend this to what he can bear is *ren*" (*ren jie you suo bu ren, da zhi yu qi suo ren, ren ye* 人皆有所不忍，達之於其所忍，仁也 7B:31). However, in the same passage, Mencius also uses the word *chong* 充: "If someone can *chong* his natural aversion to harming others, then there will be an overabundance of *ren*" (*ren neng chong wu yu hai ren zhi xin, er ren bu ke sheng yong ye* 人能充無欲害人之心，而仁不可勝用也). D. C. Lau translates *chong* as "extend to the full." But, as we shall see, in another context where Mencius talks of the heart of compassion and where the expression *kuo er chong zhi* 擴而充之 (2A:6) is used, the word "extend" may not be as appropriate as "expand." The justification for this interpretation and its significance will be discussed later.

What exactly does the principle of "extending" involve? For instance, is it a logical notion? Another related question that naturally arises is: Given the qualitative difference between affectionate attachment and social concern and the lexical priority of the former, how is "extending" possible? As may already be evident, a tension may exist between *ren* as affectionate attachment (either of parent for child or vice versa) and as social concern. As noted in the beginning, conflicts of duty can arise as a result of this tension and we shall have to investigate how Mencius deals with them.

How Is "Extending" Possible?

The problem of "extending" is illustrated in the example of King Xuan of Qi. Given that a true king is one who tends the people, King Xuan asks Mencius whether he thinks he is capable of doing so. Mencius reminds the king that he had once ordered a sacrificial ox to be spared because he could not bear to see it suffer (*bu ren* 不忍). This indicates the presence of the sprout of *ren* in his heart-mind. Thus, the king's failure to tend his people is simply due to his not acting, and not due instead to any inability. Mencius advises him to extend the treatment of his own family to others (see the passages in 1A:7 quoted above), and asks, "Why is it then that your bounty is sufficient to reach animals yet the benefits of your government fail to reach the people?"

But if we bear in mind the qualitative difference between affectionate attachment and social concern, the act of "extending" is not as easy as Mencius makes it out to be when he says, "All you have to do is take this very heart and apply it to what is over there." Actually, Mencius himself has already indicated the difficulty in his remark to the king that he simply fails to act and not because he lacks the ability (*bu wei ye, fei bu neng ye,* 不為也，非不能也). But perhaps Mencius is trying to do something else here. Given the king's failure to act, Mencius could be trying to make him see that if he can feel for the ox, he can also feel for his people, though we have to be careful how we describe this.

Thus, it is not a matter of consistency of feeling, since consistency implies only that he should feel for the people *in the same way* that he feels for the ox. Given that love of animals is the last and lowest grade of love, Mencius cannot be saying that the king should love his people in the same way. Instead, it would be more accurate to say that Mencius is trying to *induce* the king to feel for his people and hopefully, this would lead to his acting toward their well being. He does this by reminding the king of his feeling for the ox and gently rebuking that if he can feel for the animal, why not the people?

But this only reiterates the difficulty of "extending" either one's feeling or one's action. The king cannot be a very decent person if he needs this kind of reminder in the first place. Indeed, there is something disingenuous about his asking whether he is capable of tending his people.[10]

We need to enlist the help of a critic of the Confucians here, namely, the Legalist Han Fei 韓非 (d. 233 B.C.E.), author of the text *Han Feizi*. Han Fei has noted that both the Confucians and Mohists "praise the ancient kings for their universal love of the world (*jian ai tian xia* 兼愛天下), saying that they looked after the people as parents look after a beloved child." Han Fei takes issue with two assumptions here. These are the assumptions of an ideal family education, and of the family as a basic model for other relations. He puts the case eloquently:

> Now if ruler and subject must become like father and son before there can be order, then we must suppose that there is no such thing as an unruly father or son (*fu yi jun chen wei ru fu zi ze bi zhi, tui shi yan zhi, shi wu luan fu zi ye* 夫以君臣為如父子則必治，推是言之，是無亂父子也). Among human affections none takes priority over the love of parents for their children (*ren zhi qing xing, mo xian yu fu mu* 人之情性，莫先於父母). But though all parents may show love for their children, the children are not always well behaved. And though the parents may love them even more, will this prevent the children from becoming unruly? Now the love of the ancient kings for their people was no greater than the love of parents for their children. And if such love cannot prevent children from becoming unruly, then how can it bring the people to order (*jin xian wang zhi ai min, bu guo fu mu zhi ai zi, zi wei bi bu luan ye, ze min xi ju zhi zai* 今先王之愛民，不過父母之愛子，子未必不亂也，則民奚遽治哉)?[11]

Han Fei has homed in on an important aspect of what the Confucians mean by "extending" here. This is the thought that one can be educated in the family setting to be concerned about others. The close interaction one has with parents and other family members is somehow supposed to bring about an ethic of care and consideration, respect and reverence for others. Thus, for the Confucians, filial love is not merely a form of *ren*, but as stated in *Analects* 1.2, it is "the root (or beginning) of practicing *ren*." This involves what I have referred to as a "developmental" priority. However, as Han Fei so cogently puts it, there is no guarantee that there will be no unruly sons. In other words, one cannot assume an ideal family order whereby all children come to be well behaved through parental love and by extension, an ideal social order where all citizens become orderly through the *ren* of rulers. Despite this criticism, the issue is deserving of more complex treatment and I shall remark further on this in the conclusion.

Conflicts of Duty

It is not quite accurate to lump the Confucians together with the Mohists in espousing universal love, as Han Fei does in the above passage. Mencius criticizes the Mohists for assuming that it is possible for one to love members of another family as much as one's own. He accuses Yi Zhi, a Mohist, of inconsistency between holding that the practice of love begins with affectionate attachment toward one's parents on the one hand, and stating that there should be no gradations in love (*ai wu cha deng* 愛無差等 3A:5) on the other. But does Mencius's opposite insistence of there being gradations undermine the Confucian belief in the duty of having social concern? The following two examples would seem to indicate so.

Mencius is asked by Tao Ying to consider what should be done if Sage Emperor Shun's father had killed someone. Mencius replies: "The only thing to do was to apprehend him." Next, Mencius is asked whether Shun would not have tried to prevent this from happening. He replies, "How could Shun stop it? Gao Yao (the judge) had authority for what he did." Pressed to say what Shun would have done, Mencius says, "Shun looked upon casting the Empire as no more than discarding a worn shoe. He would have secretly carried the old man on his back and fled to the edge of the Sea and lived there happily, never giving a thought to the Empire" (*le er wang tian xia* 樂而忘天下 7A:35).

In another instance, Wan Zhang queries Shun's "banishing" his brother and putting him nominally in charge of a fief instead of punishing him like four others, even though the brother was the wickedest among them (*zhi bu ren* 至不仁). Mencius replies: "A *ren* person never harbors anger or nurses a grudge against a brother. All he does is to have affectionate love for him (*qin ai zhi er yi yi* 親愛之而已矣). Because he has affection for him (*qin zhi* 親之), he wishes him to enjoy rank; because he loves him (*ai zhi* 愛之), he wishes him to enjoy wealth. If as Emperor he were to allow his brother to be a nobody, could that be described as having affectionate love for him (*ke wei qin ai zhi hu* 可謂親愛之乎 5A:3)?"

The first thing that strikes us about these examples is the lexical priority Mencius seems to give to affectionate attachment. Compare them with the following example from another text, the *Lü shi chunqiu*. Fu Tun was a Mohist leader in the state of Qin. His son had murdered someone. Presumably, there were no extenuating circumstances and this was a crime deserving capital punishment. The ruler of Qin informed Fu Tun that he had ordered that his son be spared, because this was his only son and Fu Tun was too old to beget another son. Fu Tun replied that the law should be carried out because it would prevent (further) injuring and killing, and this is "the most important moral principle in the world (*fu jin sha shang ren zhe, tian xia zhi da yi ye* 夫禁殺傷人者，天下之大義也)." He had his son executed, and the text comments: "A son is what a man is most partial to. Yet Fu Tun endured the loss of what he was most partial to in order to observe his most important moral principle. The Mohist leader may properly be called impartial (*zi, ren zhi suo si ye, ren suo si yi xing da yi, ju zi ke wei gong yi* 子，人之所私也，忍所私以行大義，鉅子可謂公矣)."[12]

We learn from this example that social concern (in this case the specific concern that people refrain from killing each other) sometimes requires impartiality and strict adherence to the law. It is to the Mohist leader's credit that he was prepared to uphold the law even if it meant a tragic personal loss, and here we realize that there is an aspect of "universal love" which means taking the impartial attitude (*gong* 公) that every individual is morally equal.

Nevertheless, it would be wrong to construe Mencius as simply abandoning social concern and the impartiality that goes with it when these conflict with affectionate attachment. In the first example, his reply to the question what should be done if Shun's father had killed someone is immediate and direct: the father should be arrested. Furthermore, Shun would not stop the law from taking its course. Although Shun would run away with his father, he would do so only as a private citizen after "casting the Empire," that is, giving up the throne. Mencius is thus conscious of distinguishing between the private and the public domains and their corresponding duties. In the second example, Mencius is careful to add that Shun's brother "was not allowed to take any action in his fief. The Emperor appointed officials to administer the fief and to collect tributes and taxes. For this reason it was described as banishment. Xiang (his brother) was certainly not permitted to ill-use the people." Thus, a closer examination reveals that Mencius is concerned to balance affectionate attachment with the public standards of morality and law, consistently with (having) social concern.

But this is not to say that Mencius's attempts to balance the conflict of duties necessarily work. On the contrary, his solutions in the two examples regarding Emperor Shun are too ideal. It is almost as if he refuses to see the possibility of a tragedy, say, in the case of Shun's father. Compare his proposed solution with the case of the Mohist leader Fu Tun who refuses the royal offer to spare his son. We should not imagine that Fu Tun's decision to uphold the law is not a personally tragic one for him (although theoretically, there is no tension and no question about the course of action to be taken). We can conceive a similarly tragic scenario for Shun in the imperative that his father is to be arrested and that Shun would not interfere with the processes of the law. Nevertheless, the aplomb with which Mencius states his (hypothetical) solution to the conflict simply takes one's breath away. He assumes that Shun could drop his public persona and put on his private one—just like that! Interestingly, Mencius's statement that "Shun looked upon casting aside the Empire as no more than discarding a worn shoe" has a distinctively Yangist and Daoist flavor about it.[13]

As mentioned, the Mohists assumed that it was possible to love members of another family as much as one's own. Mencius rightly criticized this as psychologically unrealistic. However, in his anxiety to combat what he saw as the erroneous views of the Mohists, he seems to have overemphasized affectionate attachment and it appeared as if this overrode everything else. As we have just seen, this is not quite accurate. We have noted instead that Mencius is concerned to balance affectionate attachment with social concern. How successfully this can be carried out in specific cases is another matter.

So far, we have explored the problem of "extending" and how conflicts of duty occurring between affectionate attachment and social concern can be resolved. Earlier, I intimated that the word *chong* in the context of compassion could perhaps be read as "expanding" instead of "extending." This refers to the possibility of compassion as a motivational source and principle that can sometimes override the two other forms of *ren*.

Compassion

To repeat, Mencius also speaks of *ren* in terms of compassion or "a heart that is sensitive to the suffering of others," and not as the extending of affectionate attachment toward others. This suggests that compassion is a motivational source conceived independently of affectionate attachment and social concern (involving the notion of impartiality). His example of a child about to fall into a well postulates a person who witnesses this, and that this person "would certainly be moved to compassion." The common reading is that this "proves" the universal existence of a heart-mind of compassion.

But as we have seen in the previous chapter, there is another way to read Mencius. What he actually says is this: "He would certainly be moved to compassion, not because he wanted to get in the good graces of the parents, nor because he wished to win the praise of his fellow villagers or friends, nor yet because he disliked the cry of the child (2A:6)." Mencius is distinguishing compassion from the other motives described. In other words, there is such a thing as being moved by the suffering of others, and this motivation is uniquely different from all the other motivations listed, including, we might add, affectionate attachment and social concern.

This is still true, even if someone points out the inadequacy of the so-called "proof." We may appreciate Mencius's statement of a distinctive motivation if we bear in mind his debate with Gaozi (6A:1–6). To recapitulate: Gaozi insists that human beings are motivated only by appetitive desires and that this is their nature (*shi se xing ye* 食色性也 6A:4). Mencius is reminding us of the existence of moral motivations: of compassion, a sense of righteousness, shame, and a sense of right and wrong. These stand independently from appetitive desires and may in fact judge the quality and worth of our desires.

In the central 2A:6 passage, the term that Mencius uses for developing the four sprouts is *kuo chong* (*kuo er chong zhi* 擴而充之). This connotes a broadening or a filling up of the heart-mind, and unlike "extending" does not imply a movement from one grade of love to another. I have suggested that in this regard, it may be more appropriate to talk of an "expanding" of the heart-mind, instead of "extending." Someone might still ask, but how is one supposed to develop or to "expand" one's heart-mind? Mencius goes so far as to say that the person who does not do this would not be able even to serve his parents (*gou bu neng chong zhi, bu zu yi shi fu mu* 苟不能充之，不足以事父母). It might perhaps be asked whether this doesn't contradict the priority of affectionate attachment?

Behind this question, there lurks the inappropriate image of *extending* affectionate attachment toward social concern (or in the case of King Xuan, from love for animals to people). But, if we refer instead to *expanding* the sprout of compassion in the heart-mind, Mencius is reminding us that human beings are such that they can be directly moved by the plight of others, in a way that cuts across family and other loyalties and does not involve a movement from one grade of love to another. What happens in such cases is like an opening up or an original groundswell. Or as Mencius puts it, it would be "like a fire starting up or a spring coming through (*ruo huo zhi shi ran, quan zhi shi da* 若火之始然，泉之始達 2A:6)."[14]

The example of the child imminently falling into a well is also mentioned in 3A:5. In response to the Mohist Yi Zhi's comment that the Confucians approved of the ancients for acting "as if they were tending a new-born babe (*ruo bao chi zi* 若保赤子)" and that this implies no gradations in love, Mencius replies, "Does Yi Zhi truly believe that a person loves his brother's son no more than his neighbour's new-born babe? He is singling out a special feature in a certain case: when the new-born babe creeps towards a well it is not its fault (*fu Yi Zhi xin yi wei ren zhi qin qi xiong zhi zi wei ruo qin qi lin zhi chi zi hu? Bi you qu er ye. Chi zi pu fu jiang ru jing, fei chi zi zhi zui ye* 夫夷子信以為人之親其兄之子為若親其鄰之赤子乎？彼有取爾也。赤子匍匐將入井，非赤子之罪也)." The statement "*Bi you qu er ye*" is unclear, and we rely here on Lau's translation, "He (Yi Zhi) is singling out a special feature in a certain case." Nevertheless, it is clear from the context that the motivation in saving the innocent child cuts across any special affection that one may have, say, for one's nephew/niece. In other words, compassion is a distinct motive from affectionate attachment and *a fortiori* not the result of its "extending." Perhaps the example of the child in imminent danger has become something of a cliché. We need a fresh and more substantive example that will help us to see how compassion could cancel out the other motivations. The following example is from the *Gongyang Zhuan*, a text that is much earlier than the *Mencius*. This may be somewhat anachronistic, but as mentioned in the beginning, we are making a philosophical point and testing the validity of Mencius's description of a motivational source.

In their siege on the capital city of Song, Prince Zhuang of Chu and his troops had only seven days of rations left. Sima Zhi Fan of Chu climbed a hill to observe the besieged city. There he chanced upon Hua Yuan from the besieged city who informed him that his people were starved to the extent of being forced to eat each other's children, and having to use their bones for fuel. Sima asked why he was revealing this. Hua replied: "I have heard it said, the noble person seeing others in difficulties would pity them (*jin zhi* 矜之), the ignoble person would rejoice. I see in you a noble person, and thus I told you." Sima revealed that the siege could not last much longer given the insufficient rations on his own side, and added that they (the people of Song) should persevere. Returning to camp, Sima told his prince about the desperate plight of the people of Song. His prince was delighted and wanted to storm the city at once. Sima confessed that he had revealed that the siege could not last much longer. Prince Zhuang angrily insisted on storming the city at once. Sima's reply was that he would have nothing to do with it, and was leaving. Apparently having to rely on Sima, Prince Zhuang abandoned the siege.[15]

From one perspective Sima Zhi Fan's disclosure was treasonable and broke all social duties and norms (for example, the duty to one's state and loyalty to one's prince). Nevertheless, he broke them because he responded to Hua Yuan and the plight of the people of Song with compassion. This is a good example of the expansion of the heart-mind that we mentioned earlier, in discussing the phrase, *kuo er chong zhi*. To repeat Mencius's words, it is "like a fire starting up or a spring coming through."

Conclusion

Despite the Cheng-Zhu attempt to harmonize all moral motivations in terms of a metaphysically monistic principle of *ren*, we have identified at least three different motivational references of *ren* in the *Mencius*: affectionate attachment, social concern, and compassion. A tension exists between affectionate attachment and social concern and sometimes this leads to conflicts of duty. Against the background of this possibility, we discussed the following two issues: (1) How Mencius views the nature of these conflicts and how he would resolve them, and (2) How Mencius thinks that filial love or affectionate attachment can be extended. The answers to both questions have been presented in terms of examples from both the *Mencius* and other texts.

In the two examples involving Emperor Shun, there are tensions between affectionate attachment and wider considerations of duty consistent with social concern. Mencius's insistence on the gradations of love gives the impression that he would necessarily fall on the side of affectionate attachment when it conflicts with social concern. But in fact, Mencius gave proper cognizance to the duties arising out of both motivational values, despite the fact that in theory, he places affectionate attachment over social concern in a lexical ordering. In the example that we discussed, Mencius's hypothetical solution of Shun abandoning the empire and carrying his father away is due to his (perhaps naïve) belief that in a case of conflict between the public and the private, one can easily drop one's public role and the corresponding duties and responsibilities that go with that role. However, it is not due to any belief that the duties of affectionate attachment *necessarily* override those of social concern or that the duties called for by social concern are less important than the former.

Insofar as Mencius recognizes the existence of different motivational principles and the possibility that they may conflict, he can be said to be a motivational pluralist (in contrast to the Mohists). His insistence on the different grades of love means that he recognizes their conceptual differences and the possible tensions that could arise among them. These too are signs of his pluralistic tendencies and are consistent with his condemnation of the Mohists and the Yangists for singling out one thing "to the neglect of a hundred others." Mencius's statements about compassion also amount to the recognition of a motivational source and principle that is distinct from affectionate attachment and social concern. On certain occasions, compassion can erase the boundaries created by the other motivations.

We discussed how the extension of filial love or affectionate attachment is supposed to work. After surveying the logical difficulties for Mencius, we looked at how Han Fei ridiculed the seemingly naïve Confucian belief of a correlation between family love and social order. Perhaps it is a mistake to have required a solution in the logical sense. In other words, the problem of "extending" filial love is not a logical problem. In this regard, we noted that Han Fei has put his finger on an important aspect of what the Confucians mean by "extending." That is, the source and the basis of social order lies in what is learned and practiced within the family, of care and consideration, respect and reverence for others.[16]

Despite Han Fei's criticism, I indicated that the issue is more complex. Here is what I mean. There are two issues here, conceptual and empirical. *Conceptually*, the kind of love that arises out of a bonding between parent and child cannot be the same as the concern for others in general. This is why we had trouble in understanding how affectionate attachment could be extended. (The same trouble in understanding arises equally here for both the Mohists and the Confucians.) On the other hand, it is an *empirical* question whether and how far the care and consideration for others that one learns in the context of the family can result in one having an ethic of social concern.

Like Han Fei, we can see that there is no straightforward correlation between family relations/order and social relations/order. Nevertheless, we should not think that the Confucian idea of a linkage between family and social ethics is too simple. We tend to think so only because we forget that the Confucians have developed a whole ritual corpus linking family and society, and that filial love and respect as well as a host of other values and emotional attitudes are expressed through ritual and cultural forms at various levels and on various occasions. These rituals serve not only regulatory functions, but constitutive ones as well, in other words, they allow for the creation of social processes whereby the individual could be emotionally, culturally, and morally transformed.

Mencius did not pay much attention to these social processes because he was concerned to argue against people like Gaozi that there are certain basic moral predispositions that are not the result of a (seemingly arbitrary) social construction. In the absence of a discussion of the social processes involved, however, the link between family relations and the social order can seem very tenuous and this is another reason why we had some difficulty with Mencius's notion of "extending" affectionate attachment. Xunzi, coming after Mencius, could be said to have noticed this difficulty and emphasized the transformative social processes of the rites. This is the topic of the following chapters.

Xunzi's Critique of Mencius

Xunzi has traditionally been seen as disagreeing with Mencius that human nature is good, holding instead that human nature is "evil" or "bad." As we shall see, this needs to be heavily qualified, for it is only one aspect of a larger concern with social transformation. This concern is intimately tied up with the aesthetic and moral transformation of the individual through ritual, something that Confucius was himself concerned with. But first, this chapter will deal with Xunzi's critique of Mencius.[1]

According to some commentators, Xunzi's criticism of Mencius's thesis that human nature is good depends more on his legislating the meaning of *xing* 性 (nature) than on substantive argument.[2] It is also claimed that in the course of his critique Xunzi is committed to accepting Mencius's thesis that human nature is good.[3] Against these views, I shall offer what I think is a more accurate account of Xunzi's critique of Mencius's position. The account is based on an elaboration of the distinction that Xunzi makes in the *Xing E Pian* 性惡篇 ("Nature is Bad") between *ke yi* 可以 (capacity) and *neng* 能 (ability). While others have noted this distinction, I believe that it plays a greater role in making Xunzi's critique of Mencius more systematic and substantive than it is usually thought to be.[4]

It will help the reader to understand the analysis to follow if I introduce my reading of Xunzi's position first. According to Xunzi, Mencius assumes a state of nature wherein human beings have moral resources that they can voluntarily call upon at any time. This assumption is based upon certain organic analogies, for example, the capacity of the eyes to see at the same time constitutes (barring any accident or interference) the ability to see. Xunzi denies the application of this organic construal to the ability to act morally by making the distinction between having a capacity and being able to be or to do something. Thus, the ability to be a sage depends in the first place upon the fact that there is a rationale to morality that can be learned, as well as the possession of cognitive and instrumental capacities that would allow someone to learn this rationale. However, these do not necessarily translate into the ability to be a sage on the part of the individual. This is because she might not voluntarily work on the capacities that she possesses, and neither can she be forced to. Furthermore, this unwillingness may be due to certain qualities of character that may not dispose her to exerting herself toward the goal of being a sage. The transformative rationale of the rites is something that the sages cognized and worked at. They were able to transform themselves and institute processes to influence others. Even though ordinary persons too have the basic capacities, they do not have the same abilities as the sages to transform themselves, but require the force of institutions to curb their excesses and to mold their characters.

Talk of the "capacity" to be a sage might incline one to think that Xunzi's position may not be very different from Mencius's, since Mencius too claims the necessity of working at the moral "sprouts" that everyone is said to possess. Indeed, Xunzi is aware of the question, if (as he claims) nature is "evil," how can morality be instituted? If the sages were able to transform themselves and institute moral processes, does this not admit that there were certain resources that they could use in the first place, and in this sense, does it not mean that human nature is good? Xunzi's most direct reply is, "The potter molds clay to make an earthenware dish, but how could the dish be regarded as part of the potter's inborn nature?" (Knoblock 23.4a). In other words, we should not assume that any product that we make together with the constitutive structure that it has must have belonged to our nature originally. Conversely, it should not be assumed that the ingredients, capacities, and processes that go into any invention must have the same formal and constitutive structure as the final product.

Xunzi develops this point when he questions Mencius's assumption that the moral resources are ready-made or inborn. First, he adopts a deflationary strategy by saying that birth is in itself a process of moving away from any original, simple organic state. In other words, there is no such state. He also reminds us of certain ugly aspects of human nature such as self-interested tendencies and feelings of envy and hatred. Second, Xunzi goes on to expand upon the rationale of morality in terms of the necessary regulation of people's desires so as to bring about social order and the effective allocation of scarce resources. In a passage from the *Li Lun Pian* 禮論篇 ("Discourse on Ritual Principles") Xunzi argues that both the original raw material of nature (*xing*) and human artifice (*wei* 偽) are mutually necessary to bring about morality. As we shall see, this passage fits very nicely into a certain section of the *Xing E Pian*, where Xunzi goes on to argue that ritual is required to curb certain desires. At the same time, however, such rituals give rise to the expression of say, acts of deference. In the *Li Lun Pian* and the *Yue Lun Pian* 樂論篇 ("Discourse on Music") Xunzi describes the rationale of morality in terms of constitutive processes that give rise to ritual behavior. In spelling out these processes, Xunzi in effect denies that the development of morality is an organic process of nurturing certain original sprouts, even though he may admit that people have feelings of love and righteousness. Later, we shall see what this notion of "righteousness" amounts to for Xunzi. Constitutive processes are not just regulatory; they transform raw capacities into refined sensibilities, feelings, and emotions. Mencius's underlying belief in a simple organic state is therefore insufficient to account for the nature of morality, described in terms of the constitutive rationale of the rites.

Once again, it is important to understand the nature of this "insufficiency." Contrary to Mencius, it is not the failure to exercise one's moral abilities that is in question. Instead, the constitutive rationale of the rites elaborates the earlier point: just like the earthenware dish, moral and ritual rules could not have been part of original human nature. Put in terms of the capacity/ability distinction, ritual or moral ability may be the result of certain capacities. It does not follow, however, that ritual or moral ability has the same structure as the capacities that brought them about, or that such a structural ability was originally there in the first place. And it would beg the question to assume that the capacities that give rise to ritual and moral ability must themselves be ritual or moral capacities.

Capacity versus Ability

In this section, I describe Xunzi's distinction between *ke yi* or "(having the) capacity" and *neng* or "(having the) ability." The terms are discussed in two related analogies in *Mencius* 1A:7 and *Xunzi* 23.5b. A description of Mencius's analogy allows us to state his position. Comparison with Xunzi's analogy enables us to clarify the logic of his distinction.

In *Mencius* 1A:7 King Xuan of Qi asks for the difference between *bu wei* 不為 and *bu neng* 不能 or between not acting and being unable. Mencius cites "striding over the North Sea with Mount Tai under your arm" as an example of what one is unable to do. On the other hand, if one claims that one is unable to make obeisance to one's elders, one is actually not acting instead of being unable. The king's not being a (true) king does not belong to the category of "striding over the North Sea with Mount Tai under your arm" but to the category of (not) making obeisance to one's elders. No person possesses the strength to do the former. Since making obeisance to one's elders and being a true king do not require this kind of strength, one has both the capacity and the ability to do so. Similarly, given that being a true king and being a sage require the practice of compassionate government, this is a capacity that all persons have, according to Mencius, and failing to act compassionately is simply not doing so.

We discussed in the last chapter the problem of "extending" in relation to this case. For the sake of the argument in this chapter, we repeat some of the following details. King Xuan had earlier asked whether he could become a king who is able to tend and protect the people. When Mencius replies that he can, King Xuan asks how he knows this. Mencius refers to an incident in which King Xuan had spared a sacrificial ox because he "cannot bear (*bu ren* 不忍) to see it shrinking with fear, like an innocent man going to the place of execution." The term *bu ren* recurs in 2A:6 where Mencius introduces his theory of the four sprouts of the heart-mind. According to Mencius, all persons possess a heart-mind that cannot bear the suffering of others (*bu ren ren zhi xin* 不忍人之心).

This was why the Former Kings could practice compassionate government (*bu ren ren zhi zheng* 不忍人之政). In the same passage Mencius goes on to cite the example of a child about to fall into a well as evidence that "No person is devoid of a heart sensitive to the suffering of others."

Having a heart-mind that cannot bear the suffering of others is stated here as a precondition of the practice of compassionate government. If we take this practice as equivalent to the practice of being a sage, Mencius is saying that an act of sageliness is dependent upon the capacity to feel compassion for others. And his claim is that everyone is able to become sagely, since everyone has the capacity. Mencius reiterates the comparison with strength when the king asks how he knew that his heart accorded with that of a (true) king: a feather is not lifted because one does not use one's strength (*bu yong li* 不用力), and one's failure to see a cartload of firewood is because one does not use one's eyes (*bu yong ming* 不用明). Similarly, the people are not protected because one does not use one's kindness (*bu yong en* 不用恩). Mencius concludes that the reason for the king's not being a true king is that he does not act, not because he is unable. For Mencius, therefore, moral action is a matter of calling upon resources that are entirely within one's control. The same point is repeated in 6B:2 where Mencius is asked whether everyone is capable of becoming a Yao or a Shun (i.e. a sage). His reply is that there is no difficulty: all one has to do is act. The problem is not one of strength but not acting (*fu wei er* 弗為耳). The impossibility of "striding over the North Sea with Mount Tai under your arm" thus represents a strong contrast with what one has the capacity and the ability to do, that is, draw upon the moral resources at hand.[5]

Compare this with Xunzi's analogy of one's feet having the capacity to *pian xing tian xia* 遍行天下 in 23.5b. I shall leave this untranslated for the moment because it is ambiguous. The analogy comes immediately after the statement that the ordinary person *ke yi* be a Yu (a sage), but it is not necessarily the case that she *neng* be one. Xunzi adds that although she *bu neng* be a sage, this does not prevent (*wu hai* 無害) her from having the capacity. He goes on: "The feet *ke yi pian xing tian xia*, however there has never been (*wei chang you* 未嘗有) one who has done so." Given the context, we should understand this last clause as meaning to say that no one, in other words, no ordinary person, *neng* do so.

The ambiguity of *pian xing tian xia* is evident from a comparison of the different translations of Knoblock's: "across the width of the whole world," and Watson's: "to every corner of the earth" (Watson, 167–68). If we follow Knoblock, the analogy may well refer to an empirical possibility since walking across the width of the world is something that can be achieved although no ordinary person has been able to do so. (We should not have the image here of circumnavigating the globe.) This leaves room for saying that only certain persons like Yu have been able to be sages.

Watson's reading, on the other hand, is congruent with Mencius's example of something that is empirically impossible since it is as impossible to walk to "every corner" of the earth as it is to "stride over the North Sea," et cetera. However, this would not fit Xunzi's claim that some people like Yu are able to be sages. On Watson's reading too, we might have to interpret Xunzi's use of *ke yi* as "can" in the sense of a logical possibility (instead of having a "capacity"). In other words, although it is empirically impossible to walk to every corner of the earth, this would still be logically possible. But it is doubtful that this was what Xunzi had in mind. Thus, I propose that we adopt Knoblock's reading of *pian xing tian xia* as "(walking) across the width of the world."[6] This means that while Xunzi denies Mencius's claim that everyone is able to be a sage, he nevertheless does not deny that everyone has the capacity to do so. What having this capacity means is something that he discusses in 23.5a, and the reasons why the ordinary person is unable to do so—despite having the capacity—are spelt out in 23.5b.

Xunzi concludes 23.5b with the following two statements. First, having the capacity to do something or to be someone (*ke yi wei*) does not necessarily mean being able (*wei bi neng* 未必能); and contrariwise, being unable does not prevent one's having the capacity (*wu hai ke yi wei* 無害可以為). Second, and more emphatically, "'Being able or not able' and 'having the capacity or not': they are far from being the same, and it is clear that they are not interchangeable." (*Neng bu neng zi yu ke bu ke, qi bu tong yuan yi, qi bu ke yi xiang wei ming yi* 能不能之與可不可，其不同遠矣，其不可以相為明矣。) Clearly, Xunzi is asserting that a logical gap exists between "capacity" and "ability."

Explaining the Distinction

Left unexplained, it may seem puzzling that someone with the capacity is unable to do something or be somebody. Xunzi provides an explanation in terms of further requirements such as the necessity of exerting oneself in learning, so as to fulfill the capacity or capacities that one has. This explanation leads to the point that the rationale of morality and the laws are such that they require much effort to learn and to exercise. In other words, the knowledge and implementation of this rationale is not equivalent to the capacities that we all have. In this section, we look at Xunzi's explanation of the distinction.

Passage 23.5a begins with the saying, "An ordinary person[7] *ke yi* become a Yu." At the same time, it is asked, "What does this mean?" The question concerns what is involved for anyone to be a Yu or a sage. In 23.5b the question is raised: "How is it possible for the sage to reach this high state through his [cumulative] effort, but the rest of mankind cannot?" (Knoblock).[8] This poses the sage against others, in terms of what the sage alone is able to achieve.

The paradox is resolved by showing that although being a sage involves the possession of cognitive and instrumental capacities[9] for knowing and acting upon the rationale (*li* 理)[10] of morality and the laws (*ren yi fa zheng* 仁義法正 23.5a),[11] the ordinary person is either unwilling or cannot be forced to exert herself despite having these capacities (23.5b). 23.5a concludes with a further statement of what is actually required to be a Yu. This involves a process of *xue* 學 or learning the rationale of morality and the laws. This is done through concentrating one's mind and will, thinking and investigating over time, and in this way tirelessly accumulating goodness (*ji shan* 積善) and thereby achieving a spiritual clarity (*shen ming* 神明), even to the extent of forming a triad with Heaven and Earth. The last sentence of 23.5a says that the sage is one who arrives where she is through cumulative effort (*suo ji er zhi yi* 所積而致矣). In 23.5b, it is stated that the ordinary person cannot be made or forced (*bu ke shi* 不可使) to work at it. In other words, there is a strong element of voluntariness that determines whether anyone makes the effort or not. Xunzi illustrates with the following example: the ignoble person (*xiao ren* 小人) has the capacity to be a noble person, but does not want to be (*bu ken* 不肯) one. Similarly, the noble person has the capacity to be an ignoble person, but does not want to be one. In other words, each can be (like) the other (*xiang wei* 相為), but cannot be forced to do so.

Following this Xunzi says, *Gu tu zhi ren ke yi wei Yu, ze ran; tu zhi ren neng wei Yu, ze wei bi ran ye. Sui bu neng wei Yu, wu hai ke yi wei Yu.* 故塗之人可以為禹，則然：塗之人能為禹，則未必然也。雖不能為禹，無害可以為禹 "Thus, it follows (*gu . . . ze ran*) that the ordinary person has the capacity to be a Yu; even though it is not necessarily the case (*ze wei bi ran*) that the ordinary person is able to be a Yu. Although (the ordinary person is) unable to be a Yu, this does not prevent her from having the capacity to be a Yu." The word *gu* ("thus") indicates that the statement follows upon the previous one, "(A person) has the capacity but cannot be forced (*bu ke shi*)." This is taken to imply that "'Having the capacity' does not necessarily mean 'able'?" On the surface, these are two different things. The fact that one cannot be forced or does not want to do something should not imply that one may be unable. Xunzi is thinking along the following lines: "The ordinary person has the cognitive and instrumental capacities to learn the rationale of morality and the laws. In other words, the basic conditions for being a sage are there. But she is unable to be a sage because she does not work at it, and no one can force her." It might appear that Xunzi lapses into the way that Mencius talks: "People have the capacity to be a sage, except that they do not want to act on it. If they do act, however, they would be able to be a sage." But Xunzi's discussion is more complex in that he has in mind the different make-ups of different people. This comes out in the following example.

The example reads, *fu gong jiang nong gu, wei chang bu ke yi xiang wei shi ye, ran er wei chang neng xiang wei shi ye* 夫工匠農賈，未嘗不可以相為事也，然而未嘗能相為事也. That is, "The artisan, carpenter, farmer, and trader: it is not that they do not have the capacity to perform the work of the other, nevertheless, they have not been able to perform the work of the other." This implies that each category of worker has both the cognitive and instrumental capacities that would enable him or her to pick up the skills of another category, as well as the fact that the form and rationale (*wen li* 文理) of each skill is something available to anyone to learn. Nevertheless, this does not mean that each is able to perform the work of the other, presumably because (following the earlier analysis) they do not want to exert themselves to learn the skills of the other. The problem with Xunzi's way of putting it is that, as he says, "they have not been able (*wei chang neng*) to perform the work of the other," and this may not be true. One could conceive of the farmer, say, taking up the training and the work required to be a carpenter, and vice versa.[12]

Although in this example Xunzi speaks of doing the work of the other (*xiang wei shi* 相為事), the line of thought I have just offered opens up another consideration. That is, it may not be possible for one to *xiang wei*—one may just not possess the talents or distinctive qualities of another. It is in this sense that the carpenter may not have the ability to be a trader, artisan, or farmer despite having the basic cognitive and instrumental skills. This is because she might not possess some distinctive quality (say, the sagacity of a trader) that would enable her to be any of these things. Similarly, the ignoble person may be unable to be a noble person, and vice versa. Her character may be such that she is not disposed to exerting herself and to learn. The noble person, on the other hand, would be disposed to perfecting herself. In a distinctly qualitative way, she may just be different from the ignoble person.

This explanation of the distinction between "capacity" and "ability" reinforces an earlier argument in the *Xing E Pian*. In saying that certain individuals have characters and temperaments such that they exert themselves to learn and apply the rationale of morality and the laws, Xunzi is reinforcing the argument that morality and the laws do not come in a raw organic state but instead require much thought and effort.

Denying the Organic Construal of Morality

In this section, I shall show how the earlier parts of the *Xing E Pian* connect with 23.5a/b. In particular, we shall see how Xunzi attacks Mencius's picture of morality as an organic simple state we are equipped with from birth.

In the first few passages of the *Xing E Pian* (23.1a–c), Xunzi asserts that *xing* is "bad" and that rites and righteousness (*li yi* 禮義) are the result of human artifice. While nature is something we are born with, behavior according to the principles of the rites and righteousness must be learned. These principles were in fact created by the sages to "straighten out" (Knoblock, *jiao shi* 矯飾) people's characters and to set them aright (Knoblock, *zheng* 正). He goes further in 23.1d with a diagnosis of the Mencian idea that "nature is good" (*xing shan* 性善) and that badness is a result of the loss of this nature. As Xunzi sees it, this idea is due to an underlying belief in the original existence of a simple state of the human being. Presumably, beauty is thought to abide in this original simple state (*bu li qi pu er mei zhi* 不離其朴而美之). At the same time, it is also thought that there are beneficial resources lying within this simple state (*bu li qi zi er li zhi ye* 不離其資而利之也). Xunzi is referring to the beneficial resources of goodness. This inseparability of goodness from the original state is organically and functionally construed (by Mencius), just as certain natural abilities are inseparably linked with the sense organs. For example, as sight is inseparable from the eyes, and acuity of hearing is inseparable from the ears.

Evidently, Xunzi thinks that this is a naive and idealistic picture of human nature. He deflates it by saying that the moment one is born, one has already moved away from whatever original simplicity there may be. This deflationary strategy has in fact already been adopted right from the start of the chapter (23.1a), where Xunzi points to certain human tendencies such as being born with a love of benefit (*hao li* 好利). He also reminds us of the feelings of envy and hatred (*ji wu* 疾惡).[13] Later in 23.6a he has the emperor Shun saying, *ren qing shen bu mei* 人情甚不美, "Man's emotions are very unlovely!" Here, he mentions examples like a son who is no longer filial once he has started a family of his own, and people who are no longer trustworthy or loyal once they have achieved what was desired.

In mentioning these tendencies Xunzi is not asserting that human desires and emotions are intrinsically bad, despite the fact that he begins the chapter with the statement, "Nature is bad (*xing e*)." Donald Munro has recently argued that we should understand this in the context of Xunzi's macro-concern of how to match desires with scarce resources.[14] If unregulated and uncultivated, the desires of people would lead to wrangling and social disorder, resulting in a very incommodious situation for all. Further, in other chapters where Mencius is not the target of his criticisms, Xunzi does seem to allow for feelings of love for one's own kind, remembrance of and longing for the deceased, having a sense of *yi* or righteousness, and even talks of arousing one's *shan xin* 善心 or good heart when discussing the function and role of music.[15]

The admission of these feelings does not undermine Xunzi's case against Mencius. The argument is not just that Mencius's picture of an original state of simplicity is naive, and Xunzi does not just stop at providing reminders of certain self-interested tendencies. As we have seen, he further argues (in 23.1d) that goodness and morality do not come in an organically raw state. This point is reinforced through his account of the rationale of the rites and the necessity of human artifice, and it is subsequently hammered home by the capacity/ability distinction.

Before making this distinction, however, Xunzi makes a related and important point. First he posits the objection: "An inquirer says: Ritual principles, morality, accumulated effort, and acquired abilities are part of human nature, which is why the sages were able to produce them." He replies: "The potter molds clay to make an earthenware dish, but how could the dish be regarded as part of the potter's inborn nature? The artisan carves wood to make a vessel, but how could the wooden vessel be regarded as part of the artisan's nature? The sage's relation to ritual principles is just like that of the potter molding clay. This being so, how could ritual principles, morality, accumulated effort, and acquired abilities be part of original human nature?" (Knoblock 23.4a).[16] Xunzi is saying that ritual principles and morality (or rites and righteousness) are products that have a different form and structure from the original processes and ingredients that go into their construction. Given that they have a different form and structure, they cannot be said to be in one's nature from the beginning. We can construe Xunzi to be pointing to a variant of the genetic fallacy:[17] one should not assume that morality or goodness has the same form as what gives rise to them. The distinction between "capacity" and "ability" is an extension of this argument.

I have mentioned the importance of the *Li Lun Pian* and the *Yue Lun Pian* to Xunzi's whole argument. In these chapters, Xunzi describes the rationale, form, and structure of morality and the rites. There is a passage from the *Li Lun Pian* that is thought to belong to the *Xing E Pian*.[18] Here Xunzi states that *xing* or nature is the original raw material (*xing zhe, ben shi cai pu ye* 性者，本始材朴也). *Wei* or human artifice, on the other hand, is (something that can be observed in) the flourishing of the cultural form and rationale (*wei zhe, wen li long sheng ye* 偽者，文理隆盛也) of the rites. Each is a necessary condition of the other. As Xunzi says, without *xing*, *wei* would have nothing on which it can add (*wu xing ze wei zhi wu suo jia* 無性則偽之無所加). And without *wei*, *xing* would be unable to beautify itself (*wu wei ze xing bu neng zi mei* 無偽則性不能自美 ICS 19/95/1–2).

This passage can (perhaps) take its place just prior to 23.1e (ICS 23/114/2–6) where Xunzi takes the argument a step further. He reminds us of certain facts of desire that are a prominent part of our sensory and emotional nature (*qing xing* 情性),[19] and what we do to curb them in ritualistic ways. Instead of being inseparable from or abiding in our nature, these ritual practices may be said to defy our nature. Thus, we naturally desire to alleviate the sensory states of hunger, cold, and tiredness. In the presence of an elder, however, though hungry we may not eat first but *rang* 讓 or defer to her instead. Similarly, though tired, we might not seek rest but instead relieve others. This sort of deference is spelled out, for instance, in the relationships between father and son and between brothers. In this sense, we have the way or the *dao* of the filial son and the cultural form and rationale of rites and righteousness. If we simply follow the sensory and emotional aspects of our nature, on the other hand, there will be no deference. But given that there is deference, Xunzi argues, this shows that we are going against our sensory and emotional nature.

While the rules of deference are regulatory, they are at the same time, constitutive. Constitutive rules "create or define new forms of behavior."[20] In other words, such behavior would not exist without the rules that give rise to them, as opposed to the activity of say, eating, which can exist independently of rules of etiquette. The detailed attention that Xunzi gives to the rationale of the rites, in effect, spells out the constitutive processes whereby both the society and the individual are culturally transformed from a raw to a cultivated state. From this perspective, it is part of Xunzi's argument that Mencius has ignored the socially constitutive processes that are necessary for any individual to become a moral agent.

The Constitutive Rationale of the Rites

In this section, we take a closer look at these constitutive processes as described in the *Li Lun Pian* and the *Yue Lun Pian*. In the *Li Lun Pian* Xunzi describes the constitutive processes of social distinctions, hierarchy, reverence and deference, harmonious interaction, teachers and models, aesthetic refinement, and so on. It is consistent with this account of the constitutive processes of the rites and their rationale that there may be different levels of knowledge and understanding on the part of individuals. It is Xunzi's position in the later parts of the *Xing E Pian* (23.6b, 23.7) that different people may be differently inclined, or have different levels of intelligence and courage. Cumulative effort (*ji* 積) is an essential part of *wei* or human artifice. This can refer to the effort of an individual in applying himself or herself to the learning and understanding of various aspects of the rites. But consistently, it can also refer to the cumulative efforts of exemplary people and the fostering of ritual processes over time to curb the indulgence of certain motivational states, as well as to refine and transform them into more noble feelings and emotions. An important part of what it means to say that the rites are not just regulatory but constitutive is that they are, as A.S. Cua aptly puts it, "ennobling."[21] This is in effect what Xunzi means when he identifies the rites or *li* with *yang*, "nurturing" or "cultivating" (*li zhe yang ye* 禮者養也 ICS 19/90/5–6; 19.1b).

I shall discuss this and the rationale of the rites in more detail in chapter 8. Here I briefly summarize some of the rationale from a reading of certain passages in the *Li Lun Pian* and the *Yue Lun Pian*. Thus to begin with, there is the need to ensure a social and political hierarchy whereby proper relationships are established and reverence is instilled for various forms of authority such as rulers, teachers, families, and ancestors. This reverence is extended to heaven and earth, as the basis of life. While heaven and earth and ancestors provide a reverential sense of the beginnings of life and a sense of rootedness, rulers and teachers provide a reverential sense of the basis of order (families would presumably span both categories) (ICS 19/90/20–22; 19.2a).

In addition, the rites have an aesthetic rationale. Xunzi speaks of the need for individual and social harmony and elegant form wherein the emotions are also given room for refined and balanced expression. The aesthetic function of the rites serves to cultivate the desires and the emotions, resulting in beauty or refinement (*mei* 美) of conduct. The word *e* is often translated as "evil" in the context of discussions on human nature. But it should not be forgotten that it also means "ugly," the opposite of "beautiful" or "refined." Thus, when Xunzi says that "human nature is *e*," he is emphasizing that the raw material of the desires and emotions need refinement, failing which there will be disorder and impoverishment for all. As he says, "Rites trim what is too long, stretch out what is too short, eliminate excess, remedy deficiency, and extend cultivated forms that express love and respect so that they increase and complete the beauty of conduct according to one's duty" (Knoblock 19.5b; ICS 19/94/8).

In both its regulatory and aesthetic senses, the rites are complemented by music:

> Music is joy.[22] Being an essential part of man's emotional nature, the expression of joy is, by necessity, inescapable. . . . But if its form is not properly conducted, then it is impossible that disorder should not arise. The Ancient Kings hated such disorder. Thus they instituted as regulations the sounds of the Odes and the Hymns to offer guidance. This would cause the sounds to be sufficient to give expression to the joy, but not lead to dissipation. . . . It would cause . . . the rhythm and meter of the music to be sufficient to stir and move the good in people's hearts [*gan ren zhi shan xin* 感人之善心], and to keep evil and base *qi* 氣 sentiments from finding a foothold there. (Knoblock 20.1; ICS 20/98/14–18)

And further, "music embodies harmonies that can never be altered, just as ritual embodies principles of natural order that can never be changed. Music joins together what is common to all; ritual separates what is different. The guiding principles of ritual and music act as the pitch pipe that disciplines the human heart" (Knoblock 20.3; ICS 20/100/14–15).

This rationale of the rites is, at the same time, the rationale of morality and the laws.[23] As mentioned earlier, learning and imbibing them involves cumulative effort. One might think that this is too high a standard to set, since all that may be required for the ordinary person to be good or moral is that he or she obey the rules of morality and the laws without necessarily understanding their rationale. But in addition to the need for training and habituation, Xunzi is also speaking of the knowledge and transformative experience that are involved in being a sage. Given that this requires a keen perceptiveness of the rationale behind morality and the laws, not everyone will qualify. We have seen that, according to Xunzi, people have an autonomous will as well as different qualities. In this respect, there may be different levels of perceptiveness, skills, and understanding. This is precisely the point that is suggested by the example of what it is to "be another" or *xiang wei* in 23.5b and which we have already discussed.

The "Primitive Responses" Argument

It is important to note that Xunzi's disagreement with Mencius does not lie at the level of distinguishing nonmoral from moral responses, and that somehow,

Xunzi is able to connect primitive responses with moral feelings and behavior through an inherent desire of human beings for harmony. This is in fact the interpretation of David Wong.[24] Wong characterizes the difference between Mencius and Xunzi in terms of an example in *Mencius* 3A5. Presumably, in early times, the practice of burial did not exist. Mencius hypothesizes that a group of people have thrown the bodies of their deceased parents into a ditch and later observe creatures and flies eating them. They break into a sweat and hurry home for spades to bury them. Referring to this example Wong states, "Mencius describes the covering of them as right." By contrast, Xunzi "denies the Mencian claim that innate, shared reactions reveal rightness to us." Xunzi's picture of human nature is consistent with "the transformation from self interest to a love and delight in morality. On this view, we love it because it expresses, channels, and strengthens some of our natural human feelings."[25]

However, describing the action of the group of people burying their parents as "right" may still not be adequate to differentiate Mencius's position from Xunzi's. Mencius's comment on the example is, "The sweating was not put on for others to see. It was an expression of their innermost heart (*zhong xin da yu mian mu* 中心達於面目 *Mencius* 3A5)." This is a response probably having to do with the four sprouts of the heart-mind, although it is unclear which of the four Mencius may be referring to. Mencius concludes: "[If in this case] burying them is the thing to do (*yan zhi cheng shi ye* 掩之誠是也), then the burying of their own parents by filial sons and *ren* persons also must have [a] *dao* (*ze xiao zi ren ren zhi yan qi qin yi bi you dao* 則孝子仁人之掩其親亦必有道)." Note that the word "right"—which might be construed by the reader as *yi* 義—nowhere occurs in this passage. Even if "right" could be implied by the mention of "the thing to do" and of a way or *dao*, it may still not be a full-blooded moral notion of right. It could be argued that the emphasis is not so much on the "right" thing to do, as on illustrating a shared or common primitive response. This means that Mencius's position is capable of being interpreted in terms of primitive responses or predispositions that need to be developed into moral virtues. If this is possible, then the difference between Xunzi and Mencius remains unclear, and Wong's analysis would fail to dissolve the impression that their positions are not incompatible.

Throughout his essay Wong is troubled by the question, how can one move from being self-interested to having a delight in morality? According to him, Xunzi's solution is given in terms of the fact that morality allows for channeling and developing some of our natural feelings, especially the desire for harmony. Against this, however, a defender of Mencius could object that this notion of harmony and natural feelings is morally loaded. Whether this objection is valid or not, we would find ourselves back in the old debate about whether Xunzi has begged the question in his criticism of Mencius. As we have seen, it could be held that the very process of inventing morality assumes some moral capacity in the first place.

Conclusion

I have shown that Xunzi is himself conscious of this kind of objection and that his critique of Mencius does not remain at this level of debate. Instead, the distinction between "capacity" and "ability" breaks through these objections. According to Xunzi's diagnosis, Mencius assumes a simple state where, so it seems, having the necessary capacity to know and act on the rationale of morality organically translates into an ability to act morally. From Mencius's contrast of morality with the analogy of "striding over the North Sea with Mount Tai under your arm," it would seem that the moral resources are already complete within each person. He uses physical and organic analogies, such as lifting a feather and looking, to contrast the ready use of moral resources with something that it is impossible to do. Xunzi has astutely picked this up in 23.1d, where he links Mencius's thesis of human nature as originally good with the ability of the eye to see and the ear to hear.

Following this diagnosis, Xunzi's remedy consists in specifying the role of ritual processes in giving rise to a sense of morality. As we have seen, he spells out what "morality" is in terms of a social and political hierarchy, proper relationships, reverence for various forms of authority, and a sense of rootedness and order. In addition, there is the transformative influence of aesthetic devices that give rise to individual and social refinement, harmony and cultural form. All these things do not come raw but have to be cultivated. They are elaborations upon what Xunzi means by *wei* or human artifice.

From the perspective of the distinction between "capacity" and "ability," the objection that Xunzi assumes an innate moral capacity when he insists that morality is brought about by human artifice either begs the question, or misses the point. This objection begs the question because it assumes that the formal and constitutive structure of morality must have been there—in human nature—originally. As we have seen, this is in effect the point that Xunzi makes in 23.4a with his example of the earthenware dish and the potter. And it misses the point, since, instead of merely asserting that nature is evil and that goodness is constructed, Xunzi has diagnosed Mencius to have an underlying belief in a simple organic state when he claims that nature is originally good. Xunzi argues that this cannot account for the nature of morality and the laws, described in terms of their constitutive rationale.

In short, Xunzi has systematically diagnosed, analyzed, and criticized Mencius's whole picture of human nature as being too naive, idealistic, and incomplete. In doing so, Xunzi has broadened the discussion of *xing* instead of legislating what it means. He does so by giving allowance for differences in character, and an array of desires and emotions. He argues specifically against Mencius that these desires and emotions do not come to us in a morally packaged way, but require nurturance and guidance through the rites. Thus, even if there are primitive responses congenial to the development of morality in these desires and emotions, this does not ensure that people are able to be moral. We realize this especially when we come to see the underlying rationale of morality in terms of the rites and the necessity of making a cumulative effort to learn and to practise this rationale. The lack of effort could be due to various factors such as will, character, courage, intelligence, the absence of guidance or influence by teachers and models, a treacherous environment, and so forth.[26]

This completes my account of Xunzi's critique. But we should mention Mozi, too. Commentators have noted that in discussing the rites Xunzi's target is Mozi, who frowns upon the rites as lavish display.[27] According to my argument, Xunzi has in mind Mencius as well when he discusses the constitutive rationale of the rites. More intriguing, however, is the possibility that Xunzi's distinction between *ke yi* and *neng* may also be targeted at Mozi given the latter's belief in the possibility of *jian ai* (兼愛) or "universal love."[28] In the *Mozi*, someone expresses a doubt about the practice of universal love: *qi ke wei zai* 豈可為哉 or, "How can it be done?" The same person states that *bu ke wei ye* 不可為也 or, "It cannot be done," adding that it would be like picking up Mount Tai and leaping over a river with it. In reply, Mozi states that while it is impossible to pick up Mount Tai and so on, the sage kings had in fact personally practiced universal love.[29] Evidently, Mozi thinks that universal love is something that people both have the capacity and the ability to practice. The analogies of "striding over the North Sea," et cetera, and "picking up Mount Tai," et cetera, are similar and their use by both Mencius and Mozi could indicate that they were common analogies. These were used to stress that (in contrast) there are certain things that we are able to do, for example, act morally and love others universally. We cannot be sure whether Xunzi had Mozi in mind too when he offered the variation, "Travel by foot across the width of the world," to distinguish between "capacity" and "ability." In any case, his criticism of Mencius in terms of the distinction is certainly applicable to Mozi as well.

Appendix

Xunzi's two counterfactual arguments for the existence of a rationale (*li* 理) to morality and the laws in 23.5a.

These are as follows:

(1) "If morality and the laws do not have a rationale that can be known and can be practiced, then even Yu would not (be able to) know and would be incapable of practicing morality and the laws."

Although he does not spell it out, the implication is that the consequent is not the case, that is, Yu is capable of practicing morality and the laws. Therefore, the antecedent does not hold either, that is, morality and the laws *do* possess the rationale that enables them to be known and practiced. Note that this is a valid argument, in the form of *modus tollens* (if p then q, not q, therefore not p). Schematically:

If morality and the laws do not have a rationale that can be known and can be practiced, then even Yu would not (be able to) know and would be incapable of practicing morality and the laws.

But Yu is capable of practicing morality and the laws.

Therefore morality and the laws possess a rationale that can be known and can be practiced.

(2) "If the ordinary person does not have the *zhi* (cognitive capacity) to know morality and the laws, and the *ju* (instrumental capacity) to practice morality and the laws, then he does not know the righteousness of father and son or the correctness between ruler and minister."

But the consequent is *not* the case, that is, the ordinary person does know the righteousness of father and son, and so on. Therefore, it is *not* the case that the person does not have the capacities to know and to practice morality and the laws, that is, they *do* have these capacities (*ke yi zhi zhi zhi* 可以知之質 and *ke yi neng zhi ju* 可以能之具). Again, this has a *modus tollens* form:

If the ordinary person does not have the (cognitive and instrumental) capacities to know morality and the laws, then he does not know righteousness, etc.

But the ordinary person does know righteousness, etc.

Therefore the ordinary person does have the (cognitive and instrumental) capacities to know morality and the laws.

Situating Xunzi

In the last chapter, we compared the positions of Mencius and Xunzi on human nature. In the present chapter, I carry the investigation further by comparing Xunzi's position with that of Gaozi and others. In *Mencius* 6A:6, Mencius's disciple Gongduzi lists four prevalent views on the *xing* or nature of humans:

(1) Gaozi's view that it is neither good nor not-good (*wu shan wu bu shan* 無善無不善)

(2) An unattributed view that it has the capacity to become good or to become bad (*ke yi wei shan, ke yi wei bu shan* 可以為善，可以為不善)

(3) An unattributed view that there are natures that are good, and there are natures that are bad (*you xing shan, you xing bu shan* 有性善，有性不善)

(4) Mencius's view that it is good (*xing shan* 性善)

I shall show that Xunzi holds the second view. Perhaps it would be more accurate to say that Xunzi developed this view, since he came later. Related to this is the task of stating more exactly what the second view amounts to. Does it mean, for instance, that there is both good and bad in human nature? In that case, how is it different from the third view, that there are natures that are good and natures that are bad? An understanding of Xunzi's position would help us to understand the second view better. It is the task of this chapter to provide an elaboration of this second view, through an exposition of Xunzi's position.[1]

Comparisons between the second view and the other views will help to provide a clearer idea of the differences between each of them. In what immediately follows, I shall make the following comparisons, between: the first and the fourth views (Gaozi and Mencius), the first and the second (Gaozi and Xunzi), and the second and the third. I shall not compare the second and the fourth views (Xunzi and Mencius), as I have already done this in the previous chapter. However, some important differences between Xunzi and Mencius will be reiterated and developed in the course of the discussion.

The First and Fourth Views: Gaozi and Mencius

When Gongduzi asks if all the other views are mistaken, Mencius replies: "As far as what is genuinely in him is concerned (*nai ruo qi qing* 乃若其情), a person is capable of becoming good (*ze ke yi wei shan yi* 則可以為善矣). That is what I mean by good (*nai ruo wei shan ye* 乃所謂善也). As for his becoming bad, that is not the fault of his native endowment (*ruo fu wei bu shan fei cai zhi zui ye* 若夫為不善非才之罪也)."[2] Kwong-loi Shun has shown that in this passage, *qing* is interchangeable with *xing*.[3] Also, *cai* "is an endowment that enables one to attain certain accomplishments," and more specifically, that it "has to do with the emotional predispositions of the heart-mind."[4] Shun concludes that when Mencius says that nature is good and human beings *ke yi* or are capable of becoming good, he was saying that they "have a constitution comprising certain emotional predispositions that already point in the direction of goodness." Furthermore, "becoming bad is not the fault of one's constitution, but a matter of one's injuring or not fully developing the constitution in the appropriate direction."[5]

As for the first view (Gaozi's), I have argued in chapter 3 that *xing wu shan wu bu shan* should be more accurately read as "*Xing* is without good, and without not-good," instead of "*Xing* is neither good nor bad." This reading stresses that moral categories are wholly inapplicable to nature. At the same time, Gaozi agrees with Mencius's demonstration that for him (Gaozi), *xing* and *sheng* (life, life process) are tautologous (6A:3). This means that he highlights the biological instincts and desires when referring to human nature. This is reinforced by Gaozi's claim that "appetite for food and sex is *xing* (*shi se xing ye* 食色性也 6A:4)." How then do people acquire morality or *ren yi*? Gaozi's view is that this is something externally impressed upon the nature of humans. Like the willow and water, it is pliable and can be channeled. Gaozi can thus be said to hold the view that human nature is in itself neither good nor not-good and that the application of good and bad to human beings is simply an imposition, something that was not originally there.

The first and the fourth views are therefore directly opposed. While Gaozi holds the moral neutrality of nature, Mencius holds instead that nature is originally good in the sense that the heart-mind manifests the expression of some (morally oriented) emotional predispositions under certain circumstances. For Gaozi, that nature is morally neutral means that *ren yi* is an external imposition. For Mencius, on the other hand, *ren yi* is an (internal) predisposition. Mencius is alarmed by what he regards as the morally subversive implications of Gaozi's view. If *ren yi* is externally imposed, it is artificial. In other words, it may be more natural not to act in accordance with *ren yi*.[6]

The First and Second Views: Gaozi and Xunzi

This implication that *ren yi* is constructed may lead us to think that Gaozi's view is like Xunzi's. At one level, this is true. It would appear that for both, *xing* is morally neutral and *ren yi* is an (external) imposition. After all, they provide somewhat similar images of the construction of *ren yi* 仁義 or *li yi* 禮義 (I shall show later that for Xunzi these terms are equivalent). Xunzi compares the making of *li yi* to a potter's molding clay (Knoblock 23.2a, 23.4a), and Gaozi compares nature to water as amenable to being channeled in any particular direction (6A:2). But the similarity between Gaozi and Xunzi ends there.[7] Gaozi does not go on to say anything about the institutionalization of *ren yi* and we may say that his view that nature is neither good nor not-good is predicated, instead, upon the importance of the desires. In other words, moral neutrality for Gaozi means that the animal and biological desires are most characteristic of human beings. As we saw in chapter 3, Gaozi's psychological account of the human being is limited to (especially the appetitive) desires and in this regard, he cannot be said to have a "moral psychology." On the other hand, as I will show, while Xunzi notes the sensory and appetitive desires as part of human nature, he goes beyond this to describe a range of other capacities and abilities of human beings as a species, and the particular characters of individual persons. Xunzi also describes social and even metaphysical facts about the world that would allow for the individual to be able to grasp the conditions of social order. At the same time, one's ability to become orderly and to perfect oneself would also depend upon conditions such as the presence of models and teachers. Taken together, these capacities, abilities, characters, and conditions explain why it is that nature has the capacity to be good, and the capacity to be bad—the second view mentioned by Gongduzi.

Briefly, the explanation is this. Each and every individual is born with certain sensory and appetitive desires. Left unregulated, these desires (taken collectively) would lead to disorder. However, human beings also have other desires such as the desire to live in security and comfort, possess wealth, and so on. These desires are connected to the ability to make social distinctions, and every individual has cognitive and instrumental capacities to enable them to understand and to practice goodness—under a certain conception of goodness as based on order and ritual principles that give rise to order. Various other conditions both internal and external to the individual determine whether, and to what extent, someone is able to exercise these cognitive and instrumental capacities to achieve goodness. It is in this sense, therefore, that nature has the capacity to be good and the capacity to be bad. This differs from Mencius's position in that these capacities are not in themselves moral capacities and do not have any original moral structure. Instead, they are resources that go into the process of building such a structure, and it would be fallacious to assume that such resources have the same structure as the final product (as argued in chapter 5).

The Second and Third Views

This explanation of the second view also helps to distinguish it from the third (unattributed) view named by Gongduzi: there are *xing* that are good, and there are *xing* that are bad. Kwong-loi Shun has noted that this means that "people differ with regard to *xing*," and that "*xing* differs from person to person."[8] Unlike the second view, this one does not claim a common capacity or capacities and is opposed to both Mencius's and Xunzi's positions. Put simply, the third view states that some people are by nature good while others are by nature bad, and this may also imply that some people are unchangeable.[9] Lau's translation of the statement of this position is as follows: "There are those who are good by nature, and there are those who are bad by nature. For this reason, Xiang could have Yao as prince, and Shun could have the Blind Man as father, and Qi, Viscount of Wei and Prince Bi Gan could have Zhou (紂) as nephew as well as sovereign." That is, despite the rule of benevolent sage kings, some people maintained their bad nature, and despite the rule of cruel despots, some people maintained their good nature. This is the converse of the illustration of the second view, where the influence of benevolent kings led to people (in general) tending toward being good, while with the reign of tyrannical despots, they tended toward cruelty. One confirmation that Xunzi holds the second view is that he makes use of a similar illustration:

> Anciently it was said: The humane person (*ren zhe* 仁者) delights in proclaiming and manifesting it (the way of the Ancient Kings) to others. If it is proclaimed and manifested, smoothed and polished, imitated and repeated, then the myopic will suddenly become comprehensive, the uncultivated suddenly refined, and the stupid suddenly wise. If this could not be done, though a Tang or Wu held supreme power, what advantage could result, and though a Jie or Zhou Xin held supreme power, what damage could they cause? But when Tang and Wu lived, the world followed them and order prevailed (*zhi* 治), and when Jie and Zhou Xin lived, the world followed them and was chaotic (*luan* 亂). How could this be if such were contrary to [the *qing* of humans (*ren zhi qing* 人之情)] because certainly it is as possible for a person to be like the one as like the other? (Knoblock 4.10; ICS 4/15/22–4/16/3)[10]

The second last sentence of the above quotation asserts that order prevailed when the wise and benevolent kings Tang and Wu lived, while chaos prevailed during the time of the cruel and tyrannical kings Jie and Zhou Xin. This corresponds to Gongduzi's statement that the people were given to goodness or otherwise depending on whether the rulers were (the wise and benevolent) Wen and Wu on the one hand, and (the cruel and tyrannical) You and Li on the other. The last sentence of the quotation asserts a counterfactual: the influence exerted by the rulers on the people would not have been possible, if it were not the case that people have the capacity to become one way, i.e. good (*ke yu* [*yi*] *ru ci* 可

與 [以] 如此), or the capacity to become the other way, i.e. bad (*ke yu* [*yi*] *ru bi* 可與 [以] 如彼).[11] Note that in talking of these capacities, Xunzi refers to the *qing* of man. We should read *qing* here as a fact about people in general, that they have the capacity to refine the basic desires of their nature (*xing*). At the same time, however, it is a fact that some people do not exercise the capacity. Given the possibility of going either way, it would be inappropriate to translate *qing* as "essential nature" as Knoblock does.[12] This reading that I have adduced thus corresponds to the second view of nature listed by Gongduzi, that it has the capacity to become good, and the capacity to become bad (*ke yi wei shan*, *ke yi wei bu shan*). Given what we have said earlier about how Xunzi's position makes sense of the second view and helps to clarify the other views, the correspondences mentioned above would seem to be more than coincidental. In the following sections, I shall describe Xunzi's position in greater detail.

To anticipate, let us highlight some important features of this description. Xunzi has an account of *yi* 義 as the human ability to make social distinctions and which distinguishes the human species from the animals. It is crucial to the understanding of Xunzi's position as a whole that although *yi* is not an incipient moral sense in the way that it is for Mencius, and Xunzi does not speak of it as something one is born with, nonetheless, he does hold that the ability to have *yi* is what characterizes the human species. The conjunction of *yi* with *ren* and *li* gives us *ren yi* 仁義 and *li yi* 禮義. We shall have to look at the relation between these and other terms such as *qun* 群, *fen* 分, and *li* 理 to understand Xunzi's interpretation of the social and moral order. In addition, there are the capacities and conditions that he alleges would enable humans to develop and to integrate within themselves a sense of such an order. For reasons that will become evident, I will not follow Knoblock's translation of *yi* as "a sense of morality and justice." The same goes for *li yi* as "ritual and moral principles," and for *ren yi* as "the principle of humanity and justice." I shall take *li yi* as "ritual principles." As we shall see, *li yi* and *ren yi* are more or less equivalent for Xunzi.

Xunzi on Social Order

Xunzi repeatedly emphasizes the need for social order. The goal of a proper social order permeates his discussions even if it is not explicitly referred to. The presence of ritual principles constitute order, while their absence constitute disorder (*li yi zhi wei zhi, fei li yi zhi wei luan ye* 禮義之謂治，非禮義之謂亂 也 (3.7; ICS3/10/12).[13] Xunzi states the origin of ritual principles more than once (4.12, 9.3, 19.1), but the most well-known instance occurs in the first passage (19.1a) of the *Li Lun Pian*. Here, it is stated that humans are born with desires that they would seek to satisfy. Contention would arise if no limit was imposed or no restriction was set on what they desired. This would lead to disorder and a state of impoverishment all round. The Ancient Kings or sages therefore instituted *li yi* to form social divisions (*zhi li yi yi fen zhi* 制禮義以分之 ICS 19/90/4, also in 4/17/1, 9/36/2) and to nurture (*yang* 養) the desires. By creating a state of affairs where "desires did not overextend the means for their satisfaction, and material goods did not fall short of what was desired,"[14] the sages ensured that in general, the people were satisfied. In other words, by instituting ritual principles, the sages managed two things that were instrumental to establishing order. First, these principles allowed for social distinctions that laid down criteria for the distribution of goods in such terms as rank and social class, social relationships, occupational stations, and abilities. Second, these principles were at the same time educational tools of refinement that nurtured and moderated people's desires. Such moderated refinement would at the same time enable them to appreciate the need for ritual distinctions (19.1c).

Ren Yi and *Li Yi*

The guiding principles of *ren yi* (*ren yi zhi tong* 仁義之統 ICS 4/16/11) and the *fen* 分 spelled out in the *Odes*, *Documents*, *Rituals*, and *Music* are said to be important in helping one to take a long-term perspective in whatever one does (4.11). Knoblock notes that *fen* is "a technical term referring here to the patterns of life that characterize each of the classes into which the sages divided society."[15] We saw in the last section the connection between *fen* and *li yi*. The mention of *ren yi* in conjunction with *fen* as well indicates that *ren yi* and *li yi* are closely connected. The phrase *ren yi zhi tong* or the guiding principles of *ren yi* also occurs in 4.10 (ICS 4/15/20) where it is said that these are the means that make it possible for people to live together in societies, to hedge in their faults, to nurture and refine each other—the same things that are said to be brought about by the ritual principles or *li yi*. In addition, the principles of *ren yi* would bring about protection, tranquility, and security. Given these same functions, *ren yi* can be said to be equivalent to *li yi*.

If there is any difference between the two terms, it is a matter of context and emphasis. We can put the difference in the following way. The establishment of order requires humane (*ren* 仁) rulers. Besides providing the economic conditions for material prosperity, the rulers would have to win the allegiance of the people too by providing them the conditions of security and tranquility. When Xunzi uses *ren yi*, he has these additional conditions of order in mind. Thus, where *li yi* emphasizes the need for social classes and ritual distinctions, *ren yi* emphasizes the need for the wider conditions of humane rule. However, being humane for Xunzi certainly does not mean simply *ai ren* 愛人 or "loving others." It is important for Xunzi that the *ren* ruler acts rationally, taking into account the transformative influence in the long term of humane rule. What underpins this rational strategy is the abhorrence of harm to the people and the chaos that results. We see this very clearly in the reported conversations between Xunzi and two interlocutors regarding the justification of warfare under certain circumstances.[16] For Xunzi, warfare (or its deterrent threat) is justifiable on the ground that it either prevents harm to the people and hence disorder, or re-establishes order. Warfare carried out for these reasons does not constitute contention. Instead, it is one aspect of effective governance and the establishment of order. The ruler who is *ren yi* is prepared for war because he bears in mind the principle of rational order and the long-term consequences of effective governance.

Yi and Social Distinctions

As mentioned earlier, the concept of *yi* 義 is held by Xunzi to be an important distinguishing feature of human beings. In 9.16a, Xunzi compares humans and animals: they both have *zhi* 知, consciousness or "awareness" (Knoblock). The difference between them lies in humans possessing *yi* while animals are without *yi* (有 *you yi*, 無 *wu yi*). Knoblock translates *yi* as "a sense of morality and justice." The idea that humans possess "a sense of morality and justice" might lead one to think that Xunzi is conceding Mencius's belief that human beings have an incipient moral sense. But further reading of the whole passage brings out links between *yi* and other concepts. An examination of these links would not support the claim that Xunzi concedes that humans possess an incipient or an innate moral sense.[17]

In the same passage, Xunzi goes on to observe that although they are physically stronger and swifter than man, animals like the ox and the horse are nonetheless subject to being used by man. The reason for this is man's ability to *qun* 群 or to form a society. And what gives rise to this ability? The reply, in one word, is *fen* 分 or (the ability to form) social classes or distinctions. Note that *qun* and *fen* imply each other. In other words, one cannot have *qun* without *fen*, as it will result in strife, disorder, fragmentation, and hence weakness and all the consequences that entails. For this not to occur, *li yi*—or what amounts to the same thing, *fen yi*—cannot be dispensed with.

Xunzi next asks the question, How are the social distinctions put into effect (*fen he yi neng xing* 分何以能行 ICS 9/39/11)? Xunzi, again, specifies one word: *yi* 義. Thus, it is *yi* that enables social distinctions, resulting in *he* 和, concord or harmony. This in turn ultimately leads to oneness or unity *yi* 一. Unity provides the strength and power to overcome other objects and animals, and to build dwellings to ensure safety and comfort. In addition, the ability to follow the sequence of the four seasons (for instance, in farming), to exercise control over things and in general to benefit the world, are gained through *fen yi* 分義. Thus, we can say that to have *yi* in this context is to have the human ability to make social distinctions, and to adopt and apply ritual principles that would allow for the hierarchical structuring of society where everything acquires its proper place (*wan wu jie de qi yi* 萬物皆得其宜 ICS 9/39/17).[18]

Characteristics of the Species Human Being

Xunzi often refers to the appetitive and sensory desires as what a person is born with. At the same time, however, humans are said to have the capacity to arrange for the maximal satisfaction of these desires, through the ability to make social distinctions, as well as the ability to think rationally, prudently, and for the long term. This ability is necessary to the acquisition of other desires such as for security, comfort, and wealth. Xunzi tends to talk of the ability to make social distinctions not in terms of individual persons, but in terms of what it is to be human, in contrast to animals. In other words, it is characteristic of the species that it is able to make social distinctions, form social classes, think prudently, rationally, and for the long term. Whether a particular individual puts into effect these abilities of the species would depend on various factors such as whether one is prepared to make a cumulative effort to study and to apply oneself to what one has learned, whether one had good models and teachers, and one's individual character.

Let us look at some passages to illustrate the above. In 5.4, Xunzi raises the question, "What is it that makes human beings 'human beings' (*ren zhi suo yi wei ren zhe he yi ye* 人之所以爲人者何已也 ICS 5/18/13&16)?" The answer is the possession of *bian* 辨 or (the ability to draw social) boundaries or distinctions, equivalent to *fen* in this context. On the other hand, the following are what everyone is born with: the desire for food, warmth, rest, what is beneficial, and to avoid harm. Xunzi adds that these are common to Yu (the legendary benevolent king) and Jie (the cruel and tyrannical king). In other words, the sensory and appetitive desires and the desire for what is beneficial are common to each individual person, and they are also morally neutral—neither good nor bad in themselves, since they are said to be equally possessed by both a benevolent king and a cruel despot. Reiterating the ability to *bian*, Xunzi states that human beings are not just hairless bipeds (*er zhu wu mao* 二足無毛 ICS 5/18/15). The ape may also be described as a (facially) hairless biped,[19] and yet it can be made into a soup for the benefit of humans. Here, Xunzi is again stressing the fact that the species human being has the strength and power to overcome other objects and animals, and this is due to its ability to draw social distinctions and all the creative power that implies for the species a whole. Thus, although animals too have fathers and sons *fu zi* 父子, they do not have *fu zi zhi qin* 父子之親 (ICS 5/18/16–17). The word *qin* would imply here not just closeness and affection, but the relation of filial piety between father and son, and all the ritual behavior that that stipulates, including the duties and obligations governing the relationship. Similarly, animals too have sexual differences *you pin mu* 有牝牡, but lack *nan nü zhi bie* 無男女之別 (ICS 5/18/17)—the distinction between man and woman. In other words, for human beings as a species, the difference between progenitor and offspring and between the sexes is not simply biological, but has social and ritual implications. As Xunzi goes on to say, "Of

...important than that between social classes. Of ...social classes (*fen*), none is more important ...tinctive ability of human beings in a similar ...esires listed above (5.4) are stated as common ...are born with. The word *bian* is also used to ...rgans to distinguish between colors, sounds, ...though here, *bian* would clearly not amount ...nctions as in *fen*. Again, it is stated that these ...norally neutral, since there is no difference in ...king like Yu and a cruel despot like Jie. What ...someone in particular becomes a benevolent ...a farmer, or a merchant "lies entirely with the ...es, with what they concentrate on laying their ...bits and customs" (4.9). Most individuals do ...thus do not enjoy the tranquility and honor ...remain uncultivated or *lou* 陋 (4.9, repeated ...is *lou* would imply that he has not applied ...thus failed to transform himself. The passage ...were not born wholly what they became, but ...selves, brought them to perfection through ...and only after first putting forth the utmost ...' (4.9).[20] ...nan beings are born ignoble (*xiao ren* 小人). ...to do with having a nature that is inherently bad, but with what Xunzi goes on to stress, namely, that without the guidance of teachers and models, the individual is likely to think merely in terms of what is beneficial to himself. Thus, "the mouth and stomach can only lead to smacking and chewing away, feasting and gorging to satisfaction. How can they be aware of *li yi* (*an zhi li yi* 安知禮義　ICS 4/15/16)? Or know when to offer polite refusals or to yield precedence (*an zhi ci rang* 安知辭讓 ICS 4/15/16)? Or know shame more keenly or sharpen what he accumulates? If a person lacks a teacher and the model, then his mind (*xin* 心) will just be like his mouth and stomach" (4.10). It is the guiding principles of the ancient sage kings that allow for order. The passage concludes with the statement already mentioned (and which is similar to Gongduzi's illustration in *Mencius* 6A:6), that order prevailed during the rule of wise and benevolent kings, while there was chaos during the reign of cruel despots.

Yi and *Li* 理

I have described above the following facts pertaining to human beings for Xunzi: Human beings have desires that they wish to fulfill, and they also have the ability to maximize their desires through making social distinctions, thinking rationally, acting prudently, and taking the long-term perspective. The desires are said to be what one is born with or as belonging to one's nature, and although the same is not said for the abilities to make social distinctions, and so on, nonetheless these constitute what it is to be a member of the human species (*ren zhi suo yi wei ren zhe* 人之所以爲人者 ICS 5/18/13, 16).

In the *Jiebi Pian* ("Dispelling Blindness"), Xunzi talks of the *xin* in a way that is more the "mind" rather than the "heart-mind" in Mencius's sense. Not only is it the lord of the body (*xing zhi jun* 形之君, 21.6a; ICS 21/104/10) that issues commands, forbids, and so on, it also has the ability to examine the facts about things (*guan wan wu er zhi qi qing* 觀萬物而知其情 ICS 21/104/8). Through the mind, one can become conversant too with the principles and functions of things: "By laying out the warp and woof of Heaven and Earth, he tailors the functions of the myriad things. By regulating and distinguishing according to the Great Ordering Principle (*da li* 大理 ICS 21/104/8), he encompasses everything in space and time" (21.5e). Ritual principles are part of this metaphysical order that can be discerned through an investigation of its inherent rationale or *li* 理. Thus, corresponding to the species ability to make distinctions is the rationale of the conditions of the world in general and of human society in particular.

Xunzi says that "one who is *yi* accords with rational order *yi zhe xun li* 義者循理" (ICS 15/71/21&23). This highlights the fact that there is a rationale to social distinctions and ritual principles that the *yi* person is able to discern. Thus, as Xunzi says, *ren yi fa zheng you ke zhi ke neng zhi li* 仁義法正有可知可能之理 (ICS 23/116/7). Knoblock renders *ren yi fa zheng* separately as "humaneness, morality, the model of law, and rectitude (23.5a)." In the preceding chapter, I used for convenience the phrase "morality and the laws." As the above analysis has shown, however, *ren yi* is equivalent to *li yi* or ritual principles, albeit with different emphases. In any case, the emphasis in Xunzi's sentence is on the fact that there is a *rationale* to ritual principles that can be known (*ke zhi*) and can be practiced (*ke neng*). An investigation of its usage in the *Xing E Pian* reveals its close connection with the terms *zhi* 治 and *wen* 文. *Li* is often contrasted with *luan* or disorder, while *wen* is often paired with *li* as *wen li* 文理. This last term is sometimes a synonym for *li yi*, for example, when it is stated that simply following the sensory desires would give rise to *yin luan* 淫亂 or dissolute and wanton behavior and the perishing of *li yi wen li* 禮義文理 (23.1a; ICS 23/113/5). Given the social and cultural connotations of order as opposed to disorder, and the fact that *wen* connotes a cultural pattern, *wen li* can also be taken to refer to the cultured form and rationale of the ritual principles. In this sense, it draws attention to the fact that this form and rationale enables a transformation of the rudimentary or uncultivated self. For instance, Xunzi says that the way of the filial son is the cultured form and rationale of ritual principles *xiao zi zhi dao, li yi zhi wen li ye* 孝子之道,禮義之文理也 (ICS 23/114/5). Further, he says that the sage is the same with the masses in regard to his nature, but different from them in his *wei* 偽. This is because he is able to transform himself through the application of the form and rationale of the ritual principles *hua li yi zhi wen li* 化禮義之文理 (ICS 23/114/17). Thus, in addition to order, the term *li* 理 connotes the rationale of things in general, and the knowledge and practice of the socio-cultural forms and rationale behind the ritual principles. This knowledge and practice is more an aesthetic and cultural refinement, a movement from a rudimentary existence to a cultured and refined state, rather than (misleadingly) a transformation from being "evil" or "bad" to being "good."

Capacities and Character

In the previous chapter we analyzed Xunzi's claim that although an ordinary person has the cognitive and instrumental capacities for knowing and practicing the rationale of the ritual principles, she may be unwilling to do so and cannot be forced. Being a sage involves learning by concentrating one's mind and will, thinking and investigation, and making a tireless cumulative effort. In saying that the ordinary person cannot be forced, Xunzi implies that action is voluntary. As he says, the ignoble person has the capacity to be a noble person, but is unwilling (*bu ken* 不肯 ICS 23/116/18). Similarly, the noble person too has the capacity to be an ignoble person, but is unwilling. Each can be like the other (*xiang wei* 相為 ICS 23/116/18) but neither can be forced.

This implies, too, that people have different characters. Comparing people who have different skills and who are engaged in different trades, Xunzi says that they have the capacity to perform each other's work, but still, they are not able to do so. I have already mentioned a possible objection to this, namely, that one could conceive of the farmer taking up the training and work required of a carpenter and vice versa. Thus, when Xunzi says that it may be impossible for them to *xiang wei* this may be due to the fact that they may just not have certain talents or distinctive qualities. In the same way, although the ignoble person may be "unwilling" to be a noble person, a deeper explanation for this could be that she (her character) is such that she is not so disposed. Thus, if we ask why she fails to make the effort, it is possible to attribute this failure to some aspect of the character of the person.

Another explanation that Xunzi explicitly provides is the lack of the right models and teachers. Thus, environmental factors can be said to play a role here. The following example of Xunzi's is instructive: when a fragrant grass is soaked in something unpleasant, it gives an unpleasant smell. However, it is not that it does not itself have a beautiful quality (its fragrant smell) *qi zhi fei bu mei ye* 其質非不美也 (ICS 1/1/20). This example brings out the importance of environmental conditions, but at the same time, it says that there is some distinctive quality possessed by the object (or person) in question. Nonetheless, Xunzi believes in the capacity that people have to make a strong concerted effort to improve themselves. As he says, *xi su yi zhi, an jiu yi zhi* 習俗移志，安久移質 (ICS 8/34/2) which Knoblock translates: "The habituation of custom modifies the direction of will and, if continued for a long time, will alter its very substance (8.11)." The trouble with using "substance" for *zhi* in this context is that it seems too deep and unchangeable. What Xunzi is saying is that the *qualities* of a person can be changed through accumulated effort, custom, and habituation. However, some people do not make the effort, either because of some aspect of character or because of unconducive environmental conditions.

In addition to making a concerted effort, comprehensive knowledge and constancy of purpose are also necessary conditions of success in the learning of ritual principles and in their application to one's life. Thus, "one who does not fully grasp the appropriate connection between modes of behavior and the various categories of things (*lun lei bu tong* 倫類不通)" and who does not see the unity in ritual principles (*ren yi bu yi* 仁義不一) "does not deserve to be called expert in learning. The truly learned are those who make sure that their studies keep this unity (*xue ye zhe, gu xue yi zhi ye* 學也者，固學一之也). Those who leave with one principle and return with another are men of the streets and alleys. They are expert in a few things, but inexpert in many, like Jie, Zhou Xin, and Robber Zhi. Be complete and whole in it, and then you will be truly learned (*quan zhi jin zhi, ran hou xue zhe ye* 全之盡之，然後學者也" 1.13; ICS 1/4/12–14). Comprehensiveness means that one learns the rationale of the ritual principles so that "they will come to dwell within him," and such that his sensory organs would have an aversion toward whatever is contrary to them and come to delight in whatever are in accordance with them (1.14). This completeness of knowledge and internalization of ritual principles means that one does not think simply in terms of benefit, happiness, and the preservation of life. Although these are important, the way to preserve them is to act in a principled way that sometimes involves, say, being prepared to die. "Thus, if someone concentrates single-mindedly on ritual principles, then both his desires and ritual will be fulfilled (*gu ren yi zhi yu li yi, zhe liang de zhi yi* 故人一之於禮義，則兩得之矣); but if he concentrates solely on his inborn desires and emotions 情性, then both will be lost" (19.1d; ICS 19/90/17–18).[21]

Comprehensive knowledge is not a special skill that enables a person to concentrate on doing one thing. Instead, it is the ability to oversee the relations between many things so as to deploy them in the right positions. Thus: "The farmer concentrates on his fields, yet it would be inadmissible to consider him for the position of director of the fields. The merchant concentrates on the marketplace, but it would be inadmissible to consider him for director of the marketplace. The artisan concentrates on his wares, but it would be impossible to consider him for director of wares. There are men incapable of these three skills who could be commissioned to put in order any of these three offices." Such people "will treat things in all their combinations as things. Thus, the noble person is one with the Way and uses it to further his testing of things. If he is at one with the Way, then he will be right (*zheng* 正); and if he uses it to further his testing of things, then he will be discerning. If using the right frame of mind and proceeding with discernment he deploys things in their proper positions, the myriad things will perform their natural functions" (21.6b).

Conclusion

In an important paper entitled "The Ideological Background of the Mencian Discussion of Human Nature: A Reexamination," Ning Chen shows that during and even before Mencius's time, discussions about *xing* were very common and Mencius was concerned to defend what Chen refers to as an "egalitarian" as opposed to "inegalitarian" views. Interestingly, Chen attributes the third view mentioned by Gongduzi (as Chen puts it: "the nature of human beings is evil in some and good in others"), which is inegalitarian, to the Mohists, to references in the *Zuozhuan*, as well as in the *Zhuangzi*.[22] Citing some of the Guodian texts,[23] Chen shows that other Confucians before Mencius had attempted to combat these inegalitarian views, asserting instead that everyone has the same nature. According to him, Xunzi shared this egalitarianism.

For the purpose of the present discussion, I will highlight the following points that Chen makes concerning Xunzi. When Chen refers to Xunzi's position as being in tandem with the early Confucian position that nature is egalitarian, he cites passages which state that in their *xing*, the sage is identical to the common people (23.2a); the *xing* of Yao and Shun on the one hand, and Jie and Robber Zhi on the other, are the same; and both the noble person and the ignoble person share the same *xing* (23.4a). As Chen realizes, this egalitarianism does not in itself specify whether what is shared is good or bad. Comparing a passage in the *Xing zi ming chu* with the *Xunzi*, Chen notices a similarity with statements in the Xunzi about nature having to be "set aright" and being "straightened."[24] In particular, there is the passage in 23.1b which says that by instituting ritual principles, the sages intended to "straighten out" (*jiao shi* 矯飾) human nature. Chen sees in the *Xing zi ming chu*—and given the similarities, in the *Xunzi* as well—what he calls "a very negative account of nature." The implications of all the locutions about "setting aright," "straightening," and so on is that although for the author of the Guodian texts (and similarly for Xunzi) there is one universally shared nature, "the language here points to a notion of human nature as both good and evil."[25]

This is what he refers to as an "ambivalent" or "binary" account that also characterizes Gongduzi's statement of the second view. Chen also draws our attention to Wang Chong's *Lunheng*, where a view said to be similar to the second view is attributed: "Shih Shih [Shi Shi], a man of Chou, thought that there is both good and bad in human nature (*ren xing you shan you e* 人性有善有惡). If we pick out what is good in man's nature and by nourishing develop it, the good grows; if we nourish and develop the bad nature, the bad grows."[26] Chen comments: "The two accounts (Gongduzi's mention of the second view and Shih Shih's) regard human nature as binary and emphasize that education or nourishment is essential to its direction of development."[27]

According to Chen, "It is difficult to say that the Guodian text is connected with the school of Shih Shih or with the proponents of the view mentioned in Gongduzi's report to Mencius. But it certainly points to the prevalence of a conception of *xing* as morally ambivalent, with which Mencius had to take issue."[28] In the last paragraph of his paper, Chen states:

> the description of the ambivalent nature, often in strong negative terms, and the concomitant stress on the conflict between *xing* and *xin* in the Guodian texts do not mirror the view of the *Mencius*. Rather, the Guodian statements are more comparable to many statements made by Xunzi, who entertains the belief that human nature is evil, completely at odds with the learned and acquired virtues. In this regard, the Guodian position can be seen as a forerunner of Xunzi's theory of human nature as being evil.[29]

My account of Xunzi and the second view mentioned by Gongduzi differs from Chen's in the following ways. Firstly, Chen's account does not make clear what exactly is shared between the sages and others, although he thinks the statements about having to set it aright imply a negative account of nature. By a "negative account," Chen is most probably referring to Xunzi's various statements about the various desires said to be shared by all. My account of Xunzi's whole position shows that contrary to Chen, there is nothing necessarily "negative" about the various sensory and appetitive desires common to the sages and others. These desires are not "evil" in themselves. It is only when they are not collectively managed that disorder results, and it is this ugly state of affairs that the sages abhorred, not the desires themselves.

However, and this is the second point, this is not the only way in which Xunzi characterizes the human. He asks what makes human beings what they are (*ren zhe he yi wei ren* 人之所以爲人者). Thus, he contrasts the human species with animals and stresses that human beings share much more than the desires, especially the ability to make social distinctions (that is, they have *yi*). In discussing the rationale of the ritual principles, he also highlights the fact that all human beings share certain basic cognitive and instrumental capacities that enable the understanding and practice of ritual principles.

Thirdly, both Chen and Graham associate the second view mentioned by Gongduzi with Shih Shih's that "there is both good and bad in man's nature." If we take Xunzi's position as a clarification of the second view, this way of stating it is not quite accurate. For one thing, Shih Shih's view as it is reported is not precise enough: although it means to say that there is both good and bad in the nature of one person (to distinguish it from the third view), the expression "there is both good and bad in human nature" is ambiguous: it can mean good and bad "in one person" or "across persons." If so, it can be taken to be equivalent to the third view, which states that nature can be good and can be bad across different persons.[30] For another, if I am right in the claim that Xunzi's position is the same as the second view named by Gongduzi, or if I have adequately shown that Xunzi's position expands upon and makes good sense of it, then the second view cannot accurately be stated as the idea that, as Chen puts it, "there are both good and evil in human nature." For Xunzi, nature is not "bad" or "evil" in any singular sense. Instead, as I have argued in this chapter and in chapter 5, people may have various desires and they may display selfish tendencies under certain circumstances, but there is nothing intrinsically evil about these tendencies and desires. To repeat, the situation turns ugly (e) only when these desires are not refined, regulated, or controlled. It is only in this collectively consequential sense that nature may be said to be "bad."[31] Similarly, it is not accurate to say that for Xunzi, there is both good and bad in human nature. For Xunzi, "goodness" is not *in* human nature (as he argues against Mencius), and neither is there any "badness" *in* human nature as such. Xunzi holds a position of moral neutrality just like Gaozi. But, as was mentioned, Gaozi predicates this neutrality upon emphasis on the biological instincts and desires. Xunzi, on the other hand, has an account of the various resources of the species human being and of individual characters that go into the making of goodness—under a conception of goodness as based upon social order and an internalized sense of such order. It is this account that fills up the content of the second view mentioned by Gongduzi, that *xing* has the capacity to become good or to become bad.

Ritual Transformation: Emotion and Form

We have just seen that Xunzi's considered position is that human nature has the capacity to become good or bad. Xunzi has much to say about the role of ritual in transforming the individual. The term that is translated here as "transformation" is *hua* 化, and its object is nature or *xing* 性. In this chapter, we examine the exact nature of the transformation that Xunzi has in mind, and how it is possible. We shall do this by focusing, in particular, on Xunzi's response to the criticism of Confucian ritual practices put forward by Mozi.

It is well known that Mozi (墨子) criticizes the ritual practices of the Ru (儒, the Confucian school) for being wasteful. However, another criticism has been less appreciated: these practices are merely conventional habituations and violate the Ru's own moral ideals of *ren* 仁 (humanity), *yi* 義 (right, righteousness), and *xiao* 孝 (being filial). Xunzi responds to both criticisms in the *Li Lun Pian* 禮論篇 ("Discourse on Ritual Principles"). Based on an account of Mozi's arguments and Xunzi's replies, we shall discuss the significance of ritual transformation (*li yi zhi hua* 禮義之化) in Xunzi's moral philosophy. From the earlier discussion, one might think that transformation only involves the imposition of social distinctions and a hierarchical order that serves to curb the excesses of individual behavior. We shall see, however, that for Xunzi transformation involves a much more positive molding of individual character through a process of cultivation and refinement, and ultimately striving for a balance between emotion and form. In this sense, we may extrapolate Xunzi's use of the term *fen* 分 to refer to much more than (the making of) social distinctions. In other words, it could be said to include the apprehension of more subtle aesthetic and moral distinctions involved in the transformation of individual character.

Transformation (化)

Let us start by looking at analogies of transformation in the text of the *Xunzi*. The first chapter of the text begins with the admonition that learning should never cease (*xue bu ke yi yi* 學不可以已). Learning involves transformation as we see from the following analogies. Dye made from the indigo plant is bluer; ice comes from water but is colder; wood can be curved into a wheel; and metal can be sharpened (1.1, ICS 1/1/3–5).[1]

These analogies imply the change of an original state with a certain potential to another state that manifests this potential in some form. With the exception of water turning into ice under natural conditions, these changes do not occur of themselves. We see the need for effort in making the change, and this is all the more important when we think of what is involved in moral learning. As may be gathered from the previous two chapters, the overall term that signifies this in Xunzi's thinking is human artifice or *wei* (偽). This refers to the making of something requiring deliberation (*lü* 慮) and cumulative effort (*ji* 積). *Wei* can be contrasted with *sheng* (生) or what is given through "life" or "birth." Thus, a transformative moral state is thought to be the result of human effort instead of a biological feature of birth.

When Xunzi speaks of transformation through ritual practices, he has in mind a positive moral state, and not merely feeling bound by external constraints. In this regard, an important term that occurs in conjunction with *hua* is *shen* (神). This appears to refer to a state of learning and moral achievement that enables someone to influence others 'silently'. It also refers to the seemingly wondrous effect of this influence—even though the process is invisible, the effect comes through. Xunzi compares this to the following effects of natural phenomena: "The great transformations of *yin yang*, the bountiful scattering of wind and rain, each of the myriad things receiving what is agreeable to their growth, and each receiving what nurtures them to maturity (*yin yang da hua* 陰陽大化, *feng yu bo shi* 風雨博施, *wan wu ge de qi he yi sheng* 萬物各得其和以生, *ge de qi yang yi cheng* 各得其養以成)." Following this, he says: "Not perceiving the process we see the result, this is called *shen* (*bu jian qi shi* 不見其事, *er jian qi gong* 而見其功, *fu shi wei shen* 夫是謂神)" (17.2b, ICS 17/18/5–6).

Given this silent influence of *shen*, it would not be inappropriate to refer to it as a transformative moral force, and those who have been influenced as having undergone a process of *yang* or nurture (養) resulting in moral growth and maturity. This is confirmed by the association of *shen* with the moral qualities of sincerity and humanity. The noble person's nurture of a sincere heart-mind and his being humane will manifest itself in *shen*, a moral force that transforms others. (*Jun zi yang xin mo shan yu cheng . . . cheng xin shou ren ze xing* 君子養心莫善於誠 . . . 誠心守仁則形, *xing ze shen* 形則神, *shen ze neng hua yi* 神則能化矣) (3.9a, ICS 3/11/4–5). The same association between being humane and transforming others is found in the following statement: "Wherever the army of a humane person is, it has an effect like that of a *shen*; wherever it travels, it produces transformation. Like seasonable rains, it pleases and gives joy to all." (*Gu ren ren zhi bing* 故仁人之兵, *suo cun zhe shen* 所存者神, *suo guo zhe hua* 所過者化, *ruo shi yu zhi jiang* 若時雨之降, *mo bu yue xi* 莫不說喜)[2] (15.2, ICS 15/71/24).

For Xunzi, the sages have the ability to transform themselves through cumulative effort. And according to him, habitual practice can shift the will, and over time can even result in a change of substantial qualities of the person.

(*Xi su yi zhi* 習俗移志, *an jiu yi zhi* 安久移質) (8.11, ICS 8/34/2). Similarly, transformation occurs over the long-term such that the transformed object will never revert to its beginnings (*chang qian er bu fan qi chu* 長遷而不反其初, *ze hua yi* 則化矣) (3.9c, ICS 3/11/12). As he says regarding the analogy of curving wood into a wheel, "It will not return to its former straightness (*bu fu ting zhe* 不復挺者)" [3] (1.1, ICS 1/1/4).

By "beginnings" in this context Xunzi is evidently referring to human nature or *xing* (性). There is nothing *in essence* bad about human nature that prevents transformation. An appreciation of this involves understanding the contents not only of *xing* 性, but also of other general facts that Xunzi refers to as the *qing* of human beings (人之情). This has already been discussed. But briefly: *Xing* is a biological concept referring to what all persons are born with, namely, the basic sensory and appetitive desires. In addition, they are said to be born with a love of benefit, feelings of envy and hate, and pettiness. However, "the *qing* of human beings" refers to the fact that people also have wants and capacities that go beyond the basic desires and feelings. They want wealth, luxury, and a more refined life. These imply the need for security, the capacities to think long-term, to be prudent, and to establish or learn ritual principles.

The contents of *xing* are of course essential to biological life and survival. However, they are not an *essence* in the sense of being what is distinctive about a human being *qua* human being. The biological "raw material" of human beings can be transformed because in addition, their *qing* is such that they possess the capacities mentioned. However, for various reasons (see chapter 5), some people are unable to transform themselves because they do not exercise their capacities.

Thus, the object of transformation is nature (*hua xing* 化性) and the instrument of transformation is the ritual principles (*li yi* 禮義) established and taught by the sages. [4] It might be thought that they can only serve to curb the excesses of individual desires and to inculcate habits so as to establish and maintain a hierarchical social order. Although there is certainly this aspect of the rites in Xunzi's discussion of the concept, the whole educational aim of the rites is transformative in the moral sense already described. We shall be in a better position to appreciate this after an analysis of Xunzi's response to Mozi's criticisms.

Mozi's Economic Argument

Earlier, I referred to the well-known criticism of Mozi's that the Ru ritual practices are wasteful. Let us call the argument supporting this criticism the "economic argument." [5] Mozi appealed to the authority of the ancient sage kings who, according to him, acted by the law of economical use (*jie yong zhi fa* 節用之法). [6] This means the production and consumption of food, clothing, and shelter for simple utilitarian purposes. Food satiates hunger and maintains strength and health, while clothing provides warmth. Houses provide shelter against the elements. In addition, the rooms of houses are clean enough for sacrificial purposes and the partitions in the palace are high enough to separate the sexes.[7] Anything beyond these basic purposes was, according to Mozi, useless expenditure (*wu yong zhi fei* 無用之費).[8] The sage kings were economical in their use of resources (*yong cai bu fei* 用財不費),[9] and this meant too not exhausting the people unnecessarily. Artisans, carpenters, craftspeople, farmers, and other workers should therefore produce only what is necessary to satisfy the most basic desires and needs.

The aspect of Ruist ritual that Mozi is particularly critical of is its use of luxurious items that seem merely to gratify the senses. For instance, there are ceremonies that call for refined food accompanied by a variety of aesthetically pleasing utensils and decorum. Add to this the clothing, adornments, decorations, musical instruments, and other paraphernalia associated with ritual performance—the refinements of Ruist ritual must have seemed very extravagant indeed. Appealing to the law of economical use, Mozi says: "There is no need of combining the five tastes extremely well or harmonizing the different sweet odours."[10] The sage king Yao "ate out of an earthen *liu* (塯) and drank out of an earthen *xing* (形), and took wine out of a spoon. With the ceremonies of bowing and stretching and courtesies and decorum the sage-king had nothing to do."[11] In short, according to Mozi, any practice that is deemed useless (*wu yong* 無用) and of no benefit (*li* 利) should be abolished.

Xunzi on Nurture or *Yang* (養)

Certain references to Mozi and his school in the *Li Lun Pian* indicate that Xunzi is responding to Mozi's criticism. There are also passages that are a direct response to points made by Mozi, even though his name is not mentioned. In this section, we see how Xunzi responds to Mozi's economic argument through the concept of *yang* or nurture. In a single passage, Xunzi refers to various objects of nurture, and we shall analyze what "nurture" means in each case.

In chapter 6, we saw that Xunzi discusses the origin of the rites in terms of its providing the economic and social conditions for order. People are born with desires. Left unregulated, this will result in strife, disorder, and poverty. The sage kings are said to have abhorred such chaos and therefore "established the ritual principles to make normative distinctions, to nurture people's desires, and to supply what they seek (*gu zhi li yi yi fen zhi* 故制禮義以分之, *yi yang ren zhi yu* 以養人之欲, *ji ren zhi qiu* 給人之求)" (19.1a, ICS 19/90/3–5). That is, social chaos is prevented through *fen* 分, the normative distinctions established by the ritual principles. These distinctions govern relationships through norms that determine familial, social and professional status and the corresponding distribution of benefits and burdens, wealth and responsibilities. (See also 4.12, ICS 4/17/1–2.)

At the same time, the ritual principles are said to nurture people's desires (*yang ren zhi yu* 養人之欲).[12] This seems to be explained by the economic function of ensuring that desires as a whole are not left wanting because of an inadequate supply of goods (*yu bu qiong yu wu* 欲不窮於物). In this sense, the notion of *yang* would appear to be a result of *fen*. That is, people's desires and expectations would be moderated by the normative distinctions of their respective familial, social, and professional status. This moderation is implied by the converse of the statement that desires are not left wanting by an inadequate supply, namely, that supply is not exhausted by the desires (*wu bi bu qu yu yu* 物必不屈於欲) (19.1a, ICS 19/90/5).

It would seem natural, therefore, to expect that this is what Xunzi means when he next says, "Thus, ritual is nurture" (*gu li zhe yang ye* 故禮者養也). That is, ritual "nurtures" in the sense that it both curbs and moderates people's desires through the imposition of normative distinctions. However, the equating of ritual with nurture is followed by a list of refined food, flavors, fragrances, exquisite jewels, emblems, musical instruments, and bodily comforts. These items are said to nurture the various senses, namely, those of the mouth, nose, eyes, ears, and (the comforts of) the body (*yang* 養: *kou* 口, *bi* 鼻, *mu* 目, *er* 耳, *ti* 體). He then repeats, "Thus, ritual is nurture" (19.1b, ICS 19/90/8). If this is to be taken in the single sense of curbing and moderating the desires, it is puzzling why Xunzi should provide a list of refined and luxurious items that would seem instead to satisfy (or gratify) the senses to the utmost extent.

But this is resolved if we see that Xunzi is not talking about nurturing the senses *per se*. Instead, his concern is with ritual, and there is evidently some link between the nurture of the senses and ritual. Note that the things that nurture the senses are refined items of ritual. When Xunzi both prefaces and ends his remarks about the nurture of the senses with the remark that ritual is nurture, he means to associate ritual with cultivation and refinement. Thus, it would not be inappropriate to say that ritual is nurture in the sense of cultivated refinement. Elsewhere, for instance, Xunzi likens the ignorance of ritual principles to the coarse satisfaction of appetite, and in this regard the way of the tyrannical king Jie and Robber Zhi is contrasted with that of the ancient sage kings "just as the meat of pastured and grain-fed animals contrasts with dregs and husks." (See 4.10, ICS 4/15/21.) This means that to have knowledge of ritual principles is to be cultivated and refined.

Xunzi then says that the noble person who has been nurtured (in the sense of cultivated refinement) also likes the distinctions (*hao qi bie* 好其別) that this gives rise to. The emblems, regalia, and comforts of the Son of Heaven do not just satisfy the body and the senses, but they serve to nurture a sense of: trust (*yang xin* 養信), majestic authority (*yang wei* 養威), and peace/security (*yang an* 養安) (19.1c, ICS 19/90/13–14). We may understand this to mean that the refinements of ritual involve distinctions that in this instance nurture a sense of trust in and respect for authority.

With regard to *yang an* 養安, Xunzi mentions that "the horse for the Grand Chariot must be thoroughly reliable and perfectly trained before it is harnessed, to nurture a sense of security around him." While this seems to say something about the security that the ruler gains from having a reliable horse, it at the same time suggests the role of the rites in nurturing a sense of peace/security for the people. (Shortly after, for instance, the notion of *yang an* is repeated through the statement that the reverence and courtesy of ritual are means whereby peace/security is attained) (19.1d, ICS 19/90/15).

Next, Xunzi says: "Who knows that (being prepared) to go forth to one's death in the name of honor is to nurture life!" (*shu zhi fu chu si yao jie zhi suo yi yang sheng ye* 孰知夫出死要節之所以養生也!) (19.1d, ICS 19/90/14). Xunzi cannot mean by "life" here the mere maintenance of a biological and material life. The preparedness to die brings in another dimension of *sheng* 生 or "life." The term *yao jie* 要節 in this context could refer either to the duty-bound "carrying out a commission" or to "value honor."[13] In either case, we can understand Xunzi to be saying that there is a significant understanding of "life" such that in order to nurture it, one is (paradoxically) prepared to die.

Xunzi goes on to ask: "Who knows that the (seemingly wasteful) expenditures nurture wealth!" (*Shu zhi fu chu fei yong zhi suo yi yang cai ye* 孰知夫出費用之所以養財也!) (19.1c, ICS 19/90/15). This is a direct response to Mozi. Recall that Mozi had criticized the Ru for useless expenditure (*wu yong zhi fei* 無用之費) and contrasted this with the sage kings' economical use of wealth or resources (*yong cai bu fei* 用財不費). Clearly, Xunzi is denying that the use of luxurious and refined items in ritual constitute useless or wasteful expenditure.

Mozi seems to have thought of society's economic state in terms of an individual's consuming only basic necessities and limiting his or her desires to these. Xunzi, however, realizes that the economic state of a society cannot be modeled upon an individual in this way. And neither should it be thought that people only have, or should be limited to, basic desires and needs. Instead, they have a wide range of desires, wants, and needs, and it is ritual that creates the orderly conditions for the satisfaction of these. The processes of ritual also create economic activity and stimulate production. There is a cumulative network effect in the overall production and use of goods and services that promotes economic wealth.[14]

To summarize the arguments so far: Mozi stresses meeting basic desires and needs, frugality of expenditure (especially on the part of the ruler and officials), ensuring population growth, and the maintenance of peace, security, and order. In reply, Xunzi shows that the Ru ritual practices do not inhibit these goals. On the contrary, they contribute much more effectively to them. Ritual "nurtures" these goals in various ways. It brings order through normative distinctions that curb and moderate desires, ensures adequate supply of goods, and creates more economic wealth overall through its expenditures. In short, ritual nurtures activities and states of affairs that are compatible with the economic goals mentioned by Mozi.

At the same time, however, Xunzi uses "nurture" in ways that suggest the cultivation of other, noneconomic dimensions of life. For instance, he speaks of the nurture of life in paradoxical terms—being prepared to go forth to one's death because one is bound by a sense of what honorable. Similarly, when he says that "ritual is nurture," and talks of nurturing the various senses, he is suggesting that a flourishing life consists in cultivated refinement both brought about by, and engaged through, the rites.

This cultivated refinement is related to another object of nurture—the feelings or emotions, *qing* 情.[15] Xunzi asks at the end of the paragraph about nurture, "Who knows that the cultured forms of ritual principles are how to nurture the feelings/emotions?" (*Shu zhi fu li yi wen li zhi suo yi yang qing ye* 孰知夫禮義文理之所以養情也)" (K19.1d, ICS 19/90/15–16). This is an important issue that Xunzi will discuss in detail later. For now, let us note that the preceding discussion of *yang* or "nurture" is only a prelude to a wider argument: Mozi's economic argument is too narrowly focused on the biological dimension of life. Xunzi, in effect, observes that this dimension is equivalent to human *xing* or nature. It is precisely the function of ritual principles to transform this nature.

Mozi's Convention Argument

As mentioned in the introductory remarks to this chapter, Mozi's criticism that the Ru ritual practices are merely conventional habituations has been underappreciated. I shall call the argument behind this criticism the "convention argument." At first, this seems to be an extension of the economic argument. However, we shall see that the convention argument is in fact different and more forceful.[16]

Mozi begins with a statement about what the ruler would do, by analogy with the filial son (*xiao zi* 孝子). Just as the latter would look after his parents, expand the family pool, and ensure order within the family, the former would enrich the people, increase the population, and ensure order. The ruler is referred to here as the humane or the *ren* person (*ren zhe* 仁者), the emphasis being on what the *ren* person would do. Another concept that Mozi appeals to is *yi* (義) or what is "right" or "righteous." He laments that with the passing of the sage kings, *yi* has been lost and people disagree whether elaborate funerals and lengthy mourning are manifestations of *ren*, *yi*, and being filial. According to Mozi, the *ren* person would decide on the basis of whether there is devotion to three things (*san wu* 三務): actions and practices that can enrich the poor, increase population, and bring stability and order to the state would be deemed *ren* and *yi* and filial.[17]

Judging by these criteria, there is no redeeming feature of the Ru funeral rites. There is no economic gain from the elaborate and lavish funeral rites and burials. Those who cannot afford such burials but feel obliged to follow the practice will be impoverished. In the case of the funerals of rulers and ministers, there is great loss of lives in having people "accompany the dead" (*song cong* 送 從, *sha xun* 殺殉). The lengthy three-year period of mourning takes its toll on work and production, and "relations between men and women" are disrupted. All these factors lead to poverty, banditry, decline in population growth, and fewer people to guard and repair fortifications. In short, there will be disorder and inability to defend the state.[18] As a solution, Mozi advocates the following simple burial practice for all, which he claims was prescribed by the sage kings:

> The coffin shall be three inches thick, sufficient to hold the body. As to shrouds there shall be three pieces adequate to cover the corpse. It shall not be buried so deep as to reach water and neither so shallow as to allow the odour to ascend. Three feet in size shall be big enough for the mound. There shall be no extended mourning after burial, but speedy return to work and pursuit in what one can do to procure mutual benefit.[19]

Why do people maintain elaborate funerals and lengthy mourning when these were not practiced by the sage kings? Mozi's answer is that they have become accustomed to their practices and regard what is customary as right (*bian qi xi er yi qi su* 便其習而義其俗). He cites the following examples. East of the state of Yue (越) the people of Kai Shu (較沭) ate the first-born son in the belief that this would be beneficial to the next son. Upon the death of a father, the mother would be abandoned because they could not live "with the wife of a ghost." South of Chu (楚), the people of Yan (炎) considered it filial to discard the flesh of deceased parents and bury only the bones. West of Qin (秦), the people of Yi Qu (儀渠) cremated their parents' bodies to enable their ascension (*deng xia* 登遐). Mozi asks: "How can these really be the way of *ren* and *yi* (*ci qi shi ren yi zhi dao zai* 此豈實仁義之道哉)?" On the contrary, their actions are "heartless" (*bo* 薄).[20]

In sum, Mozi's criticism is: (1) The Ru practices of burial and mourning are not beneficial. (2) These practices are merely conventional and arbitrary. (3) In both these respects, they are not humane, right, or filial. Note that Mozi is not making a claim about the truth of moral relativism that all burial practices are equally "right"—this would mean that there is no absolute concept of right. Instead, there is a right way to bury one's parents, which is the utilitarian and speedy way that we have quoted above. This right utilitarian way is considered not only filial, but also humane since it does not have all the bad consequences mentioned.

Note too that Mozi's criticism is not just that the Ru ritual practices are wasteful. If this were all, it could be met by the response to the economic argument that was described earlier. Instead, there is something deeper in Mozi's second criticism. Mozi is appealing not just to benefit, but in addition, to moral criteria that are cornerstones of the Ru system of values. To put it succinctly: the Ru ritual practices are not beneficial. But the deeper point is that they have no basis in any feelings of being humane, right, and filial. Instead, they are merely arbitrary conventions, as shown by the comparison with the other burial practices described.

Xunzi: Reclaiming the Ground of Feeling

In this and the subsequent sections, we investigate how Xunzi replies to the convention argument. For the sake of clarity, I have rearranged the points made in a logical and expository sequence instead of following the order of the passages in the *Li Lun Pian*. In this regard, I shall refer to "strategies" of argument adopted by Xunzi.

One strategy is to dissociate the proper Ru ritual practices from the cruel and unnatural practices cited by Mozi. He condemns the cruel practice of sacrificing the living to "accompany the dead" (*sha sheng er song si wei zhi zei* 殺生而送死謂之賊) (19.8, ICS 19/96/1). And he castigates those who deliberately force an emaciated and starved appearance on themselves. This, he says, is the form of villains, not the form proper to ritual, and not the *qing* or feeling/emotions of the filial son (*shi jian ren zhi dao* 是姦人之道, *fei li yi zhi wen ye* 非禮義之文也, *fei xiao zi zhi qing* 非孝子之情也) (19.5b, ICS 19/94/14).

Another strategy is to stress the role of feelings in ritual and to accuse Mozi himself of a lack of feeling through his neglect of ritual. Xunzi mentions a few times the "thoughts of longing and remembrance" (*si mu zhi yi* 思慕之義 19.4c, ICS 19/94/1; 思慕未忘 19.9a, ICS19/96/7; 思慕之情 19.11, ICS 19/97/20, 19/98/1). As part of the emphasis on these feelings, Xunzi counterattacks Mozi. Xunzi first says that there is no conscious creature that would not love its own kind (*you zhi zhi shu mo bu ai qi lei* 有知之屬莫不愛其類). In the context of death, even birds and animals display some form of pining behavior. Humans have the highest consciousness and therefore would have the utmost feelings for their own deceased parents. Xunzi then refers to "depraved people who by evening have forgotten a parent who died that morning. And if we indulge in such behavior are we not lower even than these birds and beasts?" (19.9b–c, ICS 19/96/10–15). This is an oblique, *ad hominem* attack on Mozi, who recommends a quick and simple burial.

Thus, Xunzi regains the initiative by reclaiming the ground of feelings for Ru ritual. With the same objective in mind, Xunzi does not want the Ru school to seem unreasonable in failing to concede the need for some flexibility in periods of mourning. He had earlier defended the three-year period by saying that the form was established to accord with the emotions involved (*cheng qing er li wen* 稱情而立文) (19.9a, ICS 19/96/4, 5). Now he proposes an average of a year for one's closest kin, the reason being that "Heaven and Earth have completed their changes, the four seasons have come full circle, and everything under the canopy of heaven has begun anew. Thus, the Ancient Kings based themselves on this and used it for their pattern" (19.9c, ICS 19/96/23–24). Deviation from this, however, is permissible—mourning periods varying from nine months or less to three years for different ranks may be practiced.

All these points—the emphasis on proper feeling in ritual, the rejection of cruel practices, and the flexibility in periods of mourning—take the sting away from Mozi's criticism that the Ruist ritual practices are not filial, humane, or right. However, Xunzi has yet to say anything more substantial about the principles underlying the rites.

The Three Roots

Early on in the discussion, Xunzi does in fact enunciate a basic principle behind the rites. This comes directly after he mentions the difference between the Mohists and the Ruists—that the Mohists only know about satisfying basic desires of human nature and not the demands of ritual. The ignorance of ritual would lead to failure to satisfy both (19.1c, ICS 19/90/17–18). This suggests a point that will be elaborated further in the later discussion: that ritual fulfills needs belonging to other dimensions of human life. Xunzi then enunciates the following principle:

> Ritual principles have three roots (*li you san ben* 禮有三本). Heaven and Earth are the root of life (*tian di zhe* 天地者, *sheng zhi ben ye* 生之本也). Forebears are the root of kinship (*xian zhu zhe* 先祖者, *lei zhi ben ye* 類之本也). Lords and teachers are the root of order (*jun shi zhe* 君師者, *zhi zhi ben ye* 治之本也). Were there no Heaven and no Earth, how could there be life? Were there no forebears, how could there be issue? Were there no lords and no teachers, how could there be order? Were even one of these three lost, there would be no peace and security for man. Thus, rituals serve Heaven above and Earth below, pay honor to one's forebears, and exalt rulers and teachers, for these are the three roots of ritual principles. (19.2a, ICS 19/90/20–22)

In the light of Mozi's convention argument, we may read this as an assertion of the grounding of ritual in certain universal roots. Xunzi argues that the ritual practices of the Ru are not arbitrary, but rather are rooted in the relationships that human beings have with Heaven and Earth, ancestors, rulers, and teachers. Besides having to fulfill basic biological and material needs, humans have a sense of what is significant in life, and this is enacted in rituals that concern the roots mentioned.[21]

Directly after stating the principle of rootedness, Xunzi discusses the sacrifices of the king to his founding ancestor and Heaven, and at the lower levels the feudal lords, officers, and knights each perform their own sacrifices honoring their own origins (*gui shi* 貴始). This practice, according to Xunzi, is the basis of virtue (*gui shi de zhi ben ye* 貴始得 [德] 之本也). In other words, these sacrificial rituals are an educational process that brings about virtuous feelings. Thus, to have a sense of the roots of life and to pay reverence to them is a basic step toward the development of virtue.

One way to look at the development of virtue is to think of it as an acceptance of the principles of separation and hierarchy. This seems to be suggested by the following passage:

> Through rites, Heaven and Earth are [in accord] (*yi he* 以和), the sun and moon shine brightly, the four seasons observe their natural precedence, the stars and planets move in ranks, the rivers and streams flow, and the myriad things prosper. Through them, love and hate are tempered, and joy and anger made to fit the occasion (*hao wu yi jie* 好惡以節, *xi nu yi dang* 喜怒以當). They are used to make inferiors obedient and to make superiors enlightened. Through a myriad transformations nothing becomes disorderly. . . . Root and branch accord with one another; end and beginning are fitting and proper, one to the other (*ben mo xiang shun* 本末相順, *shi zhong xiang ying* 始終相應). (19.2c, ICS 19/92/4–8)

If we are not to take the above passage literally to mean that the rites regulate even the natural order, then at least Xunzi is likening the ritual to the natural order. Thus, just as the astronomical bodies and the four seasons revolve in a certain order, ritual imposes an order in human relations through its distinctions and keeping people within the bounds of these distinctions. Despite this "mirroring" of the natural order, however, some qualifications should be made.

First, even if we interpret the making of distinctions as emphasizing a hierarchical order and the sense of one's place in this order, we should note that this place is not naturally fixed. Instead, there is room for movements across positions based on accomplishment or merit, what Xunzi refers to as *ji hou* (積厚) (19.2a, ICS 19/91/5).

Second, as Xunzi constantly reminds us, human beings need to make the effort to establish and to maintain ritual principles. These are the result of constitutive activity (*qi wei* 起偽), cumulative effort (*ji* 積), and deliberation (*lü* 慮), instead of being something that we are born with. Ritual principles do not occur seemingly of their own accord just like natural events.

Third, and following upon the second qualification, some interpretation has to be made of what it means to follow the natural order and to have distinctions in human affairs. The inculcation of a hierarchical order is certainly an important part of ritual distinctions. However, there are other aspects to ritual distinctions. Note the remarks in the quotation above, following those about the natural order. It is said that through the rites, "love and hate are tempered, and joy and anger made to fit the occasion . . . end and beginning are fitting and proper, one to the other." These remarks suggest other aspects of ritual distinctions that are equally important, especially when we have in mind the moral transformation brought about by ritual learning and practice.

The Middle Course of Ritual

Thus, the making of ritual distinctions concerns, among other things, the achievement of a proper balance between: love and hate (*hao wu yi jie* 好惡以節), joy and anger (*xi nu yi dang* 喜怒以當), beginning and end or life and death (*zhong shi xiang ying* 終始相應), root and branch (*ben mo xiang shun* 本末相順),[22] and emotion and form (*qing wen ju jin* 情文俱盡) (19.2c, ICS 19/92/3–9). Besides nurturing a sense of reverence for the roots of life, a further component of the development of virtue through the rites would be to nurture principles of balance. This is what Xunzi refers to as taking the "middle course" (*zhong liu* 中流). We describe these principles below.

Evidently in response to Mozi, most of Xunzi's discussion concerns the funeral rites. Here too, we see "honoring the root" balanced with considerations of practicality. The time allowed for the deceased to be laid in state, for instance, has to be such that those who are far away can return in time to pay their last respects (19.4c, ICS 19/93/22). More interesting, however, are the following considerations that help to maintain a balance between assuaging love of the dead and feeling revulsion at the state of the corpse. Adorning the corpse disguises its hideousness, which may tend to inhibit grief (*bu shi ze wu* 不飾則惡, *wu ze bu ai* 惡則不哀). However, the ceremony should be such that one gradually comes to be separated from the deceased, and this gradual distancing enables both the proper expressions of grief and reverence on the one hand, and an eventual return to a concern with the living on the other (19.5a, ICS 19/94/3–6).

Birth and death are referred to as the beginning (*shi* 始) and the end (*zhong* 終). Beginning and end make the human way (*ren dao* 人道) complete. Thus, it is the way of the noble person (*jun zi zhi dao* 君子之道) not just to show reverence for the beginning, but equally, for the end. The failure to show reverence for the dead according to the proper ritual forms (*li yi zhi wen* 禮義之文) shows a rebellious heart (*bei pan zhi xin* 倍判 [背叛] 之心) and a lack of earnest sincerity (*bu zhong hou* 不忠厚) (19.4a, ICS 19/93/6–10). Accordingly, there are various forms to be observed in the funeral rites, and Xunzi describes the forms proper to the king, the feudal lords, and the ordinary person. There is one more category, that of the "castrated criminal." The description of the burial in this case almost exactly parallels that given by Mozi quoted earlier. Xunzi adds that this burial of the criminal "does not involve uniting his family and neighbors, but brings together only his wife and children. . . . As soon as his body is interred in the earth, everything ends as though there had never been a funeral. Truly this is the ultimate disgrace" (19.4b, ICS 19/93/15–17).

Emotion and Form

In mentioning the forms of proper burial, Xunzi is reminding his audience of the need for forms of psychological expression, a need that is fulfilled in various ways by the funeral rites.[23] We have mentioned the balance between the feelings/emotions *qing* (情) and ritual form *wen* (文).[24] As we have seen, for instance, Xunzi says of those who deliberately look emaciated and starved during the funerals that they are not taking the form proper to ritual, and that these are not the emotions of the filial son. This means that emotion and form are intimately related. Ritual is not, as Mozi claims, merely a convention, but the form in which human emotions are expressed. In the case of the funeral rites, it allows for various psychological expressions of grief. Various relations between emotion and form are possible, each with a different emphasis. However, the perfect state of ritual (*zhi bei* 至備) is when both emotion and form are fully realized (*qing wen ju jin* 情文俱盡) (19.2c, ICS 19/92/3). This proper balance between emotion and form is referred to as taking the middle course of ritual whereby one acts in an integrated manner that combines both inner and outer (*Wen li qing yong xiang wei nei wai biao li* 文理情用相為內外表裏, *bing xing er za* 並行而雜, *shi li zhi zhong liu ye* 是禮之中流也) (19.3, ICS 19/92/22 to 19/93/1).

What taking the middle course means in practice, however, would depend on the occasion. Thus, there are occasions that call for grand ritual forms, and others that call for simpler forms (*gu jun zi shang zhi qi long* 故君子上致其隆, *xia jin qi sha* 下盡其殺, *er zhong chu qi zhong* 而中處其中) (19.3, ICS 19/93/1; see Li, *Xunzi Ji Shi*, 431, note 8). Aesthetic considerations are also involved in helping one to strike a proper balance:

> Rites trim what is too long, stretch out what is too short, eliminate excess, remedy deficiency, and extend cultivated forms that express love and respect so that they increase and complete the beauty of conduct according to one's duty (*li zhe* 禮者, *duan chang xu duan* 斷長續短, *sun you yu* 損有餘, *yi bu zu* 益不足, *da ai jing zhi wen* 達愛敬之文, *er ci cheng xing yi zhi mei zhe ye* 而滋成行義之美者也). (19.5b, ICS 19/94/8)

Here, we have an interesting reference to the beauty of doing one's duty or what is right (*xing yi zhi mei* 行義之美). The beauty comes about through the expression of love and reverence according to a proper form. Thus, emotional expression should neither be deficient nor excessive, and what ensures this is a form that is guided by aesthetic criteria. Hence, the elegant adornment (*wen shi* 文飾) of ritual: "does not go so far as to be sensuous or seductive. . . . Their use of music and happiness does not go so far as to be wayward and abandoned or indolent and rude, nor do weeping and sorrow go so far as to produce despondency or injury to life. Such is the middle course of ritual" (19.5b, ICS 19/94/11–12).

The Significance of Ritual Transformation

We may now discuss the significance of ritual transformation for Xunzi by joining and reiterating some of the points made above. It should be understood that when I refer to "transformation" below, it is the process and the result of transformation through ritual or ritual principles (*li yi* 禮義) that I am referring to.

As we have seen, Xunzi speaks metaphorically of the wondrous moral force—like the bountiful effects of wind and rain—that the humane person has on others. This metaphor intimates that the effect of transformation is a positive moral state. The transformed person would act on the basis of values like humanity, righteousness and being filial, instead of being constrained by rules.

Xunzi leaves the metaphor behind when he speaks of the effort required to achieve transformation. The object of transformation is the nature that all persons are born with. Its contents are the desire for benefit, sensory desires, and dispositions to feelings such as envy and hate. There are tendencies to indulge these, with bad consequences for the individual and the society.

The sage kings therefore devised ritual principles to establish and maintain social order. Together with the influence of teachers and models, these principles impose normative distinctions that curb and moderate people's desires through a sense of hierarchy and distributional principles of rank, status, and merit.

This raises a question about the possibility of the positive moral state that was just mentioned above. If ritual serves to curb and moderate people's desires through hierarchy and distributional principles, then it seems that all it accomplishes is to make the individual feel bound by normative distinctions.[25]

I have argued, however, that we should not be too impressed by the fact that Xunzi likens the ritual order to the natural order. Thus, it might be thought that just as the astronomical bodies and the four seasons move and revolve in fixed order, ritual keeps people within the bounds of social and normative distinctions. In this respect, the daily practice of ritual serves to foster and internalize habits and customs that serve the maintenance of order.

Thus, it might appear that under the system of ritual principles that Xunzi describes, there is hardly room for the positive moral state mentioned earlier—it remains a metaphor. In reply to this, it should be admitted that moral education and moral development may begin with the imposition of social and normative distinctions and a sense of hierarchy. It does not follow, however, that the sense of morality thereafter can only be hierarchical. Xunzi stresses that ritual principles are the result of human construction. This being the case, it should not be assumed that the normative distinctions of ritual principles have a naturally set order. And in fact, Xunzi has in mind distinctions that are not just hierarchical ones.

The crux of Xunzi's reply to Mozi is that his conception of life is too narrow, since it is confined to the basic desires and needs. In his economic argument,

Mozi appeals to the law of economic use, which refers to the production and consumption of basic daily necessities. He also refers to the alleged fact that the sage kings were economical in their use of resources, which means that workers should produce only necessities that would satisfy basic desires and needs. Anything beyond this is deemed not beneficial and "useful."

To Xunzi, this is to remain at the level of human nature and its biological contents. To repeat, it is precisely the object of ritual principles to transform this nature. As we have seen, the discussion of "nurture" (*yang* 養) highlights dimensions of life beside the biological. This is perhaps summed up in the statement "ritual is nurture." This could mean bringing about a better and more refined quality of life. At the same time, however, ritual serves to nurture a sense of trust, authority, and peace/security given by the ruler. This need not be confined to the relation between ruler and subjects, however. The feelings of trust, authority, peace, and security are instilled through various forms of ritual that people tend to take for granted, and without which a society cannot properly function.[26]

Importantly, there is also the dimension of honor. Xunzi talks paradoxically of the nurture of life through being prepared to die for the sake honor. This example illustrates two remarks of Xunzi's noted earlier. First, Xunzi remarks that the substantial qualities of a person can be changed (*yi zhi* 移質). In this example, we have a person who has moved from a biological concern with the preservation of life to a moral concern with honor through the rites. Second, Xunzi remarks that transformation involves a long-term process with the result of the transformed object or person not reverting to the beginnings. It would be true of the honorable person that he will never revert to the "beginning," in that he has gone beyond his original nature. But remember that "beginning" and "end" also mean life and death. It would be literally true to say of someone that he will not revert to the beginning if he dies for the sake of honor.

Perhaps the most philosophically interesting dimension of transformation is nurture of the feelings/emotions through a balance with form. This is not just a matter of balance, but of the integration of emotion and form. The convention argument claims that the Ru ritual practices are just as arbitrary as others. There are two related assumptions behind this argument. One is that the moral values of humanity, righteousness, and being filial can have genuine expression independently of the forms of ritual practice. Another is that these values reside in spontaneous feelings that are found in human nature. To Xunzi, however, this claim of a separation between human nature and convention, or between the feelings and the forms of ritual, is spurious. As he says, "Without nature there would be nothing for constitutive activity to act on, (but) without constitutive activity nature would be unable to beautify itself"[27] (19.6, ICS 19/95/1–2). And as Antonio Cua has stated, "When the natural expression of one's feeling, such as joy or sadness, love or hate, is subjected to the regulation and transformation of *li*, it can no longer be viewed as mere natural expression, for so regulated and transformed it acquires a significance beyond its original and spontaneous untutored expression."[28]

We may elaborate upon the relation between emotion and form in terms of some examples given by Xunzi. Think of the example mentioned earlier, of those who force an emaciated and starved appearance on themselves in a funeral rite. In reference to this example Xunzi says, "This is not the form of ritual and not the emotion of the filial son" (*Fei li yi zhi wen ye* 非禮義之文也, *fei xiao zi zhi qing* 非孝子之情). This condemnation implies that there is a form or forms that would count as the proper expression of being filial. Thus, a spontaneous feeling in itself does not constitute being filial. Instead, certain forms of action would count as being filial or not. Take the speedy burial advocated by Mozi, for instance. We had said that Xunzi's oblique reference to this constitutes an *ad hominem* argument against Mozi. But putting this in the context of the relation between emotion and form, let us imagine someone following Mozi's general recommendation of a speedy burial. It may well be that this person's action is not filial because it gives the impression that he has quickly forgotten his parent, implying that he has not cared. Of course, pretense is possible while going through the motions of ritual. But this does not invalidate the integration of emotion and form. On the contrary, pretense is possible because of this integration in the first place.

We may also consider the following examples in the *Xing E Pian* ("Nature is Bad"), which follows the statement supposedly made by the sage king Shun, that human emotions are unlovely (*ren qing shen bu mei* 人情甚不美) (23.6a, ICS 23/116/25). A man who has married and built up his own family may neglect his filial duty to his parents; someone who has received what he or she desired may betray the trust of a friend; and someone may abandon loyalty to a superior after having attained a high and lucrative official post. The feelings of being filial, loyal, and trustworthy cannot be understood apart from what it means to be in the particular relationship in each case. In the case of the superior-subordinate relationship, for instance, perhaps the subordinate person no longer shows proper respect. Or perhaps not quite realizing it, he or she becomes neglectful in some way, thus indicating that he or she no longer values the relationship. In either case, the person fails to manifest loyalty. What this shows is that the feeling of loyalty is structured by certain ritual forms, and failure to maintain these forms—in the absence of some good explanation—constitutes not being loyal. Again, it is possible for one to hide one's real feelings while maintaining the form. But it is the context of events that reveals this, and the possibility of pretense does nothing to negate the integration of emotion and form.

The issue of maintaining the form and determining whether it expresses the appropriate emotion, however, is a complex one. Getting it right involves a host of factors. One has to balance simplicity, for instance, with a sense of the occasion and the need to be practical. Neither form nor emotion should be exaggerated. Wisdom is required to realize, for instance, that sometimes there is a need to maintain distance so as to perform one's duty properly. Thus, different occasions call for different combinations of emotion and form. In other words, taking the "middle course" is not a fifty-fifty matter. Aesthetic considerations may be involved since the making of distinctions in keeping a balance is a refined matter.

This elaboration of the balance between emotion and form enables us to see that what constitutes actions that are humane (*ren*), right (*yi*), or filial (*xiao*) is not something self-evident, or simply based on some feeling independent of conventional forms. As Xunzi notes, you cannot have one without the other. Even so, a proper balance has to be negotiated and it is the cultivation and refinement of ritual learning that helps one to do this successfully.

Conclusion

In his reply to Mozi's criticism, Xunzi has to concede the excesses of some Ru or Confucian ritual practices. Although he sometimes resorts to (what seems to be) *ad hominem* argument in reclaiming the ground of feeling for ritual principles, Xunzi manages to offer a more substantial reply to Mozi's convention argument. Essentially, this is that there are nonbiological dimensions of life that require to be nurtured. In particular, the emotions need to be nurtured as they cannot be totally divorced from the conventional forms of ritual through which they are expressed. These forms serve not merely to transform the person to habitually obey rules of hierarchy. Instead, through them, he or she has learned to be humane, to do what is right and to be filial according to a balanced integration of emotion and form. In these respects, such a person has gone beyond the biological dimension of human nature. As Xunzi says, this is the result of having been nurtured by ritual (*li zhe yang ye* 禮者養也).

Three Conceptions of the Heart-Mind

Xunzi, Mencius, and Confucius clearly share a central concern, namely, to identify what is distinctly human. There are variations in their accounts of the human. In this concluding chapter, we shall summarize and compare their different views. The comparisons should yield a clearer, synoptic view of the ethical philosophies of the three thinkers. Given that the detailed analytical work has been done on each of the thinkers in the previous chapters, I will not hesitate (occasionally) to make deductive and somewhat speculative remarks in the course of these comparisons.

A good focus, and one that will help to structure the comparisons, is to look at their different conceptions of *xin* or the heart-mind. For both Mencius and Xunzi, the heart-mind functions as a central human capacity and plays a theoretical role in their philosophies, although in different ways. I shall mention what I see as the weaknesses and strengths of their respective theories. For Confucius, the heart-mind plays no theoretical role. Instead, it is used to refer to (what in contemporary terms would be known as) different states of mind. Nevertheless, this is consistent with his emphasis on *ren* as an overall ethical orientation, and as the expressions of particular emotions, attitudes, and values. I shall refer to these expressions as "human expressions."

Xunzi

But let us begin by comparing Xunzi with Mencius. For Mencius, the heart-mind is incipiently moral and representative of the human insofar as the four sprouts are said to exist universally (even if not always manifested). For Xunzi, on the other hand, the cognitive function of the heart-mind is a species-ability: although each individual, qua human being, possesses the cognitive capacity, say, to discover the rationale of ritual and moral principles, not everyone has the ability to do so. We can say that for Mencius, the way or *dao* 道 is a moral *dao* that resides in the heart-mind. It is something that has to be drawn out or recovered, from within the person. For Xunzi, on the other hand, the heart-mind is distinct from the *dao*.[1] It has a cognitive function of understanding the *dao* or the way of things in the natural world, and in human affairs. This separation of the heart-mind from the *dao* enables Xunzi to allow for the fact that people differ: there are different empirical selves, each manifesting to different degrees what is distinctive of the human.

A difference between Mencius and Xunzi that is related to their different conceptions of the heart-mind concerns their different characterizations of *tian* 天 or Heaven. As we have seen (see chapter 3), Mencius speaks of *tian* as the source of the moral predispositions in the heart-mind. The realization of these predispositions means knowing and serving Heaven. Thus, Heaven not only endows one with the moral predispositions, it also provides a norm of what is properly decreed (*Mencius* 7A:1–2). By contrast, Xunzi rejects the view of a moral Heaven. For him, *tian* is "Nature" (to distinguish this from human "nature" or *xing*). This refers to the constant operations of natural events such as, say, the four seasons. Nature is morally neutral. Nevertheless, human beings should try to avoid natural disasters by acting in accordance with the patterns of Nature. Apart from this proviso, the progress of moral, social and political affairs are worked out by human beings themselves in terms of ritual principles. These principles are the result of the sages having discerned the *dao* of the human world and constitute "markers" (*biao* 表) of the *dao*. As Xunzi says, "Those who govern the people mark out the *dao*, but if the markers are not clear, then the people will fall into disorder. Ritual principles are such markers (*li zhe biao ye* 禮著表也)." (*Xunzi* 17.11).[2]

Xunzi's conception of the heart-mind is less well known than Mencius's, and will need to be described here. According to Xunzi, the heart-mind has three qualities that provide the capacity for knowledge. These are emptiness (*xu* 虛), unity (*yi* 壹), and stillness (*jing* 靜)[3] (21.5d). "Emptiness" refers to the seemingly endless absorptive capacity of the heart-mind. That is, its current store of knowledge and memory does not prevent the reception of new input. Knowledge involves the capacity to distinguish between things and to perceive different aspects of things. The heart-mind is not split or paralyzed by these distinctions and differences. Xunzi refers to this as the capacity for "unity." In other words, the heart-mind has the capacity to make sense of distinctions and differences, and to cope with them in one way or another. "Stillness" can be explained as follows. The heart-mind seems to be in a stream of perpetual movement, whether it is in a relaxed state, planning, or dreaming. Nevertheless, the heart-mind has the capacity for being unmoved or being in a state of stillness. This is likened to a pan of still water where the silt has sunk to the bottom (21.7b). The water is clear and pure enough for one to examine the lines on one's face. In other words, the heart-mind has a capacity for a clarity that allows it to outline the rationale (*li* 理) of things in the world, including the rationale of human affairs.

Xunzi is especially concerned about the latter. More specifically, the ordering of society depends on learning the rationale of ritual and moral principles that would bring about order. In spelling out the rationale, Xunzi first posits the self-interested desires and the scarcity of resources that constrain maximal satisfaction. In the absence of the right social mechanisms to regulate desires and their satisfaction, there will be disorder. Xunzi goes on to describe the necessary mechanisms that would lead to order. These include the establishment of hierarchical distinctions through ritual procedures. However, rituals are, at the same time, constitutive elements of individual aesthetic refinement, including the refinement of desires and the emotions. The cognitive capacity of the heart-mind is, therefore, matched by the corresponding existence of (apparently objective) patterns in the world, forming a rationale of ritual principles to be discovered or known.

As we have seen, Xunzi makes a clear distinction between capacity and ability and applies this to the critique of Mencius. For Mencius, the capacity and the ability to see, for instance, are held to be the same. In this regard, the eye (with its capacity for sight) is inseparable from eyesight (the ability to see). The structure that allows for the capacity to see at the same time constitutes the ability to see. Xunzi observes that Mencius talks of moral abilities in the same organic terms. Xunzi, however, questions this assumption in terms of the potter analogy: "The potter molds clay to make an earthenware dish, but how could the dish be regarded as part of the potter's inborn nature?" In other words, it is not to be assumed that before an object can be produced, its structure must have already been innately present in the producer. Similarly, it should not be assumed that the processes, rules, and structures of ritual and moral activities must already have been present innately. It might be argued that Mencius can accommodate the capacity/ability distinction since there are occasions in which the lack of appropriate circumstances may prevent a capacity from manifesting itself. What prevents the capacity from being manifested as ability is the lack of appropriate circumstances, or the interference of inappropriate circumstances. Xunzi's potter analogy, however, pre-empts this move by denying the assumption of a structural similarity between an innate capacity and its manifestation as ability. As Xunzi sees it, ritual and moral ability need not be structurally predetermined by some innate capacity. He debunks this idea in his remarks about an "original simplicity" and "childhood naiveté," adding that the moment one is born, one would have moved away from any such simple state.[4]

Another aspect of the capacity/ability distinction regards the different motivations and characters of people. Not everyone exercises the human capacities that he or she has, for various reasons. First of all, the achievement of knowledge involves a long process of cumulative hard work and learning experience. Not everyone has the motivation to go through this process, and no one can be forced to do so. Furthermore, not everyone has the ability to achieve comprehensive knowledge. Comprehensive knowledge is not the ability to concentrate on a single task. Xunzi compares this with the concentration on the respective tasks of the farmer, merchant, and artisan. The skills possessed by each are not enough to make them become a director of the field, marketplace, or of wares. Similarly, comprehensive knowledge and constancy of purpose are also necessary conditions of success in the learning of ritual principles and in their practical application.

In distinguishing capacity from ability, and in the context of describing how ritual principles and social order came to be established, Xunzi highlights two classes of people—the ordinary people and the sages. The latter, unlike the former, have worked at accumulating the knowledge of ritual principles, and possess comprehensive knowledge. They have refined themselves, and at the same time worked out the ritual principles that are necessary to the establishment of social order. We may assume that over time, these ritual procedures became institutionalized.

In chapter 6, I denied the "egalitarian" view attributed to Xunzi that all people share one and the same nature. This denial should not be taken to mean that I hold Xunzi to be an "inegalitarian," in the contemporary, social and political sense. For one thing, the belief that there are different selves with unequal motivations and talents does not necessarily mean that Xunzi is inegalitarian. For another, "equality" is itself an essentially contested term—there is much disagreement about what it amounts to. In any case, it would be unfair and anachronistic to impose a label like this on Xunzi, given that contemporary notions of equality and liberty were not options for him, or for that matter, neither were they options for Confucius or Mencius.[5]

My discussion of Xunzi has focused on his theory of human nature, and where he stands in regard to the four views of human nature listed by Gongduzi (in the *Mencius*). I have argued that Xunzi's considered position is that human nature has the capacity to become good or bad. Like Gaozi, this can be said to amount to a position of moral neutrality. Unlike Gaozi (and Mozi too), however, who sees the biological instincts and desires as distinctive, Xunzi gives an account of the species-ability to discover the principles that go into the making of goodness. And for Xunzi, the notion of goodness is based upon a conception of social order and an internalized sense of such order. In this regard, Xunzi provides what seems to have been lacking in the *Mencius*, this lack giving rise to a puzzle about how, if filial love is to have priority over other forms of love and concern, it could be extended. Xunzi helps us to see that this is in part not a conceptual problem, but an empirical one, of fostering ritual processes whereby family and social functions are integrated. From Xunzi's account, we realize that this is not a matter of the ritual processes being (purely) instruments of social order. This is a point that we have emphasized, through an account of what Xunzi means by ritual transformation, in chapter 7. For Xunzi, the ritual processes are socially constitutive. In other words, civilized and orderly forms of human life such as relations between both individuals and groups are constituted by certain rules—without these rules, these civilized and orderly forms would not exist. In this regard, Xunzi's conception of an aesthetic rationale to the rites is especially interesting. It shows how individuals can be constitutively transformed by the rites, culturally, emotionally, and morally. To say that the individual is constitutively transformed is to place a positive aesthetic/ethical value on such transformation, instead of simply regarding it as instrumental and subordinate to the need for social order. This also reminds us that Xunzi's remark that human nature is *e* should be read in the context of what is initially unconstituted, instead of being essentially bad or "evil."

The account of Xunzi's conception of the heart-mind that I have just given in this chapter is consistent with this view of goodness and social order, as objective conditions that are to be discovered and implemented. In this regard, there are other aspects of Xunzi's ethical thought that should also be mentioned. Beside his belief in the existence of objective conditions for ethical knowledge, he also gives a detailed account of various standards of argumentation, as well as the various ways in which such knowledge and judgment can be obscured given various obsessions and fallibilities of the heart-mind. These rationalistic aspects of Xunzi have been well discussed in the work of A. S. Cua.[6] In the previous chapters, I highlighted this distinctive rationalistic aspect of Xunzi through his skillful analysis of Mencius, his detection of fallacies, and his use of counterfactual arguments.

Mencius

Xunzi's focus on the *dao* as lying in certain objective conditions does not seem to have been as popular as Mencius's belief that the *dao* lies within the heart-mind. The reasons for this would be somewhat speculative. Perhaps the fact that some of Xunzi's students, such as Han Fei 韓非 (d. 233 B.C.E.) and Li Si 李斯 (d. 208 B.C.E.),[7] were Legalists did not help. Also, the notion of the objective conditions of ethical knowledge can lend itself to different interpretations by various camps, each claiming to have gotten it right. Perhaps, in this respect, placing moral faith in Mencius's notion of the internality of the heart-mind cuts off the route to such interpretations and can be regarded as more objective. Whatever may be the reasons, it is indeed the case that Mencius's view of the heart-mind has become embedded in the Chinese psyche, and has served to inspire high ideals of self-cultivation and courageous moral conduct in the face of personal, social, and political adversities. This influence is quite remarkable considering the weakness of Mencius's theory. Perhaps, then, the best way to read him is not to see him as propounding a *theory*, but as giving us a moral psychology that is both insightful and capable of inspiring the highest human ideals. Let us first describe the theoretical weakness of what Mencius says before suggesting why his ethical perspective has nevertheless endured.

There is no need to repeat Mencius's conception of the heart-mind. For the sake of the analysis, let us note the following corollary points. Mencius laments the fact that for various reasons—a failure to reflect or an inappropriate environment—some people neglect their heart-mind and fail to cultivate the moral sprouts. While knowing how to care for parts of their body, for instance, they somehow fail to nurture their heart-mind. Mencius describes this as "losing one's original heart-mind" (6A:10). Mencius also describes the heart-mind as forming the normatively "greater" or more important part of a person, while the other parts of the body and the desires for food and drink constitute the "smaller" or less important part (6A:14).

All human beings, then, share the same core identity, described in normative terms as the "original" and "greater" part of themselves. In describing the heart-mind, Mencius is describing what, to him, forms a central aspect of the human. This aspect is both identified with, and inseparable from, the moral resources that lie within it. Sometimes, distorting factors may be at work and the person is called upon to recollect the innate resources. For example, Mencius attempts to lead King Xuan to realize that he is capable of acting in a kingly way and to do the right thing for his people, by reflecting upon the fact that he had a feeling of compassion for an ox that was being led to sacrifice (1A:7).

Corresponding to the account of the heart-mind and what is centrally human, Mencius has a view about *xing* or (human) nature, which can be characterized in the following two ways. First, there is an original unspoiled, pristine nature. This pristine nature is characterized as innately moral. In his critique of Mencius, Xunzi has put it the following way: Mencius claims that nature is good, and that evil is a result of the loss of this nature. However, this idea is due to an underlying belief in the original existence of a simple and beautiful state (or what I have just referred to as a "pristine" state). As we have seen, Xunzi pours cold water on this idea by saying that the moment a person is born, he or she would have already moved away from whatever original simplicity there may be.

Second, the nature that is characterized as originally good is not unique to the individual. If we describe this nature in contemporary terms as forming what is essentially true of the "self," we may say that this is a universal self, common to all as forming the (normatively) greater part of each self. However, this gives rise to a problem that is astutely raised by Mencius's own disciple, Gongduzi. In 6A:14, Mencius has just made the distinction between greater and smaller parts of the self or person (the word used here is *shen* 身, literally, "body"). He observes that some people lose their priorities—they know how to take care of parts of their bodies, or care about food and drink, but neglect their greater part. In the next passage 6A:15, Gongduzi asks: "Though equally human, why are some people greater than others?" Mencius replies: "He who is guided by the interests of the parts of his person that are of greater importance is a great person; he who is guided by the . . . parts . . . of smaller importance is a small (ignoble) person." But Gongduzi persists: "Though equally human, why are some guided one way and others guided another way?" Mencius replies with a distinction between the heart-mind and the sensory organs. While the latter are simply led or attracted by their objects, "The organ of the heart-mind can reflect (*si* 思). But it will find the answer only if it does reflect; otherwise, it will not find the answer." As we can see, Mencius's answers are unsatisfactory and Gongduzi's question hits the nail on the head: Given that all persons are equally human, why is it that some manifest this humanity, while others do not? The reply that this is because some reflect while others do not merely repeats what was said earlier: that some manage to call up what is within them, while others fail to do so.

Given the lack of an independent, philosophical justification for his description of the universal heart-mind, Mencius can only reiterate his normative position about the existence of the original, morally pristine nature. At the same time, his conception of this universal nature cannot—from a theoretical point of view—adequately account for asymmetric, moral and immoral persons or selves. Of course, Mencius argues that environmental factors cover this pristine nature and distort its development (what we have referred to earlier as the interference of inappropriate circumstances). Nevertheless, it is insisted that the immoral person, reflecting upon his or her heart-mind, should still find what was originally there.[8]

The above analysis shows that the support for Mencius's theory is thin, and this was recognized by Xunzi as we have seen in the description of his critique. But, to do overall justice to Mencius, we should say something about the philosophical views he was up against. Gaozi, for instance, held that human nature is morally neutral and thoroughly malleable. Mozi, too, seems to have suggested the same. In arguing for the practical possibility of "universal love," Mozi tells the story of a king who loved slender waists. To please him, his subjects went to the extent of starving themselves.[9] Mozi's point is that the establishment of universal love is not an impossible task; people can be made to love others without discrimination. In contemporary terms, both Gaozi and Mozi may be said to have held a *tabula rasa* or a "blank slate" view of the human self. Mencius was alarmed by what he thought were the adverse implications of these doctrines—given the alleged malleability of nature, no form of behavior is inherently impossible, and people can be manipulated to behave in ways that are directed by a particular doctrine, or by the authorities.

If indeed Mencius had such a worry in this last regard, it would prove to have been prescient. Two excessively cruel periods of Chinese history have borne out the dangers of regarding human nature as a blank slate that can be drawn on arbitrarily and manipulated at will. The first was the *Qin* dynasty (221–206 B.C.E.), its governance being influenced by Legalist policies of manipulating behavior through the implementation of *fa* 法, usually translated as "law," but which under the Legalist philosophy was an instrument to maintain the supreme power of the ruler.[10] The second, in more recent times, was the Maoist era, especially during the period of the Cultural Revolution. Mao Zedong, interestingly, made the following metaphorical remarks that belie a belief in a malleable nature: "A blank sheet of paper has no blotches, and so the newest and most beautiful words can be written on it, the newest and most beautiful pictures can be painted on it."[11] It might be thought that the Legalist and Maoist policies were social experiments that went astray, and it is not impossible to conceive of more enlightened policies that could shape the blank nature in better ways. With the benefit of hindsight, it could be argued that Mencius would have been skeptical of this. His objection to Gaozi and Mozi (even though Mozi's theory of universal love was well-intended) was precisely that their doctrines conceived of nature as something entirely malleable or easily channeled (and here we see the force of Gaozi's water analogy), and left no room for the growth of natural moral predispositions or feelings that he saw as inherently and universally human.

The above remarks suggest that the best way to read Mencius is not as a thinker who provides strong support for a theory of human nature, but as a moral psychologist. This is to be understood in the sense of offering keen insights into various aspects of human motivation, and this is where Mencius is at his intellectual best. In the debate with Gaozi, Mencius questions Gaozi's use of the terms "internal" and "external" as applied to the concepts of *ren* and *yi*. The claim (made by Gaozi) that there is no difference in respect for an elder from my own family and an elder from outside my family does not establish the "externality" of *yi*. For by the same token, since there is no difference between enjoying my own roast or another's, it could also be argued (absurdly) that my enjoyment of roast is "external" (6A:4). Similarly, although respect may vary according to the ceremonial context, this does not establish that respect is "external." For, by the same token, one may take a hot drink in winter but a cold drink in summer, but this does not establish that one's sensation of drinking is "external" (6A:5). These logical demonstrations throw doubt upon the validity of Gaozi's use of "internal/external." Other remarks of Mencius's show that the so-called internality of the desires could just as well be external, since acquisition of what is desired are subject to various contingencies. In this regard, to make no distinction between *ren* and *yi* on the one hand, and the desires on the other, is to misunderstand the nature of *ren* and *yi* as distinctly human motives.

For Mencius, this is at the same time, a failure to understand the full potentialities of what it is to be human. These include having a sense of what it means to be related to others in certain ways, as well as having conceptions of limits on action, and what cannot be tolerated. Furthermore, in discussing *ren*, Mencius refers to a plurality of motivational sources, and recognizes the fact of motivational conflict. The conception of limits on action in turn includes not doing or accepting certain things that are humanly unworthy, and not willingly accepting certain abusive treatments of oneself. A description of these attitudes and feelings brings out what Mencius means by the internality of *yi*, a notion that he ultimately also links to a superior form of courage and vital energy, or *qi* 氣 (2A:2). In mentioning *yi*, Mencius refers to the attitude/feeling of *xiu wu*

羞惡, or shame and loathing. Kwong-loi Shun has noted that the term *xiu* is closely linked to another, *chi* 恥. The latter is "more like the attitude of regarding something as contemptible or as below oneself than like the emotion of shame." And further, "while *chi* is focused more on the thing that taints oneself, *xiu* is focused more on the way the self is tainted by that thing." The concept of *yi* is linked to these attitudes, and as such it is a self-directed term, involving "a concern to distance oneself from situations that are below oneself, as measured by certain standards to which one is committed."[12] I mention these remarks of Shun's because they add to the above, and together, these show a way of approaching the reading of the *Mencius*, in moral psychological terms. At the same time, we can see how the description of some of these human motivations is capable of being ethically inspiring, and this may help to explain why Mencius's perspective of the human has endured.

Confucius

We may now return to Confucius. Unlike Mencius and Xunzi, Confucius does not distinctly spell out what he thinks is human, and neither does he attempt to put forward a theory of what it is to be human. Nevertheless, the centrality of the concept *ren* 仁 in the *Analects*, and the association between *ren* and its homophone 人 "person" indicate a concern with the human.[13] Following the Han dynasty lexicon *Shuowen jiexi* 説文解字, it has often been pointed out that the character *ren* 仁 consists of the radical for "person," *ren* 人, and the number "two," thus stressing the fact that a person does not exist by himself or herself, but in various kinds of relations with others. This seems to imply a basic consideration of the interests of others, and caring about the general good. My reading of *ren*, however, shows that we need to go beyond this general idea, to the emotions, attitudes, and values, and an overall ethical orientation. We can connect this reading with Confucius's use of *xin*, heart or the heart-mind.

In the *Analects*, there are only five occurrences of the term. The term does not play any theoretical role as it does for Mencius and Xunzi. Instead, it appears in the contexts of describing (what we may now refer to) as various states of mind. Let us look at two of these passages, following D. C. Lau's translations.[14] In 2.4, Confucius says of himself, "At seventy, I followed my heart's desire without overstepping the line." In other words, he has integrated his motivational attitudes with ritual, is at ease with his desires, and has a sense of harmony in his life. In discussing *ren* in chapter 2, I referred to an "immediacy of ethical commitment," as opposed to thinking of *ren* in theoretical terms. This involves the expression of attitudes and values such as affection and reverence for elders, earnestness or the doing of one's best for others, sincerity, genuine feeling and lack of pretentiousness, not being glib, and so on. The "immediacy" here refers to a straightforward link between attitude and action. In other words, attitude and action are harmonized in such a way that one has a state of mind that is described as being "at home" or "at rest." A negative case of this is the person whose deeds belie his words, as in the case of Zai Wo. Confucius refuses to discuss the possibility of shortening the three-year period of mourning with him, saying of him that he is "unfeeling" (*bu ren* 不仁, literally, "not *ren*"), and that it was because of Zai Wo that he has learned to watch a person's deeds after listening to his words. In other words, Zai Wo is insincere, and lacks (genuine) feeling. He lacks the state of mind or the orientation of *ren*. Without any theoretical baggage that claims the original goodness of human nature, Confucius has no problem with the everyday fact that some people just do not express their humanity (and certainly, we know that there are worse examples than Zai Wo).[15] (Commentators who claim that Confucius holds a theory of the original goodness of human nature like Mencius does would have to bear in mind that this brings with it the problems raised, for example, by Gongduzi.)

In 6.7, Confucius says of Yan Hui, "For three months at a time Hui does not lapse from *ren* in his heart." This is a reference to Yan Hui's constancy of moral purpose, as compared to the other disciples, who are said to manifest *ren* occasionally. As we have seen, Yan Hui manifests the orientation of *ren* in the sense that he does not regard it as something that can be grasped once and for all, but as calling for constant moral learning (9.11). The fact that *ren* connotes an ethical orientation and practice is emphasized in Confucius's remark, that although Yan Hui seems stupid in not asking questions, nevertheless, he throws light upon Confucius's teachings in his daily life (2.9). Although *ren* is not referred to here, we would imagine that Confucius is pleased here with Yan Hui's expressing the particular attitudes and values that are part of *ren*, and manifesting its overall orientation.

Note that the term *zhi* 志, which has a heart radical and which I have referred to in chapter 1 as the individual's aim or direction, or what the individual has set his or her heart-mind upon, is also translated by Lau as "heart." (See 5.26, 11.26, and also 2.4.) As we have seen in discussing passage 11.26, the uninhibited statement of one's *zhi* can be revealing of one's state of mind and character. In this regard, I have spoken of a harmony between the aesthetic and the ethical parts of one's character. This is shown in the example of Zengxi, where the conjunction of ritual, music, and the Odes find delightful expression in the joyous celebration of a spring rite. In this example, we find the point of an ethico-aesthetical training, where one's emotions, motivations, and attitudes are harmonized with reasons for acting, as spelled out within the rites.

In my discussion of *ren* in the *Analects* in chapter 2, I resisted giving any translation of the term (although in the case of the *Mencius*, I did more precisely break it down into the three motivational components of compassion, social concern, and affectionate attachment). Given the overall discussion, however, perhaps we may now venture to sum up what *ren* means for Confucius: it is a fundamental ethical orientation involving human expressions of attitudes, emotions, and values that reflect the meaning and significance of modes of conduct and relationships. Given the centrality of these human expressions, the word "humanity," I think, comes closest to *ren*. The ethical significance of this description of *ren* can be seen if we distinguish it from some of the general definitions that have been given of *ren*, for example, "love for all," "the principle of love," "distinctive nature" of people, or a love that is refined into "ethical commitment and metaphysical principle," and so on (see chapter 2). These general and metaphysical definitions fail to capture the human expressions of *ren*. In other words, the value of these expressions does not reside in a concern with living up to any general or metaphysical principle, but in the expressions themselves under the appropriate behavioral contexts.[16]

Ren as a Fundamental Value

I have argued for a distinctive reading of each of the three thinkers, and noted their differences against the background of philosophical debate and development. Once this has been done, however, there is no harm in noting that they shared a concern with establishing *ren* as a fundamental value. Although we should still keep in mind the developments of this concept by Mencius and Xunzi, they were clearly inspired by Confucius and saw themselves as carrying forward and defending an ethical project that he initiated. In this regard, some central concerns of Confucius when he talked about *ren* are also valid for Mencius and Xunzi.

For instance, we have seen that for Xunzi, the ritual processes play a positively constitutive role in the aesthetic and ethical transformation of the individual. Such a transformation is consistent with Confucius's concern about the human expressions of *ren* through the educational forms of ritual. Mozi's criticism that Confucian ritual is merely conventional and goes against the Confucians's own values of *ren*, *yi*, and *xiao* compels Xunzi to account for the basis of these values. Xunzi argues that these are not spontaneous uncultured feelings. Neither are they arbitrary conventions. Ritual both cultivates the emotions and provides the form through which the emotions are properly expressed. Again, this reminds us of the stress that Confucius puts on the practice of *li* with the proper attitude of *ren*. Just as in the case of Confucius, for Xunzi, ritual is only meaningful when the appropriate emotions are expressed. But what constitutes being appropriate, however, is something that is guided by the forms. In this sense, Xunzi sees that the separation between nature and convention on the one hand, and between the emotion and form on the other, is both unnecessary and spurious.

We have also observed that for Xunzi, *ren* is a necessary part of rulership, although this is put in terms of a long-term rational strategy where the rulers have to win the people's allegiance by providing them security and tranquility. But this is in turn motivated by the abhorrence of harm to the people and the chaos that results. Xunzi is also mindful of the transformative effect on the people, through the rule of the *ren* person, which he likens to the spirit-like moral force of *shen*, and which (like both Confucius and Mencius) he speaks about in terms of the metaphor of the bountiful effects of the seasonal wind and rain. We can better appreciate this attitude of Xunzi's toward *ren* if we contrast it with the attitude of his student Han Fei, who totally rejects the value of *ren* to rulership, because he thinks of it only in terms of its negative instrumental value.[17] It is important to stress Xunzi's positive attitude toward the transformative effect of *ren*, instead of merely the need for a hierarchical social order. The sole emphasis on social distinctions and hierarchy would distort Xunzi's ethical philosophy if the intrinsic concern for *ren* is removed, making it more akin to the Legalist philosophy of Han Fei.[18] For Xunzi, a more inclusive account of what he means by social distinctions must include the refined emotions resulting from aesthetic distinctions that constitute a part of the transformed individual. The individual whose emotions are developed and expressed through the ritual forms is, in effect, the same ethico-aesthetic individual that we mentioned when discussing Confucius's ethics. This individual character is formed through the educational structure of *li* and acts in the spirit of *li* which incorporates various attitudes that amount to *ren*. He has gone through a process of self-cultivation such that his motivational attitudes and actions are harmoniously integrated.

In the case of Mencius, the moral predispositions of the heart-mind that he posits have to presuppose the human expressions that Confucius mentions. In other words, the understanding of these predispositions requires a prior understanding of the significance of appropriate human expressions. As was observed in chapter 3, Mencius would find it difficult to argue for the contents of the heart-mind without a prior picture of what it is to be human, and there are indications that Mencius shares the conception of the human expressions that Confucius describes. For example, in 7B:11, referring to someone who is out to gain a reputation for himself, Mencius observes that such a person would have no qualms about giving away "a state of a thousand chariots." However, when there is nothing to be gained in this respect from giving away rice and soup (presumably to a beggar), "reluctance would be written all over his face." This happens to illustrate something that Confucius says about *ren* in *Analects* 12.20, when he distinguishes between "getting through" and "being known." Confucius describes the latter in terms of someone "who has no misgivings about his own claim to *ren* when all he is doing is putting up a façade of *ren* which is belied by his deeds."

Although Mencius shares Confucius's concern with character, however, his concern with expounding his theory of human nature is never far away. Consider *Mencius* 4B:19, where Emperor Shun is said to have "followed the path of morality (*ren yi* 仁義). He did not put morality into practice." In other words, Shun is acting in a naturally and morally integrated manner. Confucius would have entirely approved of such a description. Note, however, that Mencius cites the example as evidence of what is distinctive of the human being, as compared to animals. The remark just cited is prefaced by the statement, "Slight is the difference between humans and brutes. The common person loses this distinguishing feature, while the noble person retains it." Thus, the example is taken as indicating Mencius's theory of the predispositions of the heart-mind. If we ignore this, however, it is a fine example of the kind of human expression that Confucius was concerned about in his teaching of *ren*.

Conclusion

Confucius had no theoretical account of the human, and he resisted any expectation of such an account—we observed in chapter 2 his reactions to some disciples who expected him to theorize about *ren*, and perhaps it was this kind of expectation that led to the remark in *Analects* 9.1, that he rarely spoke about *ren*. But the many occasions on which he was concerned with character, ethical orientation, modes of behavior, states of mind, and so on—in short, concerns with the human expressions that we have mentioned—were, in fact, concerns about *ren*, although not spoken about directly or theoretically. Subsequent intellectual challenges and social/political developments made theorizing inevitable, as our examinations of the *Mencius* and the *Xunzi* have shown in detail. Thus, although sharing Confucius's concern with the fundamental place of *ren*, Mencius was forced to develop a theory of *ren* in terms of the moral predispositions and (as revealed through our analysis) the different motivational sources and principles of compassion, social concern, and affectionate attachment. Xunzi too shared the same concern about the fundamental place of *ren*, and in response to the criticisms of Mozi, argued for a structured and objective understanding of *ren*, in terms of the balance between emotion and ritual form.

Notes

Introduction

1. I shall be studying what has come down to us as the received texts. It should be noted though, that especially in the case of the *Lunyu*, the text as we have it is the result of a long history of accretion, with layers composed by different people or groups of people. See especially E. Bruce Brooks and A. Taeko Brooks, *The Original Analects: Sayings of Confucius and His Successors* (New York: Columbia University Press, 1998). See also John Makeham, *Transmitters and Creators: Chinese Commentators and Commentaries on the Analects* (Cambridge: Harvard University Asia Center, 2003).

2. Here, I agree with the following remarks of Yuet Keung Lo: "Nevertheless, in spite of its accretional nature and questionable historicity, the *Analects* presents a coherent account of how a group of early Confucians, revolving around Confucius himself, acted, behaved, thought, and lived in a loosely organized collection of often disembodied conversations, aphoristic statements, and explorative queries. Inasmuch as the anthology consists of different layers of texts, it is possible that the images emerging therefrom of Confucius and his disciples are products of retrospective construction dictated by historical and ideological demands." See Lo, "Finding the Self in the *Analects*: A Philological Approach," in *The Moral Circle and the Self: Chinese and Western Approaches*, ed. Kim-chong Chong, Sor-hoon Tan, and C. L. Ten (Chicago: Open Court, 2003), 249–50.

3. See E. Bruce Brooks and A. Taeko Brooks, "Word Philology and Text Philology in *Analects* 9:1," in *Confucius and the Analects: New Essays*, ed. Bryan W. Van Norden (Oxford: Oxford University Press, 2002).

4. Here, too, there has been a philological attempt to show that the statements that nature is "evil" do not properly belong to the text in chapter 23 of the *Xunzi*. See Dan Robins, "The Development of Xunzi's Theory of *Xing*, Reconstructed on the Basis of a Textual Analysis of *Xunzi* 23, 'Xing E' 性惡 (*Xing* is Bad)," *Early China* 26–27 (2001–2002): 99–158.

5. This view has been clearly stated by Antonio S. Cua, "Philosophy of Human Nature," in *Human Nature, Ritual, and History: Studies in Xunzi and Chinese Philosophy* (Washington, D.C.: The Catholic University of America Press, 2005).

6. With reference to Mencius's use of the term *qing* 情 in response to a question about what he means by a person's *xing* 性 being good, A. C. Graham has given the following definition: "The *qing* of X is what makes it a genuine X, what every X has and without which would not be an X." We may break this down as follows: Take an

entity called "X" (in this instance, "a person"). There is some essential ("genuine") characteristic of X that makes it what it is. This characteristic is "essential" in the sense that each and every member of the class "X" necessarily possesses it. An entity that lacks this characteristic is not "X." According to Graham, in the *Mencius* and the pre-Qin philosophical texts in general, the term *qing* refers to this essential characteristic in the way just defined. I would deny that this is the way to read Xunzi's understanding of *qing* and *xing*. See A. C. Graham, "The Background of the Mencian Theory of Human Nature," in *Studies in Chinese Philosophy and Philosophical Literature* (Singapore: The Institute of East Asian Philosophies, 1986), 33, and 59–66. I have written on this issue in "Xunzi and the Essentialist Mode of Thinking about Human Nature," *Journal of Chinese Philosophy* (forthcoming).

7. For a comprehensive discussion of the issues surrounding the relation between the patriarchal social context of Confucianism and interpretations of Confucian philosophy, see Sor-hoon Tan, "Women's Virtues and the *Analects*," in *Conceptions of Virtue East and West*, ed. Kim-chong Chong and Yuli Liu (Singapore: Marshall Cavendish Academic, 2006). Referring to the *Analects*, Tan herself attempts to "establish a reading of the text that resists sexism and render it useful for modern society" (256).

Chapter 1: The "Basic Stuff"

1. Unless otherwise stated, quotations and passage numberings are from D. C. Lau, tr., *Confucius: The Analects* (Harmondsworth: Penguin, 1979). I have changed Lau's Wade-Giles romanizations to *Hanyu Pinyin*. I have also consulted Lau's revised bilingual edition of the same book published by The Chinese University Press (1992).

2. As noted by Chen Daqi 陳大齊, *Lunyu Yijie* 論語臆解 (Taipei: Taiwan Shangwu, 1996), 266.

3. A point made explicit by Lau in his revised translation of *hui shi hou su*: "The plain silk is there first. The colours come afterwards."

4. I shall be referring to the "Introduction" to Lau's translation of *Confucius: The Analects* (Harmondsworth: Penguin, 1979). Page references to this "Introduction" are given in parentheses, directly after quotations of Lau's remarks. Except for some translations, Lau's "Introduction" remains unchanged in the revised edition.

5. Other translations of *zhi* in this passage should be noted. Roger T. Ames and Henry Rosemont, Jr., in *The Analects of Confucius: A Philosophical Translation* (New York: Ballantine Books, 1998), translate it as "one's basic disposition." Arthur Waley, in *The Analects of Confucius* (New York, Vintage Books, 1989), translates it as "material." (Waley's passage numbering is 15.17.) These different translations should not affect my discussion, since the question remains what the "basic disposition" or "material" refers to. Edward Slingerland, in *Effortless Action: Wu-wei as Conceptual Metaphor and Spiritual Ideal in Early China* (New York: Oxford University Press, 2003), 58, translates *zhi* in this passage as "stuff," but also refers to *zhi* in other passages and in discussion as "native stuff" and "native substance." (See my discussion of Slingerland below.)

6. David L. Hall and Roger T. Ames, *Thinking Through Confucius* (Albany: State University of New York Press, 1987), make the following criticism of Lau's reading of *yi* as act-based: "If *yi* is only derivatively applicable to the person performing such *yi* acts, then any transforming effect of *yi* upon the person seems to be denied. Thus the consistently right actions performed by an individual, which lead to his being designated as righteous, are then in no real sense internal to the person. This makes *yi* an external, wholly objective measure by which actions are assessed. To whatever extent *yi* can be said to be characteristic of human conduct, its source clearly lies elsewhere. Such an analysis of *yi* leads directly to the separation of the dispositional, meaning-disclosing dimensions of moral activity from a person's actions."

7. Chung-ying Cheng, in "On *Yi* as a Universal Principle of Specific Application in Confucian Morality," *Philosophy East and West* 22 (1972), refers to *yi* as "the fundamental principle of morality" adjudicating right and wrong, and also as a "universal and total principle" that judges the worthiness of actions. (See Cheng, 269 and 270.) Like Lau, Cheng never provides any determinate criterion. It is possible that both Lau and Cheng are using "principle" more in the sense of a fundamental attitude. However, their reference to a "fundamental principle" is liable to mislead.

8. Slingerland, *Effortless Action*, 54.

9. Ibid., 55. Slingerland refers to *Analects* 3.4, where Confucius is replying to Lin Fang who asked about the root or the basis of the rites.

10. Ibid., 72. Slingerland says, "Supplementing these 'adornment' and 'root' metaphors, we can find several passages in the text that suggest the existence of some kind of innate tendency toward the good. For instance, we read in 16.9 that some are 'born knowing it,' and although Confucius does not count himself among them (7.20), it is apparent that Yan Hui, at least, has some intuitive grasp of the Way." Referring to 2.9 and 5.9, Slingerland says: "Although in these passages Yan Hui is portrayed as requiring some instruction, he seems to have been something of a moral genius naturally inclined toward the Way."

11. Ibid. Slingerland cites 19.22: "The Way of Wen and Wu has not fallen to the ground, but is in people. . . . There is no one who does not have the Way of Wen and Wu in them."

12. A problem highlighted by David Nivison, "The Paradox of Virtue," in his *The Ways of Confucianism: Investigations in Chinese Philosophy*, ed. Bryan Van Norden (Chicago: Open Court, 1996).

13. Slingerland, *Effortless Action*, 55.

14. Ibid., 53.

15. Ann-ping Chin and Mansfield Freeman, trs., *Tai Chen (Dai Zhen) on Mencius: Explorations in Words and Meaning* (New Haven: Yale University Press, 1990), 156. For the full discussion in the original Chinese, see Dai Zhen 戴震, *Mengzi Ziyi Shuzheng* 孟子字義疏證 (Beijing: Zhonghua Shuju, 1982), section on *Ren, Yi, Li, Zhi* 仁義禮智 (48–50).

16. Dai Zhen's reading goes against others such as Zhu Xi's, who reads *hui shi hou su* as the base of plain silk coming first. See Zhu Xi 朱熹, *Sishu Zhangju Jizhu* 四書章句

集注 (Taipei: Changan, 1990), 63. That Zhu Xi's reading has been highly influential is indicated not only by the fact that it is the reading adopted by Lau, but also by recent Chinese commentaries. For instance, Yang Bojun 楊伯峻, *Lunyu Yizhu* 論語譯注 (Taizhong, Taiwan: Landeng Wenhua, 1987), and Li Zehou 李澤厚 *Lunyu Jindu* 論語今讀 (Hefei: Anhui Wenyi, 1998) both read *su* as providing a white base (*bai se di zi* 白色底子 or *bai di* 白底). Chen Daqi 陳大齊, *Lunyu Yijie* 論語臆解 (Taipei: Taiwan Shangwu, 1996), however, gives a detailed critique of Zhu Xi's reading and provides an analysis of why *hui shi hou su* should be read as first applying the colors (Chen, 49–51). See also Daniel Gardner, *Zhu Xi's Reading of the Analects: Canon, Commentary and the Classical Tradition* (New York: Columbia University Press, 2003). Gardner discusses Zhu Xi's reading of this passage as a disagreement with He Yan 何晏 (*Lunyu jijie* 論語集解), and notes that for Zhu Xi, "Only when man's inner resources, the inner potential of human nature, have been properly tended, only when he knows how to be true to his endowed nature and trustworthy, will ritual not be performed without meaning. . . ." (Gardner, 93).

17. Chin and Freeman, *Tai Zhen on Mencius*, 158.

18. Ibid., 156.

19. Ibid., see 157–58.

20. Herbert Fingarette, *Confucius—the Secular as Sacred* (New York: Harper and Row, 1972).

21. See Roger T. Ames and David L. Hall, trs., *Focusing the Familiar: A Translation and Philosophical Interpretation of the Zhongyong* (Honolulu: University of Hawaii Press, 2001), 99, where we find *yi zhe*, *yi ye* 義者, 宜也, or "Appropriateness means doing what is fitting." See also their explanation of *yi* on 84.

22. Yang Bojun, *Lunyu Yizhu* (Taiwan, Taizhong: Landeng wenhua, 1987), 173.

23. Ibid., 65.

24. In a reading of 12.8, Joel Kupperman has adopted the reading of *wen* as "art" and *zhi* as "nature." This nature, however, is the result of a refined training. As Kupperman says, "The word 'art' has connotations of something that is learned; and to say that 'art is nature' suggests that what a man learns may well affect what is natural relative to him." And although it "may seem paradoxical to speak of naturalness in a sense in which 'nature is art,'" the paradox "disappears, however, once we stop thinking of education as merely placing a veneer over original 'nature.' Once we realize that education can transform what a person is, we realize that it can in a sense transform people's natures. What 'comes naturally' is very much a product of training and habit." Kupperman's remarks nicely agree with mine about there being no mystery over *zhi*, even though his rendering of *zhi* is "nature." See Joel Kupperman, *Learning from Asian Philosophy* (New York: Oxford University Press, 1999), ch. 2, "Confucius and the Problem of Naturalness," 30. Kupperman's reading of *wen* and *zhi* follows the translation of the *Analects* by W. E. Soothill (London: Oxford World Classics, 1962). See also Kupperman's more recent essay, "Naturalness Revisited: Why Western Philosophers Should Study Confucius," in Van Norden, *Confucius and the Analects*, where he takes note of the different translations of *zhi* and says on p. 45: "Soothill's 'nature' seems to me to capture the contrast between

what a person is before the educational progress is seriously underway and what then becomes second nature."

25. Again, following Soothill's reading of *he* in this passage as "naturalness," which is consistent with the tenor of my own discussion, as this naturalness is the result of ritualized practice. As he says elsewhere in the same essay, "The result of a successful training program is thus a new 'nature' and a new kind of 'naturalness.' The writer, artist, or composer who has become disciplined and skilful will in general develop something of a characteristic 'voice' or style. Modes of expression that fit this characteristic style will come to seem 'natural'; they will come to be 'natural.'" See Kupperman, *Learning from Asian Philosophy*, 31. Kupperman has taken note of the different translation of *he* as "harmony" in "Naturalness Revisited: Why Western Philosophers Should Study Confucius."

26. See Kwong-loi Shun, "*Ren* and *Li* in the *Analects*," in Van Norden, *Confucius and the Analects*, 68–69.

27. This way of characterizing the two examples was put to me by Kwong-loi Shun.

28. Susan Wolf, "Moral Saints," *Journal of Philosophy* 79, no. 8 (August 1982): 419–39. An excellent discussion of how some modern Western ethical theories fail to harmonize reasons for action with motivational attitudes is Michael Stocker, "The Schizophrenia of Modern Ethical Theories," in *Virtue Ethics*, ed. Roger Crisp and Michael Slote (New York: Oxford University Press, 1997).

29. In the words of Robert Eno, "Aesthetics was not ethically trivial for Confucius." See his *The Confucian Creation of Heaven: Philosophy and the Defense of Ritual Mastery* (New York: State University of New York Press, 1990), 39.

30. See especially Steven Van Zoeren, *Poetry and Personality: Reading, Exegesis, and Hermeneutics in Traditional China* (Stanford: Stanford University Press, 1991), 60–63. Van Zoeren discusses this passage in the context of the articulation of one's *zhi* 志. My discussion of *zhi* below is from my paper, "Autonomy in Early Confucian Thought: *Zhi, Li* and *Ren* in the *Analects*," in Chong, Tan, and Ten, *The Moral Circle and the Self*.

31. See D. C. Lau, "The Disciples as They Appear in the *Analects*," Appendix 2, *Confucius: The Analects* (Penguin: 1979).

32. See Wing-tsit Chan, *A Sourcebook in Chinese Philosophy* (New Jersey: Princeton University Press, 1973), 38, for a summary of some of the traditional answers. Thus, Zengxi was "enjoying the harmony of the universe (Wang Ch'ung)," "following traditional cultural institutions (Liu Pao-nan)," "wisely refraining from officialdom at the time of chaos (Huang K'an)," "thinking of the 'kingly way' whereas other pupils were thinking of the government of feudal states (Han Yü)," "in the midst of the universal operation of the Principle of Nature (Chu Hsi)," and "expressing freedom of the spirit (Wang Yang-ming)."

33. Julia Ching (citing Wang Chong) notes this "as a place to go in late spring in proper seasonal robes and in the company of a group of young men and children—presumably trained in the music of rain dances. There, they would bathe in the river, follow the airs of the rain dance, and return home singing, after sharing in a sacrificial meal."

Julia Ching, *Mysticism and Kingship in China* (Cambridge: Cambridge University Press, 1997), 19. For Wang Chong 王充, see *Lunheng Jiaoshi* 論衡校釋, ed. Huang Hui 黃暉 (Beijing: Zhonghua Shuju, 1996), juan 15, no. 45, Ming Yu Pian 明雩篇 (see p. 673 onwards). Note the suggested alternative reading of Zengxi's words as *yong er kui* 詠而 饋 instead of *yong er gui* 詠而歸. That is, chanting poetry and having a sacrificial meal, instead of chanting poetry and returning home.

34. A point noted by Van Zoeren, 62.

35. It might be argued that Yan Yuan or Yan Hui, Confucius's favorite disciple, could be taken as a counterexample to mine. Yan Hui was cited for his virtuous conduct (11.3), and for sustaining *ren* longer than the others (6.7). He is known also for his poverty and ascetic lifestyle (6.11, 11.19). Surely there is nothing "aesthetic" about his virtues and lifestyle? But I think that we should not neglect the fact that he is said not to allow his poverty to "affect his joy" (6.11). It would be instructive to ask, wherein lies this "joy" or "delight" of Yan Hui? A more composite picture of Yan Hui would refer to his eagerness to learn, his intelligence, and his remarks that Confucius "broadens me with culture and brings me back to essentials by means of the rites" (9.11). See Appendix 2 of Lau's translation of the *Analects* for a fuller picture of Yan Hui.

Chapter 2: The Orientation and Practice of *Ren*

1. See Wing-tsit Chan, "The Evolution of the Confucian Concept *Jên*," *Philosophy East and West* 4 (1955): 295–319. Hereafter referred to as "Evolution." The list I have given is derived from a longer list given by Chan on p. 295 of his paper. In chapter 8 below, I will say how *ren* does capture what it is to be human, in terms of certain human expressions, and given the centrality of these expressions, the term "humanity," I think, comes closest to *ren*. But before this can be established, a more detailed account of *ren* needs to be given in this chapter, and comparisons made with Mencius and Xunzi—the task of chapter 8. More recently, David Hall and Roger Ames define *ren* as "authoritative person" in *Thinking Through Confucius*. It is "the integrative process of taking in and subsuming the conditions and concerns of the human community in the development and application of one's own personal judgment." And, "because [*ren*] always entails the application of personal judgment to the concrete circumstances of environing persons, it follows that one is most fully constituted by those relationships nearest at hand in the naturally defined social structure. [*Ren*] is always immediate, that is, unmediated" (Hall and Ames, 120). I will argue that *ren* involves an "immediacy of ethical commitment." However, the stress that Hall and Ames give to considering the community in personal judgment seems to me to be a wider social consequence of the orientation of *ren*, rather than the orientation itself, which I shall be describing.

2. Chan, "Evolution," 303.

3. Ibid., 303.

4. Since this passage is central to my discussion, I have translated it myself. But

unless stated otherwise, other quotations from the *Analects* mostly follow Lau, *Confucius: The Analects*. Passage numberings are in parentheses after each quotation or reference. I sometimes modify the quotations by leaving certain words untranslated, for example, *ren*, *xiaoti*.

5. Zhu Xi 朱熹, *Sishu Zhangju Jizhu* 四書章句集注 (Taipei: Changan Chubanshe, 1990). I have translated the following passages from Zhu Xi's commentary.

6. I have translated *zhu* as "chief expression." But compare Chan, *A Source Book in Chinese Philosophy*, 560: "The *controlling factor* of humanity is love, and there is no greater love than to love parents." And Gardner, *Zhu Xi's Reading of the Analects*, 72, has: "True goodness presides over love. . . ." I have translated *shi* as "aspect" instead of "items" as Chan does on p. 559. "Aspect" will serve my later discussion of the various aspects of *ren* better than if I were to talk of the "items" of *ren*. Gardner, 72, has: "filial piety and fraternal respect are a matter of true goodness."

7. Liu Baonan 劉寶楠, *Lunyu Zhengyi* 論語正義 (Beijing: Zhonghua Shuju, 1982). He refers to 4.7, 12.1, 15.9, 19.16. We may add 14.2 and 17.6 to the list and also note that in 1.1, Confucius talks of *xi* 習 or practicing what one has learned. Liu Baonan also mentions other phrases such as *zhi yu ren* 志於仁, *qiu ren yu ren* 求仁欲仁, *yong li yu ren* 用力於仁 as instances of the practice of *ren*. The basis of my reading does not rest on these allusions alone but on the whole argument of this chapter. It should also be noted that some commentators (e.g. Lau) take *ren* to mean "man" (which I have rendered gender-neutral) thus giving us "the root of a person's character," instead of "the root of (practicing) *ren*." But Yang Bojun in *Lunyu Yizhu* argues that although this is a possible reading it would not go together with "the root established, *dao* grows."

8. Gardner, *Zhu Xi's Reading of the Analects*, provides a reading of *qi wei ren zhi ben yu* that agrees with my analysis so far and in what follows: "For Zhu, true goodness [*ren*] is foundational to human nature, endowed in man at birth. In this sense, filial and fraternal behavior [*xiaoti*] originate in it and are an expression of it. In Zhu's view . . . filial piety and fraternal respect cannot be the foundations of true goodness because true goodness is itself ontologically foundational. Zhu's commentary suggests . . . that . . . *wei* should not be read as 'to constitute,' . . . but as 'to practice.' Thus the line [*qi wei ren zhi ben yu*] means that practicing true goodness begins with the practice of filial piety and fraternal respect. In this case, consistent with Zhu's metaphysical understanding, true goodness is identical with human nature (and substance), and filial piety and fraternal respect are its function" (Gardner, 73).

9. As noted by Chan, "Evolution," 301.

10. Quotations from the *Mencius* follow with modifications D. C. Lau, tr., *Mencius* (Hong Kong: The Chinese University Press, 1984).

11. See also 4A:11, 4A:19, 5A:3, 6B:3, and 7A:15. In 7A:46, *qin xian* 親賢 is applied to intimacy with the wise and virtuous. Note that in *Analects* 1.6 where *qin ren* occurs, *ren* could be read either as "people" or as a virtue.

12. Lau's translation here does not differentiate between *qin* and *ai* and both are translated as "love" in this passage. While *qin* is to love a parent or a relative, *ai* can, for instance, refer to the love of animals. See passage 7A:45 quoted above. I shall discuss

this in more detail in chapter 4. With reference to the example under discussion (5A:3), Mencius is careful to add that the "banishment" of his brother was not unqualified: "Xiang was not allowed to take any action in his fief. The Emperor appointed officials to administer the fief and to collect tributes and taxes. For this reason it was described as banishment. Xiang was certainly not permitted to ill-use the people." See also the hypothetical example in 7A:35 where according to Mencius, if Shun's father has (wrongly) killed someone, although Shun would not (as Emperor) forbid his arrest, personally he "would have carried the old man on his back and fled to the edge of the Sea and lived there happily, never giving a thought to the Empire."

13. See Chan, "Evolution," 302: "It is love that embraces all relations, but it is righteousness that distinguishes them."

14. *Yishu* 遺書, 18/1a of the *Er-Cheng quanshu* 二程全書, SPPY 四部備要 edition (1933). Quoted in Chan, "Evolution," 306.

15. Chan, "Evolution," 306.

16. See the discussion in Wing-tsit Chan, *Zhu Xi: New Studies* (Honolulu: University of Hawaii Press, 1989), ch. 15, "Substance and Function," and ch. 11, "Zhu Xi's '*Ren-shuo*' 仁説 (Treatise on Humanity)."

17. Chan, "Evolution," 306–9.

18. The passage 17.2 has been discussed in chapter 1. Chan refers to Zhu Xi's interpretation of 6.17 where the word *sheng* 生 occurs, as "man is born upright," to imply that "human nature is originally good." But Chan admits that "although the Confucian tradition in general holds that human nature is originally good, Confucius's own position is not clear." Chan, *A Source Book in Chinese Philosophy*, 29. Lau's translation of the same passage (6.19 in Lau) makes no mention of "nature." In 5.13, Zigong states that "One can hear about the Master's accomplishments (*wen zhang* 文章), but one cannot get to hear his views on human nature [*xing*] and the Way of Heaven." Instead of Lau's "accomplishments" for *wen zhang*, Ames and Rosemont has "cultural refinements." They also translate *xing* here as "natural disposition." See also Philip J. Ivanhoe, "Whose Confucius? Which *Analects*?" in Van Norden, *Confucius and the Analects*. Ivanhoe describes various interpretations of 5.13 in the commentarial tradition. Some commentators (e.g. He Yan) attribute to Confucius a metaphysical understanding of human nature, while others (e.g. Zhang Xuecheng) denied this and emphasized instead Confucius's practical teachings. Ivanhoe notes that "these disagreements often reveal deep, complex, and subtle philosophical differences." One lesson to be drawn is that "if a translator has a clear and comprehensive theory about what a given text means, then relying on different commentaries may be warranted and effective. But in the absence of a guiding theory, such a practice tends to produce translations that are montages of unrelated views. This may well contribute to the mistaken impression that Chinese thought is strongly unsystematic." See Ivanhoe, "Whose Confucius? Which Analects?" 129.

19. Chan, "Evolution," 296–97. See also Chan, *A Source Book in Chinese Philosophy*, 34–35.

20. Chan, "Evolution," 297. Among the explanations that Chan finds unacceptable

is Derk Bodde's, the idea that *yu* 與 in the relevant passage is not the conjunction "and" but instead means "give forth," thus interpreting Confucius to have indeed held forth on *ren*. See Derk Bodde, "A Perplexing Passage in the Confucian *Analects*," *Journal of the American Oriental Society*, 53 (1933): 350. E. Bruce Brooks and A. Taeko Brooks, "Word Philology and Text Philology in *Analects* 9:1," in Van Norden, *Confucius and the Analects*, argue that "the sense 'and' for *yu* 與 before a noun is well established. . . . The natural reading of 9:1 would thus be 'The Master seldom spoke of *li* 利 ("profit") or *ming* 命 ("fate; that which is ordained") or *ren* 仁. The problem arises because this grammatically natural reading is unacceptable to *Analects* readers" (164). (I have replaced Brooks and Brooks's romanizations with *hanyu pinyin*.) Brooks and Brooks themselves propose the philological solution that 9.1 as we have it is the insertion of a school that holds a *li*-centered doctrine (as opposed to a *ren*-centered one).

21. James Legge, tr., *The Chinese Classics* (Taipei: Southern Materials Center, Inc., 1985), 216.

22. Yü-sheng Lin, "The Evolution of the Pre-Confucian Meaning of *Jen* 仁 and the Confucian Concept of Moral Autonomy," *Monumenta Serica (Journal of Oriental Studies)* 31 (1974-75): 185.

23. Ibid., 179–81.

24. Ibid., 188.

25. Ibid. Lin admits on the same page that "Confucius did not discuss explicitly the generic nature of man and his statement concerning *xing* is so laconic as to be very vague."

26. See the next chapter for a discussion of Gaozi. Mencius's concerns about the Mohists and the Yangists have been fully discussed, for example, by Angus Graham, *Disputers of the Tao: Philosophical Argument in Ancient China* (La Salle: Open Court, 1989), chs. 2 and 3; and Kwong-loi Shun, *Mencius and Early Chinese Thought* (Stanford: Stanford University Press, 1997), ch. 2.

27. See also 9.19: "As in the case of making a mound, if, before the very last basketful, I stop, then I shall have stopped. As in the case of levelling the ground, if, though tipping only one basketful, I am going forward, then I shall be making progress."

28. Lau, *Analects*, 97, n. 7. Hall and Ames appropriately state that *ren* "is a process term that has no specific *terminus ad quem*" (Hall and Ames, *Thinking Through Confucius*, 115).

29. Confucius says of Yan Hui in 6.7, "In his heart for three months at a time he does not lapse from *ren*. The others attain *ren* merely by fits and starts." The "fits and starts" is Lau's rendition of *riyue* 日月, literally, "day-month." As Yang Bojun notes in his commentary, the "three months" and "day-month" should not be taken literally, but as relatively longer and shorter periods of time. See also Confucius's ambivalent attitude toward Guan Zhong in 3.22, 14.9, 14.16, and 14.17.

30. Lau, *Analects*, "Introduction," 16. The passages usually cited are 4.15, 6.30, 12.2, and 15.24.

31. Fingarette has noted the notorious difficulties with the principle of (as Lau puts it) "asking what one would like or dislike were one in the position of the person at the

receiving end." Perhaps therefore one should take *shu* more as an ethical *attitude* of taking into consideration the feelings of others than as a *principle*, although of course such an attitude would still not guarantee doing the right thing. In this regard, *shu* would also be congruent with the *attitude* of doing one's best for others, as Lau's interpretation of *zhong* would have it. The seeing of *shu* and *zhong* as ethical attitudes rather than (taken together) as a principle or method does not mean that one would need to regard these as constituting "one thread" of Confucius's thinking. I would agree with Bryan Van Norden about the danger of trying to "systematize" Confucius's thinking in regard to the "one thread" of Confucius's *dao* that is mentioned in *Analects* 4.15. It would take us too far to go into this, since there is a vast literature on this issue. Van Norden's essay has a very succinct critique of some of the more prominent works. See "Unweaving the 'One Thread' of *Analects* 4:15," in Van Norden, *Confucius and the Analects*. Van Norden details problems with Lau's reading of *zhong* as "doing one's best"; Fingarette's linking of *zhong* with *zhong-xin* 忠信 as "commitment to preserve integrity"; Nivison's hierarchical reading of *shu* as "reciprocity directed toward social equals or subordinates," and *zhong* as "the corresponding principle of reciprocity directed toward social equals or superiors"; and Ivanhoe's reading of *zhong* as being closer to Fingarette's than he thinks. See Herbert Fingarette, "Following the 'One Thread' of the *Analects*," *Journal of the American Academy of Religion* 47, no. 3, Thematic Issue S (September 1980): 373–405; David S. Nivison, "Golden Rule Arguments in Chinese Moral Philosophy," in his *The Ways of Confucianism*; Philip J. Ivanhoe, "Reweaving the 'One Thread' of the *Analects*," *Philosophy East and West* 40, no. 1 (January 1990): 17–33. Chan Sin Yee, "Disputes on the One Thread of *Chung-Shu*," *Journal of Chinese Philosophy* 26, no. 2 (June 1999): 165–86, develops and defends Lau's reading of *zhong* and *shu*. She holds that "there is support for Lau's idea that *chung* (*zhong*) means exerting one's best efforts in serving others and that *shu*, as analogical thinking, has an unrestricted scope of application" (177). Andrew Plaks's comments should also be noted: "D. C. Lau's translation of these terms . . . as 'doing one's best' and 'using oneself as a measure to gauge others' shows that the semantic value of these words is much richer than their common colloquial sense of 'loyalty' and 'consideration' (or 'reciprocity') would indicate." See Andrew Plaks, tr., *Ta Hsüeh and Chung Yung* [*Daxue and Zhongyong*] (London: Penguin Books, 2003), 108. See also Bo Mou, "A Re-examination of the Structure and Content of Confucius's Version of the Golden Rule," *Philosophy East and West* 54 (April 2004): 218–48.

32. Xinzhong Yao, "*Jen*, Love and Universality: Three Arguments Concerning *Jen* in Confucianism," *Asian Philosophy* 5 (1995): 185.

33. I have preferred Legge's translations of 12.3, 12.4, and 13.3 (below). Note that the *ren* person and the *junzi* 君子 (noble person) seem to be interchangeable in some contexts. See Lau, *Analects*, 15, for some instances.

34. A chain of consequences follows: "If language be not in accordance with the truth of things, affairs cannot be carried on to success . . . proprieties and music will not flourish . . . punishments will not be properly awarded . . . the people do not know how to move hand or foot. Therefore a noble person considers it necessary that the names he uses may be spoken appropriately, and also that what he speaks may be carried out

appropriately. What the noble person requires, is just that in his words there may be nothing incorrect."

35. Regarding this problem, Irene Bloom perceptively notes that it "is plausibly, if only partially, explained by the fact that his disciples questioned him so persistently about *jen*, undeterred and perhaps even impelled by his spare, laconic responses to their inquiries. They may have become aware that *jen* was fundamental to his thinking about what it means to be human. And Confucius, many of whose utterances seem to have been conditioned by awareness or anticipation of their impact on his interlocutors, may have been restrained by a kind of psychological insight from allowing *jen* to become too accessible" (Bloom, "Three Visions of *Jen*," in *Meeting of Minds: Intellectual and Religious Interaction in East Asian Traditions of Thought*, ed. Irene Bloom and Joshua A. Fogel [New York: Columbia University Press, 1997], 11).

36. See Qian Mu (Ch'ien Mu) 錢穆, *Lunyu Xinjie* 論語新解 (Taipei: Dongda, 1988), 641.

37. Compare Yü-sheng Lin's reading of *ren* in 4.7, mentioned above. Note that translators do not agree whether to read *ren* in this passage as 仁 or 人 (man or person). Thus, while Lau reads it as the latter, Ames and Rosemont (*The Analects of Confucius: A Philosophical Translation*) read it as the former. Compare also *Mencius* 2A:2, 6A:6, and 7A:21.

38. Compare *Mencius* 4A:10: "Benevolence (*ren*) is man's peaceful abode and rightness (*yi*) its proper path." The almost tautologous nature of *ren* and "not *you* 憂" has been noted by Fingarette, *Confucius—the Secular as Sacred*, 43. Indeed, he states on the same page, "*Yu* [*you*], it is fair to presume, is the opposite of *jen* [*ren*]."

39. Fingarette, *Confucius*, 41–42.

40. Ibid., 14. In a note on this page, Fingarette lists two trends: the positivistic trend of the Vienna Circle interested in formal languages, and the trend fostered by those more interested in natural languages, for example, Wittgenstein, Gilbert Ryle, J. L. Austin, P. F. Strawson, and John Wisdom. Fingarette's analysis is inspired by this second trend. It would not be exact to claim that they were all concerned to "exorcise the ghost of Descartes" as I said above, but nonetheless, because of the style of a public criterial analysis shared by them, this is not an inappropriate phrase to apply here. Gilbert Ryle, *The Concept of Mind* (London: Hutchinson, 1949), is directly concerned with Descartes and a good example of this criterial analysis.

41. For example, Charles Wei-hsün Fu, "Fingarette and Munro on Early Confucianism: A Methodological Examination," *Philosophy East and West* 28 (1978), 187. Also, Shu-hsien Liu, "Sinological Torque: An Observation," *Philosophy East and West* 28 (1978): 203–4.

42. Fingarette, *Confucius*, 42.

43. Mary Bockover, "The Concept of Emotion Revisited: A Critical Synthesis of Western and Confucian Thought," in *Emotions in Asian Thought: A Dialogue in Comparative Philosophy*, ed. Joel Marks and Roger Ames (New York: State University of New York Press, 1995), 169–70.

44. The idea of this spirit as approaching others "empathetically and to treat them

with the dignity they deserve" has Kantian overtones. Bockover recognizes this problem, and in a note, qualifies what she says: "I am not trying to suggest that Confucius was espousing an egalitarian philosophy where all humans were considered worthy of respect. To the contrary, this would depend upon the person, that is, on how one carries out one's various roles and responsibilities." See Marks and Ames, *Emotions and Asian Thought*, note 15, 177–78.

45. Benjamin Schwartz, *The World of Thought in Ancient China* (Cambridge, MA: Harvard University Press, 1985), 82.

46. Kwong-loi Shun, "*Ren* and *Li* in the *Analects*," *Philosophy East and West* 43 (1993): 457–79. See also the slightly modified version of this essay in Van Norden, *Confucius and the Analects*.

47. Shun, "*Ren* and *Li* in the *Analects*," 471; in Van Norden, *Confucius and the Analects*, 66.

48. See, for example, Shun, "*Ren* and *Li* in the *Analects*," 469, where the definitionalist is described as holding "that the general observance of *li* is, at least in part, constitutive of *ren*"; in Van Norden, *Confucius and the Analects*, 61.

49. Shun, "*Ren* and *Li* in the *Analects*," 472; in Van Norden, *Confucius and the Analects*, 67. Wei-ming Tu, "*Jen* as a Living Metaphor in the Confucian *Analects*," in *Confucian Thought: Selfhood as Creative Transformation* (New York: State University of New York Press, 1985), also argues that puzzlement over the relationship between *ren*, *li* and *zhi* 智 can be overcome "if *ren* is conceived of as a complex of attitude and disposition in which the other two important concepts are integral parts or contributing factors." However, Tu emphasizes the priority of *ren* over the other concepts. As he says, "*ren* is unquestionably a more essential characterization of the Confucian Way." See pp. 86–87 of his book. Yü-sheng Lin also argues for the priority of *ren* over *li*, "in spite of the necessity of *li*. For *ren* is an end; while *li* is a means. The significance of *li* resides in its function of assisting the cultivation and development of *ren*; *li* itself has no meaning, whereas *ren*'s value and meaning is independent of *li*" ("The Evolution of the Pre-Confucian Meaning of *Jen* 仁 and the Confucian Concept of Moral Autonomy," 194). In this respect, *li* is seen as merely providing a nonchaotic environment wherein *ren* can be developed.

50. Shun, "*Ren* and *Li* in the *Analects*," 471; in Van Norden, *Confucius and the Analects*, 66.

51. This idea was anticipated by Wei-ming Tu in "The Creative Tension Between *Jen* and *Li*," *Philosophy East and West* 18, no. 1-2 (January-April 1968): 29–39. Also published in his *Humanity and Self-Cultivation: Essays in Confucian Thought* (Berkeley: Asian Humanities Press, 1979). See p. 12 of the latter, where he says, "a Confucianist may very well refute an established *li* by exposing its incompatibility with *jen* (*ren*)." The possibility of argumentation and change in Confucian ethics has been discussed in great detail by Antonio Cua, who refers to the various kinds of "appeal" that can be made in ethical argumentation, besides the appeal to *ren*. For example, appeal can be made to "moral notions of particular virtues," to *li*, to "living or historical persons," to "*sheng-ren* or the sage," to "*chün-tzu* (*junzi*) or [noble person]," and to "the *time* in

exigent situation." See A. S. Cua, "Reasonable Action and Confucian Argumentation," in *Moral Vision and Tradition Essays in Chinese Ethics* (Washington, D.C.: The Catholic University of America Press, 1998), 11–12.

52. My description of *ren* as an ethical orientation and an ethical commitment is anticipated by Antonio Cua in some of the essays in his *Moral Vision and Tradition*. Speaking of *ren* as an "ideal theme" rather than as an "ideal norm," Cua says: "an ideal may be construed as a sort of *theme* that endows the life of a commitive agent with a certain quality of excellence. In this sense, it offers not normative or preceptorial guidance, but a focal point of orientation for conduct. It is a perspective that gives a significance or quality to an individual's life. *Jen* [*ren*] may be taken thus as an ideal theme, as a focal point of attention for achieving a meaning or significance in an agent's life. The stress on self-cultivation in accordance with *jen* [ren] is a central feature in Confucian ethics" (Cua, "Reasonable Action and Confucian Argumentation," 14). See also "Confucian Vision and Experience of the World," in the same book, 30: "An ideal theme is neither a typal conception nor an archetype that establishes a pattern of behavior. It is a vision that focuses upon the gestaltlike character of a way of life. It functions as a standard of inspiration, not by providing an articulate norm or set of action guides to be complied with, but by providing a point of orientation. The achievement of an ideal theme does not depend on prior knowledge of directives that issue from it. One can comport to an ideal theme in various ways. Much depends on the creative development of the individual in his life and conduct. It is the action and experience of individual agents that furnish the content of the ideal theme."

Chapter 3: Debating Human Nature: Mencius and Gaozi

1. I shall again be referring to the bilingual edition of D. C. Lau, tr., *Mencius*, previously cited. Passage numberings follow those given in this edition. I have modified some of Lau's translations. Apart from the debate in Book 6, Mencius also discusses Gaozi in 2A:2, where he is said to have achieved an "unmoved mind" (*bu dong xin* 不動心) even before Mencius. In Gaozi's case, this is explained as: "If you fail to understand words, do not worry about this in your heart; and if you fail to understand in your heart, do not seek satisfaction in your *qi* 氣." Kwong-loi Shun has explained that Gaozi believed in shaping one's motivations by first adopting and being committed to certain doctrines, in this way attaining an "unmoved mind." Mencius's criticism of Gaozi in 2A:2 is that Gaozi did not know *yi* "because he regarded it as external and was therefore mistaken about its source, and he was not good at nourishing *ch'i* (*qi*) because he was helping *ch'i* grow by imposing a mistaken conception of *yi* from the outside." See Kwong-loi Shun, *Mencius and Early Chinese Thought* (Stanford: Stanford University Press, 1997), 119. I shall not be discussing 2A:2. However, I shall be concerned to explicate the sense in which Gaozi holds *yi* to be external, as it is very much an issue in Book 6. Discussions of 2A:2 can also be found in Whalen Lai, "Kao Tzu and Mencius on Mind: Analyzing

a Paradigm Shift in Classical China," *Philosophy East and West* 34 (April 1984): 147–60, and Jeffrey Riegel, "Reflections on an Unmoved Mind," *Journal of the American Academy of Religion* 47, no. 3, Thematic Issue S (September 1980): 433–57.

2. Mencius saw it as his mission to combat the egoism (*wei wo* 為我) of Yang Zhu and the doctrine of universal love or impartial caring (*jian ai* 兼愛) of Mozi, and his theory may be said to have been developed or at least sharpened with this mission in mind. This was to him an urgent task given the popularity of the idea that *xing* 性 or nature merely refers to *sheng* 生 the process of life, and the Yangist recommendation of its nurturance in individualistic terms. The Mohist challenge of particularistic concern and the gradations of love, too, had to be met. In *Mencius* 3B:9, Mencius says that he has no alternative but to dispute Yang and Mo. "The teachings current in the Empire are those of either the school of Yang or the school of Mo. . . . If the way of Yang and Mo does not subside and the way of Confucius is not proclaimed, the people will be deceived by heresies and the path of morality [*ren* yi] will be blocked. When the path of morality is blocked, then we show animals the way to devour humans, and sooner or later it will come to humans devouring each other. Therefore, I am apprehensive. I wish to safeguard the way of the former sages against the onslaughts of Yang and Mo and to banish excessive views." For detailed discussions of these challenges, see especially A. C. Graham, "The Background of the Mencian Theory of Human Nature," in his *Studies in Chinese Philosophy and Philosophical Literature* (Singapore: Institute of East Asian Philosophies, 1986) and Shun, *Mencius and Early Chinese Thought*. See also my "Egoism in Chinese Ethics," in *Encyclopedia of Chinese Philosophy*, ed. A. S. Cua (New York: Routledge, 2003). In chapter 4, I shall discuss how the Mencian theory of motivation is opposed to the Mohist's.

3. The affiliation of Gaozi is not important to my discussion, although I shall be concerned to explicate his views on human nature more fully in this and a subsequent chapter, where I compare him with Xunzi. Paul Rakita Goldin has noted that the idea that "morality must be obtained from outside of the self, is common to Gaozi, Xunzi, and the Guodian manuscripts—and to virtually no other known members of the Confucian school." See Goldin, "Xunzi in the Light of the Guodian Manuscripts," *Early China* 25 (2000): 120, and also 139–46. In other words, Gaozi may have belonged to an early branch of the Confucian school. The view that Gaozi belongs to the Confucian school is shared by Maurizio Scarpari. See "The Debate on Human Nature in Early Confucian Literature," *Philosophy East and West* 53 (July 2003): 336, note 5. A. C. Graham notices parallels between Gaozi and the *Jie* 戒 section of the *Guanzi* 管子. See Graham, "The Background of the Mencian Theory of Human Nature," *Studies in Chinese Philosophy and Philosophical Literature*, 22–23. David Nivison, "Philosophical Voluntarism in Fourth Century China," in his *The Ways of Confucianism*, says, "We must take seriously . . . the possibility that Gaozi as a very young man was a disciple of Mozi" (130). Shun, *Mencius and Early Chinese Thought*, investigates the various possibilities, but concludes that "Based on the available evidence, I do not think it is possible to determine Kao Tzu's (Gaozi) affiliation, whether as Confucian, Mohist, or Taoist . . . the content of his thinking does not point clearly in any one direction. Indeed, since this distinction between philosophi-

cal schools is drawn retrospectively, it is quite possible that they were not distinguished clearly during that period, and that Kao Tzu's thinking drew upon ideas from different philosophical movements. If so, this might well explain why his thinking is resistant to classification into our standard categories" (126).

4. Arthur Waley, *Three Ways of Thought in Ancient China* (New York: Doubleday & Company, 1956), 145. Originally published by George Allen and Unwin (London, 1939).

5. D. C. Lau, "On Mencius' Use of the Method of Analogy in Argument," in Lau, *Mencius*, vol. 2, 334.

6. Chad Hansen, *A Daoist Theory of Chinese Thought: A Philosophical Interpretation* (New York: Oxford University Press, 1992), 188.

7. Graham, "The Background of the Mencian Theory of Human Nature," in Graham, 27.

8. See especially Whalen Lai, "Kao Tzu and Mencius on Mind, and Huang Min Hao 黃敏浩 (Simon Wong), *Mengzi, Gaozi Bianlun de zai quan shi* 孟子, 告子辯論的再詮釋, *Tsinghua Journal of Chinese Studies*, New Series 32, no. 1 (June 2002): 117–44. Both Lai and Huang analyze the debate in detail and argue that Gaozi has been much misunderstood and unjustifiably maligned. Paul Rakita Goldin, *Rituals of the Way: The Philosophy of Xunzi* (Chicago: Open Court, 1999), realizes that "the crux of the debate between Mencius and Gaozi is the question of the source of morality—is it internal or external?" (32). But he states that "Gaozi's recurrent obstacle in the discussion is his inability to marshal his images; he is outwitted at every turn by Mencius" (33), although he attributes this to Mencius's sometimes engaging in "legerdemain" and "sophistry" (34). See also Shun's examination of the debate in *Mencius and Early Chinese Thought*.

9. This follows Lau's translation of *ren yi* as "morality." In the context of the present chapter, *ren* itself means "love," especially the love of kin. In one instance (7B:24), I have translated it as "filial love" which I think is more appropriate than Lau's "benevolence" since the context is the relation between father and son. Note, however, that *ren* in the *Mencius* has other meanings that I will discuss in the next chapter. The term *yi* itself pertains to the virtue of righteousness or dutifulness that has its basis in the sprout of loathing and shame in one's heart-mind (*xiu wu zhi xin* 羞惡之心).

10. Zhu Xi, *Sishu Zhangju Jizhu* 四書章句集注 (Taipei: Changan Chubanshe, 1990), 325.

11. See Donald J. Munro, "A Villain in the *Xunzi*," and David B. Wong, "Xunzi on Moral Motivation," both in *Chinese Language, Thought, and Culture: Nivison and his Critics*, ed. Philip J. Ivanhoe (Chicago and La Salle, Illinois: Open Court, 1996).

12. Shun, *Mencius and Early Chinese Thought*, 88.

13. A point made by Goldin, *Rituals of the Way*, 33: "A willow does not turn into so many cups and bowls *naturally*; one must chop the tree and work its wood to *create* cups and bowls." I wonder what the *qi* willow or *qi liu* 杞柳 is or was like. Was it necessary to cut the whole trunk or just its branches to make cups and bowls? If the former, perhaps it would have been killed, if the latter, then not necessarily.

14. Lau, "On Mencius' Use of the Method of Analogy in Argument," 336.

15. Donald Munro, in personal correspondence, comments: "Chinese thinkers of many schools use the behavioral implications of a doctrine as grounds for accepting or rejecting it (i.e. the psychological impact it is likely to have on people who hear it). The behavioral implication of saying that it is unnatural to be moral (or a violation of the nature) is that people will not act morally, namely, they will have no incentive to do the right thing."

16. Lau, "On Mencius' Use of the Method of Analogy in Argument," 338.

17. For instance, Sarah Allan, *The Way of Water and Sprouts of Virtue* (Albany: State University of New York Press, 1997), 42.

18. A comparison may be made here with Xunzi's image of molding clay when describing the production of *li yi*. Gaozi's image of water, however, is more dynamic and implies that nature is more easily influenced or directed. See the chapter on "Man's Nature is Evil" (性惡) in John Knoblock, tr., *Xunzi*, vol. 3 (Stanford: Stanford University Press, 1994), 157.

19. Lau, "On Mencius' Use of the Method of Analogy in Argument," 340: "If we insist on saying that this [the appetite for food and sex] constitutes the whole of human nature then we will have to accept the logical conclusion that the nature of a man is no different from that of a dog or an ox and this not even Gaozi was prepared to accept." Graham, "The Mencian Theory of Human Nature," 46: "Gaozi has committed himself to much more than he has bargained for; if *xing* in general is merely *sheng* there is no inherent tendency in the development of any specific thing, and nothing to distinguish the natures of ox, dog and man."

20. Whalen Lai says: "If nature is just food and sex, then man is no better than a dog (6A:3). Kao Tzu (Gaozi) would have agreed, but with this qualification: by *hsing* (*xing*) is meant what pertains to life, but above that is *jen-hsing* [*ren xing*] (specific human nature). Compare this with 'All men are mortal; Socrates is a man; Socrates is mortal.' It does not mean that that is all Socrates is." See Lai, "Kao Tzu and Mencius on Mind," 148. Except for the idea that above *xing* is *ren xing*, I would agree with the logical tenor of Lai's remarks.

21. My rendering of *yue* as what "pleases" is contextual, and I believe it captures what Gaozi is thinking of in his explanation of "*ren* is internal." Lau translates *yue* as "explanation" here in the sense of *shuo* 説, thus rendering *shi yi wo wei yue zhe ye gu wei zhi nei* 是以我為悦者也故謂之內 as "This means that the explanation lies in me. Hence I call it internal." And similarly, a few sentences later, *shi yi zhang wei yue zhe ye gu wei zhi wai ye* 是以長為悦者也故謂之外也, as "This means that the explanation lies in their elderliness. Hence I call it external." The first use of *yue* as "the explanation lies in me" is consistent with my rendering of it as what "pleases," although not the second "the explanation lies in their elderliness." Note that in 6A:7, we have *gu li yi zhi yue wo xin you chu huan zhi yue wo kou* 故理義之悦我心猶芻豢之悦我口 which Lau renders as "Thus reason and rightness please my heart in the same way as meat pleases my palate." Although both instances of *yue* are translated as "please(s)," I show below that the pleasure that the heart-mind takes in *li yi* is different in kind from the sensory pleasure of taste.

22. After providing this example, and anticipating what Mengjizi would say, Mencius says to Gongduzi: "You can then say, "[In the case of the person from my village] it is also because of the position he occupies. Normal respect is due to my elder brother; temporary respect is due to the person from my village." I cannot make sense of this. But this should not affect the logical point that is at work in the ensuing exchange between Gongduzi and Mengjizi, after the former conveys Mencius's example to the latter.

23. Shun, *Mencius and Early Chinese Thought*, 106. A similar explanation is given by Huang Min Hao 黃敏浩 (Simon Wong), *Mengzi, Gaozi Bianlun de zai quan shi* 孟子, 告子辯論的再詮釋131.

24. Shun, *Mencius and Early Chinese Thought*, 109.

25. Ibid., 108.

26. Lai, "Kao Tzu and Mencius on Mind," 148.

27. Ibid.

28. Lau, "Mencius' Use of the Method of Analogy in Argument," 351.

29. David Nivison states, "Gao and Mencius are agreed about *ren*, exemplified by loving: I won't show love unless I am disposed to, in virtue of the relation of the object to me. They disagree about *yi*, exemplified by behavior showing respect for elderliness, because Gao thinks of the occasional cause as the decisive one: It is what is 'out there' that counts, every time, no matter where, including the applicable public standard." See Nivison, *The Ways of Confucianism*, 162–63. Nivison notes the absurd consequence of Gaozi's having to say that his enjoyment of roast is external, but does not make the point that Mencius is rejecting the internal-external distinction that Gaozi is working with. Xiusheng Liu, "Mengzian Internalism," in *Essays on the Moral Philosophy of Mengzi*, ed. Xiusheng Liu and Philip J. Ivanhoe (Indianapolis: Hackett Publishing Company, 2002), 115, says that "Mengzi and Gaozi agree on the meanings of 'internal' and 'external.' This is shown by the fact that they do not even try to correct each other's use of those terms. What they dispute is whether *yi* is internal or external. Gaozi insists that it is external; Mengzi disagrees. We therefore can derive the meaning of 'internal' from either Mengzi's or Gaozi's statements."

30. Modifying Lau's "Only this has never dawned on me" for *fu si er yi* 弗思耳矣. Bryan Van Norden has noted the psychological importance of *si* for Mencius. He notes "8 occurrences in which *si* clearly is a technical term of Mengzian psychology referring to the psychological act that I label 'concentration': 4A1, 6A6, 6A13, 6A15 (four occurrences), and 6A17" (Van Norden, "Mengzi and Xunzi: Two Views of Human Agency," in *Virtue, Nature, and Moral Agency in the Xunzi*, ed. T. C. Kline III and Philip J. Ivanhoe [Indianapolis: Hackett Publishing Company, 2000], 112).

31. Lau translates *bu ren ren zhi xin* 不忍人之心 in 2A:6 as "a heart sensitive to the suffering of others," and "a sensitive heart." Wing-tsit Chan translates this as "the mind which cannot bear to see the suffering of others." Mentioning the example, Mencius attributes this capacity to something more basic, *ce yin zhi xin*. Lau translates this as "compassion," and Chan as "a feeling of alarm and distress." It could be argued that Lau's "sensitive heart" and "compassion" are no different, and one cannot as such be the basis of, or serve as evidence for, the other. On the other hand, Chan's "feeling of

alarm and distress" could be seen as a more rudimentary form of response, necessary (but not sufficient) for the "heart which cannot bear to see the suffering of others." See Chan, *A Source Book in Chinese Philosophy*, 65.

32. For a detailed discussion of the nontransferability of compassion or concern, see my book *Moral Agoraphobia: The Challenge of Egoism* (New York: Peter Lang, 1996), 50–51, where the case of Dorothea is described more fully. The example is from George Eliot, *Middlemarch* (Harmondsworth: Penguin, 1976), 103. To obviate any misunderstanding, consider also the following case: I see a child killed in a car accident; contrary to what I normally do, I might give some money to a child begging further down the road. There is no denying that this constitutes a psychological phenomenon of "transference," but it should not affect what I mean by the "nontransferability" of compassion or concern.

33. See Shun, *Mencius and Early Chinese Thought*, 137; Ann-ping Chin and Mansfield Freeman, tr., *Tai Chen on Mencius: Explorations in Words and Meaning* (New Haven: Yale University Press, 1990), 74.

34. Shun, *Mencius and Early Chinese Though*, 150, 265. According to Tang Junyi (T'ang Chün-i) 唐君毅, the pre-Qin thinkers largely used *li* in the sense of *wen li*, or pattern. See his study of the concept of *li* in "Lun Zhongguo zhexue sixiangshi zhong (li) zhi liu yi 論中國哲學思想史中 (理) 之六義 in *Xinya Xuebao* 新亞學報, vol. 1, no. 1 (1995): 45–98. See p. 47. The three passages where *li* occurs are 5B:1, 6A:7, and 7B:19. In the last we have someone called Mo Ji saying, *Ji da bu li yu kou* (稽大不理於口) which Lau renders as "I am not much of a speaker." Yang Bojun 楊伯峻 takes *bu li* as *bu shun* (不順) or "not agreeable." As such, he gives the modern Chinese equivalent of the passage as "I am badly spoken of by others." See Yang Bojun, *Mengzi Yizhu* 孟子譯注 (Hong Kong: Zhonghua zhuju, 1984).

35. Lau's translation of the relevant passage in 5B:1 reads, "Confucius was the one who gathered together all that was good (*ji da cheng* 集大成). To do this is to open with bells and rally with jade tubes. To open with bells is to begin in an orderly fashion (*shi tiao li ye* 始條理也); to rally with jade tubes is to end in an orderly fashion (*zhong tiao li ye* 終條理也). To begin in an orderly fashion pertains to wisdom while to end in an orderly fashion pertains to sageness." Note Wing-tsit Chan's and Chin and Freeman's translation of *ji da cheng* as a "complete concert." See Chan, *A Source Book in Chinese Philosophy*, 711; Chin and Freeman, *Tai Chen on Mencius*, 69.

36. See David Wong, "Is There a Distinction between Reason and Emotion in Mencius?" *Philosophy East and West* 41, no. 1 (1991): 31–44, for an extended argument of this point. An earlier argument of the same point is Donald Munro, *The Concept of Man in Contemporary China* (Ann Arbor: The University of Michigan Press, 1977). See especially ch. 2, p. 26 ff.

37. Translation my own. Compare Lau: "If it was truly right for them to bury the remains of their parents, then it must also be right for all dutiful sons and benevolent people to do likewise." As Lau often uses "right" for a translation of *yi* 義, and *yi* does not occur in this passage, it is better not to use the term "right" here.

38. A similar point is noted by Confucius's disciple, Gongduzi in 6A:15, when

he asks, "Though equally human, why are some people greater than others?" Bryan Van Norden notes the persistence of Gongduzi in the same passage. Commenting on Mencius's final answer that if you don't *si* (Van Norden: "concentrate") then you won't get it, Van Norden says: "This passage . . . confirms the importance of concentration in Mengzi's picture of self-cultivation, but it fails as an altogether satisfactory answer . . . since we may go on to ask why some people concentrate and others do not" (Van Norden, "Mengzi and Xunzi: Two Views of Human Agency," 115). I discuss this problem further in chapter 7.

39. In addition to the view that "All humans are capable of becoming good," Bryan Van Norden finds in the *Mencius* a view of human agency with various claims, perhaps the most central of which is that "Humans must do that which they believe will obtain for them what they most desire." See Van Norden, "Mengzi and Xunzi," 116–17. This is debatable, given the fact that Mencius often laments that although people know how to tend to the various things cited, they nevertheless neglect what is most important. However, I totally agree with Van Norden's view that Mencius has a "deep" point, that "humans are, intrinsically, evaluative animals. We are not just creatures who desire to satisfy our desires for food, sex, etc. We are creatures who desire to feel worthy, to be esteemed, to lead lives which have moral value" (114).

40. The original text has *sheng ren* (sage), instead of *sheng* (sageness). I have adopted "sageness" instead of "sage," because it allows for a more consistent reading of *ren*, *yi*, *li*, *zhi*, *sheng*. This is a possible reading as noted after the Chinese text of 7B:24 in Lau. Lau cites Pang Pu 龐樸. The full bibliographic reference is given by Kwong-loi Shun in *Mencius and Early China*: *Boshu wuxing pian yanjiu* 帛書五行篇研究 (Jinan: Qilu shushe, 1988), 19–21. As Shun notes, "Pang Pu argues for the emendation on the grounds that *sheng* is grouped along with *ren*, *yi*, *li*, and *zhi* in the 'Essay on the Five Processes' in the Mawangdui silk manuscripts." See Shun, *Mencius and Early Chinese Thought*, 203–4.

41. The distinction between the descriptive and normative senses of *ming* is made by Shun, 78–79. Shun gives quite an exhaustive discussion of different possible interpretations of 7B:24, on pp. 203–5 of his book.

42. Lau makes a related distinction between instrumental and constitutive means in his discussion of *Mencius* 4A:17, although I would not describe what I have said as a constitutive relation between seeking and getting in terms of "means." Asked why he would save a drowning sister-in-law (contrary to the rites of *nan nü shou shou bu qin* 男女授受不親) but not the Empire, Mencius replies: "When the Empire is drowning, one helps it with the Way; when a sister-in-law is drowning one helps her with one's hand. Would you have me help the Empire with my hand?" To Waley, this is a "cheap debating point" (Waley, *Three Ways of Thought in Ancient China*, 146). Lau replies that one may use anything to save a drowning woman, the means is purely instrumental. But one may only save the Empire through the proper way, the *dao*. He adds that the way "becomes part of the end it helps to realize, and the end endures so long as the means remains a part of it. Remove the Way at any subsequent time, and the Empire will revert to disorder" (Lau, "On Mencius' Use of the Method of Analogy in Argument," 341–42.

43. Roger Ames, "The Mencian Conception of *Ren Xing*: Does it Mean 'Human Nature'?" in Henry Rosemont, Jr., ed., *Chinese Texts and Philosophical Contexts: Essays Dedicated to Angus C. Graham* (La Salle: Open Court, 1991), argues for an understanding of *xing* as not given and essentialistic but instead, creatively and existentially achieved and maintains that it should be more accurate to translate it in terms of character, personality, and constitution rather than "nature." Ames also stresses the distinction between *xin* and *xing* in that *xing* is something creatively achieved out of *xin* (see 143–45). Ames is correct, insofar as the contents of *xin* (and not *xing*) denote a *potential* that need to be worked upon, creatively. At the same time, however, Mencius says that if someone becomes bad, it is not the fault of his native endowment *cai* (6A:6). Ames's denial of an essentialistic "nature" has been controversial on precisely this point, as he seems to deny something which Mencius has explicitly stated. See Irene Bloom, "Mencian Arguments on Human Nature (*Ren-Xing*)," *Philosophy East and West* 44, no. 1 (1994): 19–53; and "Human Nature and Biological Nature in Mencius," *Philosophy East and West* 47, no. 1 (1997): 21–32.

Chapter 4: Mencius on *Ren* and the Problem of "Extending"

1. See C. L. Ten, "The Moral Circle," in Chong, Tan, and Ten, *The Moral Circle and the Self*, for a discussion of the problems facing various "monistic" moral theories (including, for example, utilitarianism) that seem to stress only one ultimate value and one motivational source.

2. See especially the more recent essays by David B. Wong, "Reasons and Analogical Reasoning in Mengzi," and Philip J. Ivanhoe, "Confucian Self Cultivation and Mengzi's Notion of Extension," both in Liu and Ivanhoe, *Essays on the Moral Philosophy of Mengzi*. The debate seems to have been set off by David Nivison's "Mencius and Motivation," *Journal of the American Academy of Religion*, Thematic Issue S, 47, no. 3 (1980): 417–32, subsequently revised and published as "Motivation and Moral Action in Mengzi," in his *The Ways of Confucianism*. Subsequent debate involves papers by Kwong-loi Shun, "Moral Reasons in Confucian Ethics," *Journal of Chinese Philosophy* 16, no. 3-4 (1989): 317–43; Bryan Van Norden, "Kwong-loi Shun on Moral Reasons in Mencius," *Journal of Chinese Philosophy* 18, no. 4 (1991): 353–70; David B. Wong, "Is There a Distinction Between Reason and Emotion in Mencius?" *Philosophy East and West* 41, no. 1 (January 1991): 31–44; Craig K. Ihara, "David Wong on Emotions in Mencius," *Philosophy East and West* 41, no. 1 (January 1991): 45–53.

3. A point that has been recognized by others such as Julia Po-Wah Lai Tao, "Two Perspectives of Care: Confucian *Ren* and Feminist Care," *Journal of Chinese Philosophy* 27, no. 2 (June 2000): 215–40, 236; and David Wong, "Reasons and Analogical Reasoning in Mengzi," in Liu and Ivanhoe, *Essays on the Philosophy of Mengzi*, 209–10. Both Tao and Wong make this point through a discussion of the dilemma in *Mencius* 7A:35, which I shall also be discussing later.

4. For convenience, I shall use "filial love" for *xiaoti*, which was rendered more fully as "being filial toward parents and respectful of elders," in chapter 2.

5. See chapter 2.

6. Bloom, "Three Visions of *Jen*," 24–25.

7. Nivison, in "Motivation and Moral Action in Mencius," also discusses the problem of "extending" in terms of the model of individual moral failure. But note that Mencius treats the failure to act not as a logical puzzle in the way philosophers in the Western tradition do. Instead, he puts it in terms of the fact that people neglect the 'greater' part of themselves (the heart-mind) for the 'lesser' parts. See for instance 6A:11–12 and 6A:14.

8. `Lau says, "Throughout this passage Mencius is exploiting the fact that the word *ai* means both 'to love' and 'to be sparing, to be frugal.'" Lau, *Mencius*, vol. 2, 285, n.17.

9. The idea of a "lexical" order of priority was made popular by John Rawls, *A Theory of Justice* (Oxford University Press, 1972). As Rawls stipulates, a serial or lexical order is one "which requires us to satisfy the first principle in the ordering before we can move on to the second, the second before we consider the third, and so on. A principle does not come into play until those previous to it are either fully met or do not apply. A serial ordering avoids, then, having to balance principles at all; those earlier in the ordering have an absolute weight, so to speak, with respect to later ones, and hold without exception" (43). As will be evident, I do not hold that Mencius gives absolute weight to filial affection, despite stipulating its lexical priority. I use "lexical priority" more to differentiate it from the "ethical priority" of Zhu Xi, as discussed earlier.

10. As noted earlier, there has been a debate about the nature of the reasons that Mencius reminds the King of, for extending his compassion from the ox to his people. However, whatever the nature of these reasons that the King is brought to acknowledge, a good question is whether he would finally be motivated to *act*, to bring relief to his people, not engage in war that involves bringing suffering to them, and so on.

11. Burton Watson, tr., *Han Fei Tzu*, "The Five Vermin" (*Wu Du* 五蠹), in *Basic Writings of Mo Tzu, Hsün Tzu, and Han Fei Tzu* (New York: Columbia University Press, 1963), 101. For the Chinese, I have quoted from Fu Wu Guang 傅武光 and Lai Yan Yuan 賴炎元 ed., *Xinyi Han Feizi* 新譯韓非子 (Taipei: Sanmin shuju, 1997), 715.

12. Lin Pin Shi 林品石 ed., *Lü shi chunqiu jin zhu jin yi* 呂氏春秋今註今譯 (Taipei: Taiwan shangwu yinshuguan, 1985), 31, chapter on "*Qu Si* 去私." See also John Knoblock and Jeffrey Riegel, tr., *The Annals of Lü Buwei* (Stanford: Stanford University Press, 2000), book I, ch. 5, sec. 5.

13. I am referring to the Yangist and Daoist avoidance of and even disdain for public office. See Graham, *Disputers of the Tao*, 53–64, for a discussion of the Yangists.

14. Bloom, "Three Visions of *Jen*," 19, contrasting Confucius's metaphorical image of a difficult journey in which one is required to endure and persevere with Mencius's use of organic metaphors in their separate discussions of *ren*, says: "Mencius' organic metaphors imply concomitant notions of enlargement, fulfillment, growth, and maturation; the images are of an individual who, being fully contextualized in nature, finds

fulfillment within the natural process. His course may not be easy, but he has a lot of life's energies working within and for him. . . . Other metaphors, such as the fire and spring employed in 2A:6, are suggestive of a dynamic and growing energy: each rereading of that familiar passage must re-evoke a vision of the faintly flickering flame beginning to burn brightly and the trickle of water bursting into a bubbling torrent."

15. I have benefited from the discussion of this incident in 林義正 (Lin Yih-jing), "*Chunqiu gongyang zhuan sixiang zhong daode juezhe de wenti* 春秋公羊傳思想中道德抉擇的問題," in *Proceedings of the International Conference on Chinese Philosophy*, National Taiwan University, Taipei, R.O.C., November 3–7, 1985. I have consulted the following edition of the *Gongyang Zhuan*: *Xin yi Gongyang Zhuan* 新譯公羊傳, ed. Xue Ke 雪克 (Taipei: Sanmin shuju, 1998). The incident is recorded under the fifteenth year of Xuan Gong 宣公 or 594 B.C.E.

16. We should also not neglect the emotional and psychological role of the family in the moral development of the individual. See David Wong, "Universalism Versus Love With Distinctions: An Ancient Debate Revived," *Journal of Chinese Philosophy* 16 (1989): 251–72, for an account of the emotional and psychological processes involved in this regard.

Chapter 5: Xunzi's Critique of Mencius

1. Passage numbers such as 23.5a, 23.5b in this chapter are John Knoblock's in his *Xunzi: A Translation and Study of the Complete Works*, 3 vols. (Stanford: Stanford University Press, 1988,1990,1994). Other texts consulted: *Xunzi: A Concordance to the Xunzi*, The Chinese University of Hong Kong Institute of Chinese Studies Ancient Chinese Texts Concordance Series (Hong Kong: The Commercial Press, 1996) cited as ICS, with chapter/page/line number; Li Disheng 李滌生, *Xunzi Ji Shi* 荀子集釋 (Taipei: Xuesheng Shuju, 1994); Burton Watson, *Hsün Tzu: Basic Writings* (New York: Columbia University Press, 1963).

2. Nivison, "Xunzi on 'Human Nature'," in *The Ways of Confucianism: Investigations in Chinese Philosophy*, 212, states that Xunzi resorts to "linguistic legislation" about the difference between *xing* and *wei* 偽 (human artifice). Graham, "The Background of the Mencian Theory of Human Nature," 56, holds that it is because of a "shift" in the sense of *xing* in Xunzi's *Xing E Pian* that, "although its theory is as coherent in terms of its own definitions as Mencius's in terms of his, [it] never quite makes contact with the Mencian theory which it criticises." Goldin, *Rituals of the Way*, 11, 13, agrees with Graham. He locates Xunzi's disagreement with Mencius in terms of the former's stress on *wei* or human artifice. Goldin refers by analogy to the "policies" as against the "resources" of a state: "Success or failure rest with the policies; the resources play no appreciable role in the determination of the state's ultimate fate" (16).

3. Graham, "The Background of the Mencian Theory of Human Nature," 56–57, finds Xunzi (23.5a) "remarking incidentally that man has 'the equipment by which he

may become capable of benevolence and duty, the standard and the correct' (可以能仁義 法正之具), without noticing that as Mencius uses the term *xing* this amounts to admitting that human nature is good." D. C. Lau, "Theories of Human Nature in Mencius and Xunzi," in Kline and Ivanhoe, *Virtue, Nature, and Moral Agency in the Xunzi*, 208, argues that the capacity of inventing morality must belong to human nature: "There is no reason why we should not extend the name human nature to cover the capacity of invention possessed by the mind which is part of it." Nivison notes that when Xunzi argues (in 23.2b) that we desire goodness because we lack it, a Mencian could reply that this is evidence of a good human nature ("Xunzi on 'Human Nature'," 211–12). (A. S. Cua, "The Quasi-empirical Aspect of Hsün Tzu's Philosophy of Human Nature," *Philosophy East and West* 28 (1978): 4–5, however, does not see this as central to Xunzi: "All that follows from the conceptual point [that we desire what we lack] is that given a man desiring goodness, he lacks goodness in some sense to be specified under a certain description, but this throws no light upon the character or nature of the man.")

4. Lau, "Theories of Human Nature in Mencius and Xunzi," 204–5, takes Xunzi to be making a distinction between being "capable" and "succeeding." But it is unclear why success should come into the picture. Given various contingencies, someone who is able to be or to do something might not succeed. David Nivison's most recent view is that there is more to Xunzi's critique of Mencius than earlier thought. He analyzes the distinction between *ke yi* and *neng* in Knoblock 23.5b, noting that it is a discussion of "kinds of ability" that is "intended as a correction of Mengzi's distinction between 'not doing' and 'not being able to do' (*bu wei* 不為 vs. *bu neng* 不能) in *Mengzi* 1A7 to King Xuan of Qi, and 6B2 to the doltish Cao Jiao." See his "Mengzi: Just Not Doing It (不為)," in Liu and Ivanhoe, *Essays on the Moral Philosophy of Mengzi*. Shun, *Mencius and Early Chinese Thought*, is much clearer about the distinction between "capacity" and "ability." (See in particular pp. 218 and 225 of his book.) I first learned the distinction from Shun, and I owe much to Shun's clarification. However, unless the significance of the distinction is elaborated upon in terms of the whole argument in the *Xing E Pian*, Shun's account is still open to the objection that Xunzi admits that human nature is good since it is admitted that everyone has the capacity to be good.

5. David Nivison and Kwong-loi Shun have noted the above points. See Nivison, "Weakness of Will in Ancient Chinese Philosophy," and "Motivation and Moral Action in Mencius," in his *The Ways of Confucianism*, 83–84 and 94–95, respectively. See Shun, *Mencius and Early Chinese Thought*, 217–18. See also Nivison's "Mengzi: Just Not Doing It."

6. Nivison, "Just Not Doing It," 135, has a different reading of what is going on in 23.5b. He compares Watson's and Knoblock's translations of 23.5b and says that "apparently both have the same distinction in mind: *ke yi* . . . is merely theoretical possibility, while *neng* . . . indicates effective and practical ability." But, Nivison continues, "This interpretation has been forced on both by their misunderstanding of Xunzi's example of being able to use one's feet to walk anywhere in the world, apparently contrasted with the obvious impossibility of anyone's actually being able to walk everywhere. But this is not what Xunzi is saying. An artisan, or carpenter, or farmer, or trader, could (perhaps with

retraining) adopt one of the other modes of livelihood, but will not be able to—what? Adopt all of them? This would be ridiculous: He will not, because he would choose not to. Likewise, with two feet, I could walk anywhere 'walkable;' but—what? I would not be able to walk everywhere? Just as ridiculous: Surely Xunzi is saying that there are places I will not walk to, because my good sense makes this impossible; I would be unwilling to, could not be induced to."

7. *Tu zhi ren* 塗之人, rendered by Watson and Knoblock as "the (a) man in the street." "Ordinary person" is less cumbersome.

8. Knoblock translates *ji* as "accumulated effort" and Watson as "accumulation of good acts." Sometimes "cumulative effort" may be more appropriate.

9. I take the *zhi* 質 of the capacity to know morality and the laws (*you ke yi zhi ren yi fa zheng zhi zhi* 有可以知仁義法正之質) to refer to a cognitive capacity, ruling out the following other senses for 23.5a. (1) Some "distinctive quality" as in *qi zhi fei bu mei ye* 其質非不美也 (ICS 1/1/20). Instead of this, Xunzi requires a shared condition that constitutes the capacity to have knowledge of morality and the laws. (2) Some aspect of "character," as in *xi su yi zhi, an jiu yi zhi* 習俗移志，安久移質 (ICS 8/34/2), implying that it can be changed through cumulative effort, custom and habituation. (Knoblock's "substance" in 8.11 seems inappropriate.) But Xunzi is referring to a precondition of *knowing* morality and the laws in 23.5a. (3) Moral qualities of a *ren* person 仁人之質 (ICS 13/65/18) such as being loyal or trustworthy. This is ruled out since in 23.5a Xunzi is talking of the conditions for knowing these qualities instead of the qualities themselves. It seems fair to conclude that when Xunzi says that ordinary persons have the *zhi* that would allow them to know morality and the laws, he is referring to a cognitive capacity.

Xunzi also says that everyone *you ke yi neng ren yi fa zheng zhi ju* 有可以能仁義法正之具. The term *ju* 具 refers to the conditions for doing something or being someone. (See ICS 4/15/13, 9/37/16. In 9/40/18 we have *ju ju er wang . . . er ba . . . er cun . . . er wang* 具具而王，具具而霸，具具而存，具具而亡. Li Disheng, *Xunzi Ji Shi*, notes that the first *ju* in these pairs refers to 具備 *ju bei* "having" or "possessing" while the second refers to *tiao jian* 條件 or "conditions.") Given that Xunzi had just mentioned *ke yi zhi* or the capacity to know as a precondition of being a sage, it would be fair to render *you ke yi neng . . . zhi ju* as "possessing the condition of the capacity to practice." In short, "having an instrumental capacity."

10. In using "rationale" for 理 I follow A. S. Cua, *Ethical Argumentation: A Study in Hsün Tzu's Moral Epistemology* (Honolulu: University of Hawaii Press, 1985), even though earlier in my discussion of Mencius, I adopted the more common translation of "pattern." Cua says, "I take this passage [23.5a] to mean that *jen* [*ren*], *i* [*yi*], and standards of proper conduct can be understood in terms of their rationales. In other words, they are proper objects of knowledge. An understanding of their rationales is a precondition for moral practice" (26). For Xunzi morality and the laws have a rationale that can be known and practiced: *ke zhi ke neng zhi li* 可知可能之理. Since he argues next that the ordinary person is unable to become a sage we should not claim that *ke neng* here means that people in general are actually *able* to practice morality and the laws.

Instead, the claim is that there is a rationale and people have the capacity to know and to *practice* it. This is emphasized counterfactually: "If morality and the laws do not have a rationale that can be known and practiced, then even Yu could not know and practice morality and the laws." Eric Hutton has objected to Cua's use of "rationale" for *li*, on the grounds that "it positively obscures important aspects of Xunzi's thought rather than illuminating them. With regard to the . . . reading of *li* as a 'capacity' or 'power' of the heart-mind (*xin*), there is simply no strong evidence in the text for Cua's interpretation." See Eric Hutton, "Moral Reasoning in Aristotle and Xunxi," *Journal of Chinese Philosophy* 29, no. 3 (September 2002): 368. But we can see the appropriateness of "rationale" for *li* in the present context if we understand that Xunzi is talking of certain enabling conditions that allow for people to know and to practice morality and the laws. The statement of these enabling conditions is put in terms of two counterfactual arguments, which makes the use of "rationale" even more appropriate here. See the appendix at the end of this chapter for the details of these counterfactual arguments.

    11. Watson (166) translates *ren yi fa zheng* as benevolence, righteousness, proper rules, and standards; Knoblock (23.5a) as humaneness, morality, the model of law, and rectitude. Both take *ren yi fa zheng* as four separate items. I render it as two: *ren yi* as morality, and *fa zheng* as the laws. It does not matter to my whole argument which of these we follow. "Morality and the laws" is shorter and makes for a less cluttered exposition. Li Disheng (*Xunzi Ji Shi*, 552, note 2) comments that *ren yi* refers to external regulations and is like *li yi*, rites, and righteousness (*wai zai gui fan*, *you yan li yi* 外在規範，猶言禮義). It is different from Confucius's and Mencius's sense of *ren yi*.

    12. A point noted by Nivison, "Mengzi: Just Not Doing It," 135–36.

    13. There is another reading of 疾惡 meaning the hatred of or aversion to what is harmful. This means that Xunzi does not say that people are born with the negative emotions of envy and hatred. See Deng Xiaohu 鄧小虎, *Xiandaixing yu Xunzi*: *Daode Zizhu de Keneng* 現代性與荀子：道德自主的可能, paper presented at the conference *Xunzi Yanjiu de Huigu yu Kaichuang* 荀子研究的回顧與開創 (National Yunlin University of Science and Technology, Taiwan, February 18–19, 2006).

    14. Munro, "A Villain in the Xunzi." According to Munro (199) the core issue is not evil *per se* but the problem of how to manage the surfeit of desires with the scarcity of goods through ritual enforcement and rank-orderings. A similar view is taken by Philip. J. Ivanhoe, *Confucian Moral Self Cultivation* (Indianapolis: Hackett Publishing Company, 2000), 32. After arguing against reading Xunzi's view of human nature as fundamentally and incorrigibly evil, or in terms of "the Augustinian notion of sin as an intentional rejection of God's will," Ivanhoe says: "In a world of limited goods, inhabited by creatures of more or less unlimited desires, it is inevitable that the result is destructive and alienating competition. This is what Xunzi means by his claim that human nature is bad." A different, philological approach is taken by Dan Robins, "The Development of Xunzi's Theory of *Xing*, Reconstructed on the Basis of a Textual Analysis of *Xunzi* 23, 'Xing E' 性惡 (*Xing* is Bad)," *Early China* 26-27 (2001-2002): 99–158. He argues that the view that human nature is bad or evil is an "interpolation," and is not central to the *Xunzi*.

15. Love of one's own kind: ICS 19/96/10 愛其類. Remembrance and longing for the deceased: 19/97/20 思慕. People's good hearts: 20/98/18 人之善心. Righteousness: 9/39/10 人 . . . 有義. Nivison (*The Ways of Confucianism*, 210) reads *yi* here as "a sense of duty," holding that "there is still a problem of reconciling this view with Xunzi's view that 'human nature is evil.'" More recently, however, he reads *yi* in the sense of *li yi*, as "an institutional feature exhibited by humans as a species." See James Behuniak, "Nivison and the 'Problem' in Xunzi's Ethics," and Nivison's "Response to James Behuniak," in *Philosophy East and West* 50, no. 1 (2000): 97–110 and 110–15, respectively. Shun, *Mencius and Early Chinese Thought*, 226, thinks *yi* "in the present context is probably a capacity to draw social distinctions and to abide by and be transformed by the norms governing such distinctions; it does not involve prior inclinations of the kind Mencius highlighted." Eric Hutton, "Does Xunzi Have a Consistent Theory of Human Nature?" in Kline and Ivanhoe, *Virtue, Nature, and Moral Agency in the Xunzi*, 224, argues that *you yi* 有義 or "having *yi*" in 9.16a does not have to be read as "having innately." See also Wong, "Xunzi on Moral Motivation," 215, and Munro "A Villain in the Xunzi," 198.

16. The analogy of the potter and the wood carver appeared earlier in 23.2a (ICS 23/114/8–10). There, Xunzi asserts that their *products* are a result of their 偽, and not born of their 性.

17. I thank one of the anonymous referees for *Philosophy East and West*, where the paper on which this chapter is based originally appeared, for pointing this out.

18. Knoblock, 19.6. See vol. 3, 322, note 96. Also Watson, 102, note 16.

19. Knoblock (23.1e) translates *qing xing* as "essential qualities inherent in his nature"; Watson (159) as "emotional nature." Since the context refers to physical sensations such as hunger and tiredness instead of just emotions, it is more appropriate to use "sensory and emotional nature" for *qing xing*.

20. John Searle, "How to Derive 'Ought' from 'Is'," *Philosophical Review* 73 (1964), quoted in A. S. Cua, "Basic Concepts of Confucian Ethics," in his *Moral Vision and Tradition*, 295.

21. Cua, "Basic Concepts of Confucian Ethics," 292–95.

22. Music *yue* and joy *le* share the same character 樂.

23. The *li* 理 or rationale of morality and the laws are intimately connected with *li* 禮 the rites. *Wen* is often paired with *li* as *wen li* 文理 which can be synonymous with *li yi* 禮義 rites and righteousness, e.g., when it is stated that simply following the desires of the senses would give rise to *yin luan* 淫亂 dissolute and wanton behavior and the perishing of *li yi wen li* 禮義文理 (ICS 23/113/5). In the sense of *zhi* 治 order and governance, *li* 理 is contrasted with various forms of disorderliness (*luan* 亂). *Wen li* connotes being cultured and acting according to reasonable form, and it is this attention to cultural form and the rationale of *li yi* that enables a transformation of character. For instance, Xunzi says that the way of the filial son is the cultural form and rationale of rites and righteousness *xiao zi zhi dao, li yi zhi wen li ye* 孝子之道，禮義之文理也 (23/114/5). Similarly, the sage has the same nature as the masses but differs in his *wei* 偽 because he has been transformed by the cultural form and rationale contained in rites and righteousness *hua li yi zhi wen li* 化禮義之文理 (23/114/17). Tang Junyi, "*Lun zhongguo zhexue sixiangshi*

zhong (li) zhi liu yi 論中國哲學思想史中 (理) 之六義," *Xinya Xuebao* 新亞學報, vol. 1, no. 1 (1995), notes that *wen li* 文理 is the sense of *li* most emphasized in the *Xing E Pian* and that it is closely connected with its homophone 文禮.

24. David B. Wong, "Xunzi on Moral Motivation," 215.

25. Ibid., 218.

26. See 23.8, the last passage of *Xing E Pian*.

27. See Munro, "A Villain in the Xunzi," and Scott Cook, "Xunzi on Ritual and Music," *Monumenta Serica* 45 (1997): 1–38.

28. I thank Professor Ikeda Tomohisa of Tokyo University for this suggestion. David Nivison and Kwong-loi Shun have also noted the similarities between Mozi and Mencius. See Nivison, "Weakness of Will in Ancient Chinese Philosophy," 83–84 and "Motivation and Moral Action in Mencius," 94–95. See Shun, *Mencius and Early Chinese Thought*, 217.

29. See Sun Yirang 孫詒讓 *Mozi Xiangu* 墨子閒詁 (Beijing: Zhonghua Shuju, 1986), vol. 1, p.111 (卷四, 兼愛下第十六). See Burton Watson, *Mo Tzu: Basic Writings* (New York: Columbia University Press, 1963), 44.

Chapter 6: Situating Xunzi

1. Shun, *Mencius and Early Chinese Thought*, 261, n. 88, refers to a "parallel" between the statement of the second view and Xunzi's statement that everyone *ke yi* become a Yao or Yu and everyone *ke yi* become a Jie or Zhi, and says that this "shows that a proponent of [the second view] may well have a view of *hsing* similar to Hsün Tzu's." My argument that Xunzi can be said to adopt the second view was developed prior to my noticing Shun's observation.

2. Lau, *Mencius*.

3. Shun, *Mencius and Early Chinese Thought*, 215–16.

4. Ibid., 219.

5. Ibid., 219–20.

6. As noted by Lau, "On Mencius' Use of the Method of Analogy in Argument," in Lau, *Mencius*, vol. 2, 336.

7. One could make something out of the point that Gaozi's image of the channeling of water implies that human nature is more easily directed or influenced, and that Xunzi's image of clay implies a more difficult working material. But there are different views in the literature of the relation between Xunzi and Gaozi. I shall just note two. Bryan Van Norden states that although there are similarities between them, Xunzi "repudiated the voluntarism of Gaozi, holding that more than a simple act of choice is needed in order to become moral. We must, Xunzi claimed, engage in the moral equivalent of war against our desires, and submerge ourselves in ritual (under the guidance of a good teacher), for a large part of our lives, before we will truly be fully moral. Had Xunzi stated that human nature is morally neutral, given the background of the debate between

Mengzi and Gaozi, the claim would have been understood by Xunzi's contemporaries as an endorsement of Gaozian voluntarism. Hence, Xunzi denied that human nature is morally netural in the Gaozian sense" (Van Norden, "Mengzi and Xunzi: Two Views of Human Agency," 127). Goldin, "Xunzi in the Light of the Guodian Manuscripts," observes (120) that the idea that humanity is internal and morality external, "namely that morality must be obtained from outside the self, is common to Gaozi, Xunzi, and the Guodian manuscripts—and to virtually no other known members of the Confucian school" (120).

8. Shun, *Mencius and Early Chinese Thought*, 220.

9. Shun, ibid., notes this as an implication drawn by Tang Junyi in his *Yuanxing pian* 原性篇. See Shun, 260, n. 84.

10. I have substituted *qing* for Knoblock's "essential nature" for reasons discussed below. As in the preceding chapter, passage numbers follow John Knoblock, trans., *Xunzi: A Translation and Study of the Complete Works*, and references prefixed with "ICS" refer to *A Concordance to the Xunzi*.

11. Li Disheng, *Xunzi Jishi*, 68, n. 23, reads *yu* 與 as *yi* 以. Similarly, Jiang Nanhua 蔣南華, Luo Shuqin 羅書勤 and Yang Hanqing 楊寒清, eds., *Xunzi Quanyi* 荀子全譯 (Guizhou Renmin Chubanshe, 1995), 62, n. 21.

12. *Qing* can refer to the desires and feelings of *xing*, and in this regard, Xunzi sometimes uses the more inclusive *qingxing*. However, "the *qing* of man" for Xunzi also refers to other general facts about people: they have wants and capacities that go beyond the basic desires and feelings. Thus, people also want surplus items of wealth and luxury, and these at the same time imply the need for security, and the capacities for prudence, refinement and hence for establishing ritual principles. I argue for this distinction between *xing* and *qing* more fully in "Xunzi and the Essentialist Mode of Thinking about Human Nature," *Journal of Chinese Philosophy* (forthcoming).

13. But see 9.15 where *li yi* is said to be the "beginning of order."

14. Watson, *Hsün Tzu: Basic Writings*, 89.

15. Knoblock, vol. 1, 292, n. 87.

16. In 15.2, Chen Xiao refers to Xunzi having said in discussion that *ren yi* constitutes the fundamental basis of the principles of warfare (*chang yi ren yi wei ben* 常以仁義為本). If one who is *ren* loves others (*ai ren*), and one who is *yi* accords with rational order (*yi zhe xun li* 義者循理), why then engage in warfare—after all, doesn't warfare mean contention (and hence disorder)? Xunzi replies, "That *ren* of which I spoke does indeed involve loving others, but it is just such love for others that causes a hatred of whoever does injury to them. That *yi* of which I spoke does involve acting in accord with rational order (*yi zhe xun li* 義者循理), but it is precisely according with rational order that causes a hatred of whoever disrupts it (*xun li gu wu ren zhi luan zhi ye* 循理故惡人之亂之也). The military principles of which I spoke are just the means whereby to prohibit violent and aggressive behavior and to prevent harm to others; they are not the means to contention and confiscation." Xunzi goes on to describe the transforming spirit of a strong and humane army such that those near and far would be drawn toward the good governance protected by it. In 15.3 Li Si (Xunzi's famous pupil) refers to the

military successes of the state of Qin and its hegemony and asserts that this is not due to *ren yi* but to its "taking advantage of opportunities" (*bian* 便). Xunzi's reply is that what Li Si describes as "opportunities" are not real opportunities (*bu bian zhi bian* 不便之便). What he himself means by *ren yi*, on the other hand, are "real opportunities of the greatest magnitude (*da bian zhi bian ye* 大便之便也)." Xunzi explains that *ren yi* is the means "to reform the government (*suo yi xiu zheng zhe ye* 所以脩政者也). If the government is reformed, then the people will feel kinship with their superiors (民親其上), will delight in their lord, and will think little of dying for him." Xunzi adds something that to us now, was prescient: "Although for four generations Qin has been victorious, it has been constantly seized with fear and apprehension lest the whole world unite together in concerted action to crush Qin with their collective power. This corresponds to what I have described as the armies of decadent times, for they have never possessed the fundamental principles and guiding norms (*wei you ben tong ye* 未有本統也)." See ICS 15/71/21–15/72/7.

17. Munro, "A Villain in the Xunzi," 198, interprets Xunzi to be saying that "people are born with an innate moral sense (*yi*)."

18. One can speak of different types of *yi* but with the understanding that this refers to what it would be appropriate to do or how it would be appropriate to act under different circumstances. For example, "When such a person [of various virtuous qualities] unexpectedly encounters his lord, he devotes himself to observing the protocol appropriate to a minister and subject (*chen xia zhi yi* 臣下之義). When he meets a fellow villager, he makes it his object to employ all the courtesy due age and accomplishment (*zhang you zhi yi* 長幼之義). When he encounters an older person, he devotes himself to observing the demeanor of a son or younger brother (*zi di zhi yi* 子弟之義). When he meets a friend, he devotes himself to showing the appropriate courtesies and rules, polite refusals, and yielding precedence (*li jie ci rang zhi yi* 禮節辭讓之義). When he encounters someone of lower station or younger than himself, he devotes himself to the manner appropriate to guidance, instruction, magnanimity, and tolerance (*gao dao kuan rong zhi yi* 告導寬容之義)." See 6.10; ICS 6/23/15–17.

We should also note another set of words that are also associated with *yi*: *dang* 當, *bian ying* 變應, and *zhong* 中. *Dang* and *zhong* (the mean) connote doing what is appropriate and reasonable or nonexcessive. Thus, "in matters of conduct the noble person does not esteem indecorous, though difficult, feats; in his explanations he does not prize improper investigations; and in matters of reputation he does not value unsuitable traditions. Rather, only what is fitting to the occasion does he esteem *wei qi dang zhi wei gui* 唯其當之爲貴" (3.1; ICS 3/9/4–5). Xunzi disapproves the act of drowning on the part of one named Shentu Di: "To be sure 'carrying a stone on one's back and drowning oneself in the Yellow River' is a difficult feat, but Shentu Di was capable of it. Nonetheless, the noble person does not esteem his feat because it is contrary to the mean of behavior prescribed by ritual principles and by a sense of what is right *fei li yi zhi zhong ye* 非禮義之中也" (3.1; ICS 3/9/1, 3, 4). The same passage refers to the paradoxes of Hui Shi and others: "the noble person does not prize their feats of sophistry because they are contrary to the mean of behavior prescribed by ritual principles *fei li yi zhi zhong ye* 非

禮義之中也." Similarly the noble person does not value the reputation of Robber Zhi. Xunzi concludes: "In matters of conduct the noble person does not esteem indecorous, though difficult, feats; in his explanations he does not prize improper investigations; and in matters of reputation he does not value unsuitable traditions. Rather, only what is fitting to the occasion does he esteem *wei qi dang zhi wei gui* 唯其當之爲貴" (ICS 3/9/5). Also, "the Way of the Ancient Kings lay in exalting the principle of humanity and in following the mean in their conduct. What is meant by the 'mean (*zhong*)'? I say that it is correctly identified with ritual principles (*li yi*)" (8.3; ICS 8/28/15). For *bian ying* we have the following: "His (the noble person's) use of his sense of what is right to change in response to every situation is because of knowledge that is precisely fitting for every occasion, whether curved or straight. 以義變應，知當曲直故也" (3.5; ICS 3/10/2). The passage continues with a quotation from the Odes which is explained: "This says that the noble person is able to employ his sense of what is right to bend or straighten, changing and responding to every occasion."

19.　The ICS text has *yi er zu er mao ye* 亦二足而毛也 for the ape, that is, that it also has two feet with hair. I follow the amendation adopted by Li Disheng, adding the negation *wu* 無 before *mao*. Li follows Wang Xianqian's explanation that it is not that the ape has no hair, but that both human being and ape share a hairless face. To avoid the problem, Knoblock has "featherless biped" for both human being and ape.

20.　In the Wang Xianqian edition (荀子集解) of the *Xunzi* there are twenty-three words which are excised from this passage (4.9; ICS 4/15/7–14) in the *Rong Ru Pian* 榮辱篇 ("Of Honor and Disgrace"). See Li, 66, n. 6. The passage begins with "凡人有所一同 . . ." (Knoblock: "All people possess one and the same nature . . ."). The twenty-three words are: 是又人之所生而有也，是無待而然者也，是禹桀之所同也 ("Again, such is the nature that men are born possessing. They do not have to await development before they become so. It is the same in the case of a Yu and in that of a Jie.") Except for the 是又 ("Again"), these words repeat what comes earlier in the passage. In an essay entitled "荀子人性論新詮——附 (榮辱) 篇 23 字衍之糾謬 Xunzi renxinglun xin quan—fu (Rongru) pian 23 zi yan zhi jiu miu," 馮耀明 Feng Yaoming (Fung Yiu-ming) argues that these words should not have been excised. (See *NCCU Philosophical Journal* 14 (July 2005): 169–230.) They emphasize the capacities of *zhi* 知 and *neng* 能 possessed by human beings. Feng cites the authority of Pang Pu (龐樸) to show that there are two senses of *wei* 偽. One is the notion of what is made by humans, and another is the notion of their capacities. These capacities are designated by the character of *wei* 為 with the heart radical *xin* 心 below it. See Pang Pu, "郢燕書說——郭店楚簡中山三器心旁字試說 Yingyan Shushuo—Guodian Chujian Zhongshan sanqi xinpangzi shishuo," 武漢大學中國文化研究院編, 郭店楚簡國際學術研討會論文集 Wuhan Daxue zhongguowenhua yanjiuyuan bian, *Guodian Chujian Guoji Xueshu Yantaohui Lunwenji* (Hubei: Renmin Chubanshe, 2000).

21.　Xunzi does not scoff at *li* 利 (benefit or profit) per se. As we have seen, the aim of social order and the internalization of a sense of social order is to maximize the well-being of everyone concerned. However, many passages contrast *li* 利 with *yi*. See 2.3;

ICS 2/6/2, 2.5; ICS 2/6/13, 3.2; ICS3/9/7–8, 4.4; ICS 4/13/16, 4.6; ICS 4/14/3, 8.2; ICS 8/28/9, 11.2c; ICS 11/51/14–15.

22. Ning Chen, "The Ideological Background of the Mencian Discussion of Human Nature: A Reexamination," in *Mencius: Contexts and Interpretations*, ed. Alan Chan (Honolulu: University of Hawaii Press, 2002), 21.

23. Jingmenshi bowuguan 荊門市博物館, *Guodian Chumu zhujian* 郭店楚墓竹簡 (Beijing: Wenwu Chubanshe, 1998). Chen discusses in particular the Confucian texts in this collection: *Xing zhi ming chu* 性自命出, *Cheng zhi wen zhi* 成之聞之, and *Yucong er* 語叢二. Goldin, "Xunzi in the Light of the Guodian Manuscripts," also discusses the parallels between Xunzi and some of the Guodian texts, although in a different way. He notes the following "platform" that Xunzi shares with some of these texts: (1) "*Xing* refers to what is inborn in an organism, and thus to the features that all members of a certain species hold in common—rather than the features that distinguish a certain species from all other species," (2) "Humanity is internal; morality is external," (3) "While the *xing* is morally indeterminate, people can make themselves good through self-cultivation. The method to become good is to follow the Way (which is established by Heaven), and the Sages transmitted rituals and canonical texts in order to help us in this process. People can also be led to evil if they are given destructive examples to follow. The ruler, consequently, must be careful about the rightness of his own actions," (4) "Music is especially useful in the project of self-cultivation, because the sounds and tones of appropriate music can inspire human beings to emulate the virtues expressed in them" (145–46).

24. Chen, "The Ideological Background of the Mencian Discussion of Human Nature." He is referring to slips 9–14 of the *Xing zi ming chu*.

25. Ibid., 26.

26. Ibid., 26–27. The quotation is from Graham, "The Mencian Theory of Human Nature," 21. According to Graham, Shih Shih's [Shi Shi] 世碩 statement "is clearly a justification" of the second view. See Wang Chong 王充, Huang Hui 黃暉, ed., *Lunheng Jiao Shi* 論衡校釋 (Beijing: Zhonghua Shuju, 1996), juan 3, no. 13, *Ben Xing Pian* 本性篇, 132.

27. Chen, "The Ideological Background of the Mencian Discussion of Human Nature," 27.

28. Ibid.

29. Ibid., 25.

30. Interestingly, Graham notes that Wang Chong himself means *ren xing you shan you e* or "there is both good and bad in man's nature" to refer to the third view. As he puts it, Wang Chong "uses the formula for Position C," that is, the third view. See Graham, "The Mencian Theory of Human Nature," in 21. Graham (20) says also, "The last position [the third view] had many supporters during the next thousand years [after Mencius], for example Wang Ch'ung [Wang Chong] 王充. (A.D. 27–c.100) and Han Yü 韓愈 (768–824)."

31. See Antonio Cua, "Philosophy of Human Nature," in *Human Nature, Ritual, and History: Studies in Xunzi and Chinese Philosophy* (Washington, D.C.: The Catholic

University of America Press, 2005) for an analysis of the consequentialist sense in which according to Xunzi, nature is "bad." I confirm this reading in "Xunzi and the Essentialist Mode of Thinking about Human Nature."

Chapter 7: Ritual Transformation: Emotion and Form

1.	As in the previous chapters, the first passage numbering refers to Knoblock's translation. The second ICS numbering refers to the Institute of Chinese Studies *A Concordance to the Xunzi*. I have modified Knoblock's translations and sometimes provided my own.

2.	The same metaphor of the wondrous effect of wind and seasonal rain in the context of moral force can be found in the *Mencius*. In 3A:2, Mencius quotes Confucius: "The virtue of the noble person is like the wind; the virtue of the ignoble person is like grass. Let the wind blow over the grass, and it is sure to bend" (君子之德，風也：小人之德，草也。草尚之風，必偃). In 7A:13 we find words that are similar to Xunzi's in 15.2: "A noble person transforms where he passes, and works wonders where he abides" (夫君子所過者化，所存者神). In 7A:40 Mencius states that the first way in which a noble person teaches (教) is "by a transforming influence like that of timely rain" (如時雨化之者). Scott Cook, "Xun Zi on Ritual and Music," *Monumenta Serica* 45 (1997): 28, note 66, citing the *Maoshi zhengyi* [Sibu beiyao ed.], p. 12 [juan 1.1, p. 3a], notes the line in the "Da xu" 大序 of the *Shijing* 詩經: "'*Feng*' means the wind; it means teaching. With the wind, [things or people] are moved; with teaching, [things or people] are transformed (*hua*)" (風，風也，教也。風以動之，教以化之). Note that in contemporary Chinese, we have the idiom "spring wind transforms (into) rain" (春風化雨), which is a metaphor for the influence of a good teacher.

3.	The two statements of Xunzi just cited might seem to contradict another passage from the *Zheng Ming Pian* (正名篇 "On the Correct Use of Names"): 狀變而實無別而為異者，謂之化。有化而無別，謂之一實 (ICS 22/109/12–13). Antonio Cua, in correspondence, has suggested a translation, which I have modified: "The form/appearance changes but the substantive entity (*shi* 實) remains the same (*wu bie* 無別), even though it may seem to be different—this is called transformation *hua* 化. There is transformation but (something) remains the same—this is called one substantive entity" (compare Knoblock 22.2h). Cua suggests that if we read *xing* 性 as *shi* 實, *hua xing* 化性 is the 性 transformed. Thus, the object of *hua* is (in many contexts) *xing*. Xunzi uses the analogy of a potter's molding clay into a vessel, and so on; and *xing* provides materials for beautification. Thus, Cua understands "transformation" as giving shape or form to original and given materials in nature. This, according to Cua, seems consistent with Xunzi's definition of *hua* in the above passage. In view of Cua's remarks, I would say that there should be no contradiction as well with the two statements of Xunzi's that I have just cited in the discussion. That is, it is possible for nature to be transformed such that it will not return to what it was before—like the wheel not returning to its former quality of being straight. In this sense, it has become different. But at the same time, the substantive entity—say, the basic material of wood—remains the same. This analogy cannot be applied exactly to the transformation of human nature. But hopefully, our later discussion of the integration between emotion and form will help to make some sense of this. Cua himself relies on the distinction between second-order desires and first-order desires. Although first-order desires remain, the second-order desires are able to control how and whether they operate. See his discussion in "Dimensions of *Li* (Propriety)," in his book *Human Nature, Ritual, and History*, 49–51, and notes 28 and 29.

4. We earlier referred to analogies of transformation. Some of these such as the shaping of wood and the sharpening of metal are repeated in the *Xing E Pian* 性惡篇 ("Nature is Bad") (23.1b, ICS 23/113/9). In addition, there is the analogy of shaping clay to make a vessel (23.2a, ICS 23/114/9). The contexts of these analogies are the roles of learning and of ritual principles in transforming human nature (化性 23.2a, ICS 23/114/14). Quite clearly, the transformation is said to be effected through the form and principles of ritual (化禮義之文理 23.2a, ICS 23/114/17) and through the guiding influence of teachers and models (化師法 23.1b, ICS 23/113/12).

5. See chapters 20 and 21 of the *Mozi*, "Economy of Expenditures" (I, II) 節用上 and 節用中. References are to Yi-pao Mei, tr., *The Works of Motze* (台北: 文致出版社 [Confucius Publishing Co.], 1977) bilingual edition, and Sun Yirang 孫詒讓, 墨子閒 詁 (北京: 中華書局, 1986). I have also consulted Watson, *Mo Tzu: Basic Writings*.

6. Mei, 241; Sun, 149.

7. This indicates that the Mohists did practice some minimal forms of ritual.

8. Mei, 235; Sun, 145.

9. Mei, 235; Sun, 145.

10. Mei, 240; Sun, 149 (不極五味之調, 芬香之和).

11. Mei, 242; Sun, 151 (俛仰周旋威儀之禮, 聖王弗為). Cook, "Xunzi on Ritual and Music," gives a very good account of the apparent extravagances of ritual that Mozi was critical of. See, for instance, the account of the costs in material and personnel involved in the grand musical performances during Mozi's time on p. 11.

12. Antonio Cua reads 養人之欲 as suggesting "refinement of desires, which involves reflection and insight in moral learning." He cites as support the distinction made by Liang Qixiong 梁啓雄 "between *tianxing yu* 天性欲 (desires as endowed by nature or natural desires) and *lixing yu* 理性欲 (desires guided by reason or reflective desires)." See Cua, "The Virtues of *Junzi*," note 54, paper read at the "International Conference on Confucianism: Retrospect and Prospect," University of Toronto, Canada, September 1–2, 2005. This paper will be published in a forthcoming issue of the *Journal of Chinese Philosophy*. See also, Cua, "Dimensions of *Li* (Propriety)." See 梁啓雄, *Xunzi Jianshi* 荀 子簡釋 (台北: 台灣商務, 1978), 323. Both Cua and Liang are referring to the passage in the *Zhengming Pian* 正名篇 ("On the Correct Use of Names"), which reads: 所受乎 天之一欲，制於所受乎心之多，固難類所受乎天也 (ICS 22/11/7–8). Cua translates: "A single desire which one receives from nature (*tian*) is regulated and directed by the mind in many different ways, and thus it is difficult to assign it to the same class as those which we receive from nature (*tian* 天)."

13. Burton Watson, *Hsün Tzu: Basic Writings*, 90, translates the sentence as "[As for the king's officials] let them understand clearly that to advance in the face of death and to value honor is the way to satisfy their desire for life"; while Knoblock has it as "Who understands that risking death in carrying out a commission is how an officer cares for his life?" I follow Watson and also Li Disheng, who understands 要節 in the sense of 立名節, which is equivalent to establishing or maintaining honor. See Li Disheng 李滌生, 荀子集釋 (台北: 學生書局, 1994 edition), 420, note 8.

14. Scott Cook, "Xun Zi on Ritual and Music," 14–15, offers a slightly different but not incompatible explanation, that for Xunzi "ritual divisions promotes the structured and restrained use of limited economic resources, without which economic deprivation cannot but ensue. He addresses a Mohist concern, and criticizes the Mohists for their failure to see it through. His main argument, here and elsewhere, seems to be that the cost of the sometimes lavish ritual expenditures that Ruism entails more than pays for itself in the long term by virtue of its effect upon the continuing stability of society and the plenitude of its resources." In other words, ritual provides the conditions of stability that enables the restrained use of resources, instead of the creation of more wealth.

15. We discussed this term earlier in its context of the "facts." However, the term in other contexts refers to the "emotions," "feelings," or more generally, the "passions." A. C. Graham has maintained, "Although the word *ch'ing* [*qing*] is very common in pre-Han literature I should like to risk the generalization that it never means 'passions' even in *Hsün-tzŭ*, where we find the usage from which the later meaning developed." See Graham, "The Background of the Mencian Theory of Human Nature," 59. Anthony Yu disagrees with this claim in his book *Rereading the Stone: Desire and the Making of Fiction in Dream of the Red Chamber* (Princeton: Princeton University Press, 1997), ch. 2, "Desire," much of which is devoted to the concept of *qing* in the *Xunzi*. It is difficult to see the basis for Graham's assertion, especially in the context of the *Lilun Pian* where Xunzi discusses the balance between emotion and form or *qing* and *wen* 文.

16. See chapter 25 of the *Mozi*, "Simplicity in Funeral" (III) 節葬下, with reference to both Yi-pao Mei's bilingual edition and Sun Yirang as cited above.

17. Mei, 246; Sun, 154.

18. Mei, 250–56; Sun, 156–63.

19. Mei, 260; Sun, 164–65.

20. Mei, 264–66; Sun, 170–72. Note the striking similarity of the examples to that given by the ancient Greek historian Herodotus (5th century B.C.E.), as recounted by James Rachels, *The Elements of Moral Philosophy* (Boston: McGraw Hill, 2003), 16. Darius, a king of ancient Persia was impressed by the variety of cultural practices. For instance, the Callatians (a tribe of Indians) customarily ate the bodies of their dead fathers, while the Greeks regarded cremation as natural. He asked the Greeks and Callatians at his court, respectively, what they would take (as a reward) to adopt the other's practice. Both parties were equally horrified by the suggestions. This example is cited by Michel de Montaigne, "On Habit: And on Never Easily Changing a Traditional Law," in M. A. Screech, tr., *The Essays of Michel de Montaigne* (Harmondsworth: The Penguin Press, 1991), 130–31. I thank Cecilia Wee for this reference.

21. It is not difficult to accept the idea that one is rooted to ancestors and family. Without these roots—the identity and places that they give us, the relations engendered, the nurturance and education received, and so on—there would be no human life to speak of and no order to life. The sense of rootedness brings with it feelings of reverence and ritual is the form by which these feelings are expressed. On the other hand, it may or may not be difficult for people in contemporary times to accept Xunzi's assertion of people's being rooted in and having a reverence for Heaven and Earth. This may be a religious belief that some would not find it difficult to relate to, according to their own belief system.

22. According to Li Disheng, the term *ben* 本 (root) refers to the emotions 情, while *mo* 末 (branch) refers to the cultural form *wen* 文. See Li, *Xunzi Ji Shi*, 428, note 6.

23. For an interesting account of some of these forms in the contemporary context of the Chinese in Hong Kong, see Peter Cheung, Cecilia Chan, Wai Fu, Yawen Li, and Grace Cheung, "'Letting Go' and 'Holding On': Grieving and Traditional Death Rituals in Hong Kong," in *Death, Dying and Bereavement: A Hong Kong Chinese Experience*, ed. Cecilia Chan and Amy Chow (Hong Kong: Hong Kong University Press, 2006).

24. Cua, "Dimensions of Li (Propriety)," discusses the balance between emotion and form, the beautification of original nature and character, the emotional quality involved in ritual performance, and so on. See especially pages 49–57, which are devoted to the aesthetic dimension of ritual. 陳昭瑛 (Zhao-ying Chen), 儒家美學與經典詮釋 (台北: 台灣大學出版社中心, 2005), ch. 3, [情] 概念從孔孟到荀子的轉化, lists the various meanings of 情 in the Xunzi, including those which include a contrast and balance between 情 and文 or emotion and form.

25. Cook, "Xun Zi on Ritual and Music," contrasts the functions of ritual and music. Ritual serves to maintain hierarchical distinctions that are internalized and seen as "virtually inescapable natural laws" (16). Music, on the other hand, serves to harmonize. But as Cook describes it, music is an instrument of the ruler to "harness human sentiments and carry great masses of people forward in even uniformity to an obedient and willing submission to the ruler's will" (23). Even though Cook qualifies this to say that the ruler is exerting moral influence in transforming the people, there still seems to be a strong hierarchical element in this description. My account of ritual differs from Cook's in that I hold ritual to have more than the function of inculcating a sense of hierarchy.

26. See John Kekes, "Pluralism and Moral Authority," in Chong, Tan, and Ten, *The Moral Circle and the Self*, for an account of the various kinds of authority and their legitimate roles in our lives.

27. In the light of Mozi's convention argument and Xunzi's response in terms of the relation between emotion and form, perhaps the paragraph in which this passage occurs (19.6) should no longer be considered as not properly belonging to the *Lilun Pian*. On the contrary, the paragraph (or at least the passage cited) seems crucial to the chapter/book. Knoblock, for instance, says, "It is apparent . . . that it is unconnected with the content of this Book and rather belongs to Book 23 [*Xing E Pian* "Nature is Bad"]." See Knoblock, vol. 3, 322, note 96. Watson, *Hsün: Tzu Basic Writings*, says: "This paragraph seems to have little to do with what goes before or after and almost

certainly does not belong here. In wording and thought it is most closely allied to sec. 23, 'Man's Nature is Evil.' Probably five or six of the bamboo slips upon which the text of that section was originally written dropped out and were mistakenly inserted here." See Watson, 102, note 16. Influenced by these views, I noted in chapter 5, "This passage can (perhaps) take its place just prior to 23.1e." But even though the passage in question (故曰：性者，本始材朴也；偽者，文理隆盛也。無性則偽之無所加，無偽者性不能 自美) may fit in nicely before 23.1e, I am unsure that it does not belong to the *Lilun Pian* at all. In fact, there is another similar passage that occurs in the *Ru Xiao Pian* (儒 效篇, "Teachings of the Ru"): "Nature is insufficient by itself to establish order. Nature is what I cannot bring about. However, it can be transformed." (性不足以獨立而治。 性也者，吾所不能為也，然而可化也) (8.11, ICS 8/33/20). Masayuki Sato provides the following information that may help to resolve the textual problem. Recompiling the text around 818 A.D., Yang Liang 楊倞 moved the "Discourse on Ritual Principles" from its original position in chapter 23 to chapter 19. See Sato, *Confucian State and Society of Li: A Study on the Political Thought of Xun Zi* (Leiden: Brill, 2003), 23.

28. Cua, "Dimensions of *Li* (Propriety)," 49–50.

Chapter 8: Three Conceptions of the Heart-Mind

1. This way of characterizing the difference between Mencius and Xunzi in terms of their conceptions of the *dao* follows Li, *Xunzi Jishi*. See 484, n. 1; and 489, n. 2.

2. Confucius was more ambivalent than Mencius and Xunzi in his attitude toward Heaven. See Lau's discussion in the introduction to his translation of the *Analects*. See also Ning Chen, "Confucius' View of Fate (*Ming*)," *Journal of Chinese Philosophy* 24 (1997): 323–59.

3. Xunzi seems to have been responding to Zhuangzi, in the way he interprets these terms. See Goldin, *Rituals of the Way*, 22 onwards; and Aron Stalnaker, "Aspects of Xunzi's Engagement with Early Daoism," *Philosophy East and West* 53, no. 1 (2003): 87–129.

4. For a more detailed discussion of the philosophical import of Xunzi's capacity/ ability distinction, see my essay "Xunzi on Capacity, Ability and Constitutive Rules," in the forthcoming anthology *Searle's Philosophy and Chinese Philosophy*, ed. Bo Mou.

5. My reference to unfairness in bringing the charge of inegalitarianism to bear on Xunzi's position does not deny the validity of current attempts to reconstruct classical Confucianism so as to seek the resources for a fresh understanding of democracy and other concepts such as equality, moral autonomy and civil liberties in contemporary East Asian societies. See, for instance, A. T. Nuyen, "Confucianism and the Idea of Equality," *Asian Philosophy* 11, no. 2 (2001): 61–71; Sor-hoon-Tan, *Confucian Democracy: A Dew-eyan Reconstruction* (Albany: State University of New York Press, 2004); Joseph Chan, "Moral Autonomy, Civil Liberties, and Confucianism," *Philosophy East and West* 52, no. 3 (July 2003): 281–310; and Wm. Theodore de Bary, *The Trouble with Confucianism*

(Harvard: Harvard University Press, 1996). Chan, for instance, argues that "there is a good case for a contemporary Confucianism to downplay, if not abandon, the moral elitism in the classical period." He gives two reasons for this. First, "a contemporary Confucian perspective retains the classical view that human beings are born equal in their capacity to become moral and that ideally people should receive an education that equips them with learning and self-cultivation skills. This egalitarian principle clearly supports equal opportunity of education and offices in society." Second, and with reference to Wm. Theodore de Bary, "classical thinkers link moral education to the task of training political leaders for society, and thus the kind of learning for the gentleman [noble person] becomes very demanding and difficult for ordinary people to attain." See Chan, 292–93, and De Bary, 37–39. Chan also directly cites de Bary: "In [Confucius's] day it is a simple fact that most people do not have the means or the leisure to pursue learning, and especially learning of a kind indispensable to the gentleman [noble person] as a social and political leader" (De Bary, 37–38; Chan, 293). For a comprehensive study of the social and political thought of Xunzi in the context of his times and its influence on the Han dynasty, see Sato, *The Confucian Quest for Order*.

    6. See, for instance, Cua, *Ethical Argumentation*. For a brief overview of some of these aspects of Xunzi, see Cua's essay "Xunzi (Hsün Tzu)," in *Encyclopedia of Chinese Philosophy*, 821–29.

    7. Li Si became the prime minister of the Qin dynasty (221–206 B.C.E.). See Goldin, *Rituals of the Way*, xii; and Knoblock, *Xunzi* , vol. 1, ch. 3, "The Influence of Xunzi's Thought." Although the thought and policies of both Han Fei and Li Si had their merits, their philosophical and actual links with the Qin dynasty seems to have had a negative historical effect on their reputations, and by association, Xunzi's reputation as well. As Knoblock says (37), "That Xunzi was the teacher of both Han Fei and Li Si greatly damaged his reputation in later centuries when they were officially anathematized."

    8. Roy Perrett, "Evil and Human Nature," *Monist* 85, no. 2 (April 2002): 315, comments: "Mencius freely acknowledges, of course, that humans frequently perform wrong actions. But his explanation that this is because their original good nature has been corrupted is entirely compatible with his theory that human nature is good, provided the wrongdoer still knows she is doing wrong and feels ashamed of herself. What would be inconsistent with Mencius' theory of human nature would be for a wrongdoer to approve of doing something that she believed to be wrong. But Mencius' internalism rules out this possibility as incoherent, or at least wildly implausible."

    9. Watson, *Mo Tzu: Basic Writings*, chapter on "Universal Love," 47–48: "So I cannot understand how the people of the world can hear about this doctrine of universality and still criticize it! In the past King Ling of the state of Ching loved slender waists. During his reign, the people of Ching ate no more than one meal a day, until they were too weak to stand up without a cane, or to walk without leaning against the wall. Now reducing one's diet is a difficult thing to do, and yet people did it because it pleased King Ling. So within the space of a single generation the ways of the people can be changed, for they will strive to ingratiate themselves with their superiors."

10. A good account of this is given in Zhengyuan Fu, *China's Legalists: The Earliest Totalitarians and Their Art of Ruling* (New York: M.E. Sharpe, 1996). See ch. 4, "Law as the Penal Tool of the Ruler."

11. Quoted in Steven Pinker, *The Blank Slate: The Modern Denial of Human Nature* (New York: Viking, 2002), 156. According to Fu, *China's Legalists*, 129, Mao openly professed admiration for the Legalists.

12. Shun, "Self and Self-Cultivation in Early Confucian Thought," 236. For other readings of the *Mencius* in terms of moral psychology, see for example Philip J. Ivanhoe, "Mengzi's Conception of Courage," *Dao: A Journal of Comparative Philosophy* 5, no. 2 (June 2006): 221–34; Yang Xiao, "When Political Philosophy Meets Moral Psychology: Expressivism in the *Mencius*," *Dao: A Journal of Comparative Philosophy* 5, no. 2 (2006): 257–71; Manyul Im, "Emotional Control and Virtue in the *Mencius*," *Philosophy East and West* 49, no. 1 (January 1999): 1–27, and "Moral Knowledge and Self Control in *Mengzi*: Rectitude, Courage, and *Qi*," *Asian Philosophy* 14, no. 1 (2004): 59–77. The study of moral psychology in Confucianism is not restricted to Mencius, however. See, for instance, Antonio S. Cua, "The Ethical Significance of Shame: Insights of Aristotle and Xunzi," *Philosophy East and West* 53, no. 2 (April 2003): 147–202; and Jane Geaney, "Guarding Moral Boundaries: Shame in Early Confucianism," *Philosophy East and West* 54, no. 2 (April 2004): 113–42.

13. Yuet Keung Lo has put the search for the human in the *Analects* perceptively: "The *Analects* perhaps can be viewed as a record of collective strivings for self-fulfillment, independence, and happiness primarily within a small community of educated scholars who took Confucius as their teacher. The endless process of collective strivings reveals a deep underlying concern with the problem of human self-identity, or to put it differently, the problem of human being qua human and qua being. We can see a concerted, if anxious, effort to define who we are as persons. Clearly, the anthology makes human expression central to this relentless pursuit of self-definition." I am happy to note that Lo, too, uses the term "human expression" in his account. See Lo, "Finding the Self in the *Analects: A Philological Account*," in Kim-chong Chong, Sor-hoon Tan, and C. L. Ten, *The Moral Circle and the Self*, 250.

14. Beside 2.4 and 6.7, which I discuss below, the other three passages in which *xin* appears are as follows: In 14.39, a passerby hears Confucius playing the stone chimes and comments that the sound is "fraught with frustrated purpose (*you xin zai* 有心 哉)." Whether the passerby's description is accurate or not, this refers to a particular state of mind that is unconsciously revealed through some activity. In 17.22, Confucius remarks, "The person who . . . does not put his mind to some use is sure to meet with difficulties." Lau's translation of *xin* as "mind" here is a reference to concentration and devotion to some useful end. In 20.1, there is an unattributed remark in the context of good governance, that "the hearts of all the common people in the Empire will turn to you." This refers to the loyal devotion of subjects to a ruler who manifests *ren*.

15. Wittgenstein: "I often cannot discern the *humanity* in a man." See Ludwig Wittgenstein, *Culture and Value*, tr. Peter Winch (Chicago: University of Chicago Press, 1980), 1.

16. The same idea has perhaps been put in different ways by other authors. Commenting on *Analects* 2.10 ("Look at the means someone employs, observe the path he takes and examine where he feels at home. In what way is a person's true character hidden from view?"), Stephen Owen says, "what is manifest is not an idea or a thing but a situation, a human disposition, and an active relation between the two. What is manifest is ongoing and belongs entirely to the realm of Becoming." See Stephen Owen, *Readings in Chinese Literary Thought* (Cambridge: Council on East Asian Studies, Harvard University 1992), 20. And according to Vincent Shen, Chen Daqi "differs from Mou Zongsan, a contemporary Neo-Confucian who, in developing a 'moral metaphysics' of Confucianism, neglected the importance of praxis in Confucian ethics. Chen takes ethics as the core of Confucius's thought—which he sees not as a theoretical philosophy but rather as a practical philosophy." Shen also notes that for Chen, "*an* (calm happiness) is Confucius's ultimate value." See Vincent Shen, "Chen Daqi (Ch'en Ta-ch'i)," in Cua, *Encylopedia of Chinese Philosophy*, 30. Shen also details Chen's interest on logical aspects of Xunzi and his pioneering work in interpreting Confucian ethics as a virtue ethics.

17. Han Fei says: "As for the ruler's shedding tears when punishments are carried out in accordance with the law—this is a fine display of *ren* but contributes nothing to the achievement of order. *Ren* may make one shed tears and be reluctant to apply penalties; but law makes it clear that such penalties must be applied. The ancient kings allowed law to be supreme and did not give in to their tearful longings. Hence, it is obvious that *ren* cannot be used to achieve order in the state" (Watson, *Han Fei Tzu*, "The Five Vermin," 101–2).

18. For Sato, *The Confucian Quest for Order*, *ren* is central to the *Xunzi* (198). According to him, there are two aspects of *ren* in Xunzi's thought: (1) "Conventional" in which *ren* and *ren yi* denote an indispensable moral quality of the ruler and (2) "Analytical and theoretical" where *ren* is combined with other terms. Sato claims that *ren* occupies a higher position than *li* even when combined since *ren* "designates the purpose of the moral society" whereas *li* constitutes "the means [to] establish it" (201). See also the section entitled "Xun Zi's Firm Belief in the Predominance of Morality over Real Politics" (314).

Bibliography

Allan, Sarah. *The Way of Water and Sprouts of Virtue*. Albany: State University of New York Press, 1997.

Ames, Roger T. "The Mencian Conception of *Ren Xing*: Does it Mean 'Human Nature'?" In Rosemont, *Chinese Texts and Philosophical Contexts*.

Ames, Roger T., and Henry Rosemont, Jr., trs. *The Analects of Confucius: A Philosophical Translation*. New York: Ballantine Books, 1998.

Ames, Roger T., and David L. Hall, trs. *Focusing the Familiar: A Translation and Philosophical Interpretation of the Zhongyong*. Honolulu: University of Hawaii Press, 2001.

Behuniak, James. "Nivison and the 'Problem' in Xunzi's Ethics." *Philosophy East and West* 50, no. 1 (January 2000): 97–110.

Bloom, Irene. "Mencian Arguments on Human Nature (*Ren-Xing*)." *Philosophy East and West* 44, no. 1 (January 1994): 19–53.

——. "Three Visions of *Jen*." In Bloom and Fogel, *Meeting of Minds*.

——. "Human Nature and Biological Nature in Mencius." *Philosophy East and West* 47, no. 1 (January 1997): 21–32.

Bloom, Irene, and Joshua A. Fogel, eds. *Meeting of Minds: Intellectual and Religious Interaction in East Asian Traditions of Thought*. New York: Columbia University Press, 1997.

Bockover, Mary. "The Concept of Emotion Revisited: A Critical Synthesis of Western and Confucian Thought." In Marks and Ames, *Emotions in Asian Thought*.

Bodde, Derk. "A Perplexing Passage in the Confucian Analects." *Journal of the American Oriental Society* 53 (1933): 347–51.

Brooks, E. Bruce, and A. Taeko Brooks. *The Original Analects: Sayings of Confucius and His Successors*. New York: Columbia University Press, 1998.

——. "Word Philology and Text Philology in Analects 9:1." In Van Norden, *Confucius and the Analects*.

Chan, Alan, ed. *Mencius: Contexts and Interpretations*. Honolulu: University of Hawaii Press, 2002.

Chan, Cecilia, and Amy Chow, eds. *Death, Dying and Bereavement: A Hong Kong Chinese Experience*. Hong Kong: Hong Kong University Press, 2006.

Chan, Joseph. "Moral Autonomy, Civil Liberties, and Confucianism." *Philosophy East and West* 52, no. 3 (July 2003): 281–310.

Chan, Sin Yee. "Disputes on the One Thread of *Chung-Shu*." *Journal of Chinese Philosophy* 26, no. 2 (June 1999): 165–86.

Chan, Wing-tsit. "The Evolution of the Confucian Concept *Jên*." *Philosophy East and West* 4, no. 4 (1955): 295–319.

——. *A Sourcebook in Chinese Philosophy*. New Jersey: Princeton University Press, 1973.

——. *Zhu Xi: New Studies*. Honolulu: University of Hawaii Press, 1989.

Chen Daqi 陳大齊. *Lunyu Yijie* 論語臆解. Taipei: Taiwan Shangwu, 1996.

Chen, Ning. "Confucius' View of Fate (*Ming*)." *Journal of Chinese Philosophy* 24 (1997): 323–59.

——. "The Ideological Background of the Mencian Discussion of Human Nature: A Reexamination." In Chan, *Mencius*.

Chen Zhao-ying 陳昭瑛. *Rujia Meixue yu Jingdian Quanshi* 儒家美學與經典詮釋. Taipei: Taiwan Daxue Chubanshe Zhongxin, 2005.

Cheng, Chung-ying. "On Yi as a Universal Principle of Specific Application in Confucian Morality." *Philosophy East and West* 22, no. 3 (July 1972): 269–80.

Chin, Ann-ping, and Mansfield Freeman, trs. *Tai Chen on Mencius: Explorations in Words and Meaning*. New Haven: Yale University Press, 1990.

Ching, Julia. *Mysticism and Kingship in China*. Cambridge: Cambridge University Press, 1997.

Chong, Kim-chong. "Autonomy in Early Confucian Thought: Zhi, Li and Ren in the Analects." In Chong, Tan, and Ten, *The Moral Circle and the Self*.

——. "Egoism in Chinese Ethics." In Cua, *Encyclopedia of Chinese Philosophy*.

——. *Moral Agoraphobia: The Challenge of Egoism*. New York: Peter Lang, 1996.

——. "Xunzi and the Essentialist Mode of Thinking about Human Nature." *Journal of Chinese Philosophy* (forthcoming).

Chong, Kim-chong, S. H. Tan, and C. L. Ten, eds. *The Moral Circle and the Self: Chinese and Western Approaches*. Chicago: Open Court, 2003.

Chong, Kim-chong, and Yuli Liu, eds. *Conceptions of Virtue East and West*. Singapore: Marshall Cavendish Academic, 2006.

Cook, Scott. "Xunzi on Ritual and Music." *Monumenta Serica* 45 (1997): 1–38.

Crisp, Roger, and Michael Slote, eds. *Virtue Ethics*. New York: Oxford University Press, 1997.

Cua, A. S. "Basic Concepts of Confucian Ethics." In Cua, *Moral Vision and Tradition*.

——. "Confucian Vision and Experience of the World." In Cua, *Moral Vision and Tradition*.

——. "Dimensions of Li (Propriety)." In Cua, *Human Nature, Ritual, and History*.

——, ed. *Encyclopedia of Chinese Philosophy*. New York: Routledge, 2003.

——. *Ethical Argumentation: A Study in Hsün Tzu's Moral Epistemology*. Honolulu: University of Hawaii Press, 1985.

——. "The Ethical Significance of Shame: Insights of Aristotle and Xunzi." *Philosophy East and West* 53, no. 2 (April 2003): 147–202.

——. *Human Nature, Ritual, and History: Studies in Xunzi and Chinese Philosophy*. Washington, D.C.: The Catholic University of America Press, 2005.

——. *Moral Vision and Tradition: Essays in Chinese Ethics*. Washington, D.C.: The Catholic University of America Press, 1998.

——. "Philosophy of Human Nature." In Cua, *Human Nature, Ritual, and History*.

———. "The Quasi-empirical Aspect of Hsün Tzu's Philosophy of Human Nature." *Philosophy East and West* 28, no. 1 (January 1978): 3–19.

———. "Reasonable Action and Confucian Argumentation." In Cua, *Moral Vision and Tradition*.

———. *The Virtues of Junzi. Journal of Chinese Philosophy*. Forthcoming.

———. "Xunzi (Hsün Tzu)." In Cua, *Encyclopedia of Chinese Philosophy*.

Dai Zhen 戴震. *Mengzi Ziyi Shuzheng* 孟子字義疏證. Beijing: Zhonghua Shuju, 1982.

De Bary, William Theodore. *The Trouble with Confucianism*. Harvard: Harvard University Press, 1996.

Deng, Xiaohu 鄧小虎. *Xiandaixing yu Xunzi: Daode Zizhu de Keneng* 現代性與荀子: 道德自主的可能, paper presented at the conference *Xunzi Yanjiu de Huigu yu Kaichuang* 荀子研究的回顧與開創 (National Yunlin University of Science and Technology, Taiwan, February 18–19, 2006).

Eliot, George. *Middlemarch*. Harmondsworth: Penguin, 1976.

Eno, Robert. *The Confucian Creation of Heaven: Philosophy and the Defense of Ritual Mastery*. New York: State University of New York Press, 1990.

Feng, Yaoming (Fung Yiu-ming) 馮耀明. "荀子人性論新詮——附 (榮辱) 篇23字衍之糾謬 Xunzi renxinglun xin quan—fu (Rongru) pian 23 ziyan zhi jiu miu." *NCCU Philosophical Journal* 14 (July 2005): 169–230.

Fingarette, *Herbert. Confucius—the Secular as Sacred*. New York: Harper and Row, 1972.

———. "Following the 'One Thread' of the *Analects*." *Journal of the American Academy of Religion* 47, no. 3, Thematic Issue S (September 1980): 373–405.

Fu, Charles Wei-hsün. "Fingarette and Munro on Early Confucianism: A Methodological Examination." *Philosophy East and West* 28, no. 2 (April 1978): 181–98.

Fu, Wuguang 傅武光, and Lai, Yanyuan 賴炎元, ed. *Xinyi Han Feizi* 新譯韓非子. Taipei: Sanmin shuju, 1997.

Fu, Zhengyuan. *China's Legalists: The Earliest Totalitarians and Their Art of Ruling*. New York: M.E. Sharpe, 1996.

Gardner, Daniel. *Zhu Xi's Reading of the Analects: Canon, Commentary and the Classical Tradition*. New York: Columbia University Press, 2003.

Geaney, Jane. "Guarding Moral Boundaries: Shame in Early Confucianism." *Philosophy East and West* 54, no. 2 (April 2004): 113–42.

Goldin, Paul Rakita. *Rituals of the Way: The Philosophy of Xunzi*. Chicago: Open Court, 1999.

———. "Xunzi in the Light of the Guodian Manuscripts." *Early China* 25 (2000): 113–46.

Graham, A. C. "The Background of the Mencian Theory of Human Nature." In Graham, *Studies in Chinese Philosophy and Philosophical Literature*.

———. *Disputers of the Tao: Philosophical Argument in Ancient China*. La Salle: Open Court, 1989.

———. *Studies in Chinese Philosophy and Philosophical Literature*. Singapore: Institute of East Asian Philosophies, 1986.

Hansen, Chad. *A Daoist Theory of Chinese Thought: A Philosophical Interpretation*. New York: Oxford University Press, 1992.

Hall, David L., and Roger T. Ames. *Thinking Through Confucius*. Albany: State University of New York Press, 1987.

Huang Hui 黃暉, ed. *Lunheng Jiaoshi* 論衡校釋. Beijing: Zhonghua Shuju, 1996.

Huang, Minhao 黃敏浩 (Simon Wong). *Mengzi, Gaozi bianlun de zai quan shi* 孟子, 告子辯論的再詮釋. *Tsinghua Journal of Chinese Studies*, New Series 32, no. 1 (June 2002): 117–44.

Hutton, Eric. "Does Xunzi Have a Consistent Theory of Human Nature?" In Kline and Ivanhoe, *Virtue, Nature, and Moral Agency in the Xunzi*.

———. "Moral Reasoning in Aristotle and Xunxi." *Journal of Chinese Philosophy* 29, no. 3 (September 2002): 355–84.

Ihara, Craig K. "David Wong on Emotions in Mencius." *Philosophy East and West* 41, no. 1 (January 1991): 45–53.

Im, Manyul. "Emotional Control and Virtue in the *Mencius*." *Philosophy East and West* 49, no.1 (January 1999): 1–27.

———. "Moral Knowledge and Self Control in *Mengzi*: Rectitude, Courage and *Qi*." *Asian Philosophy* 14, no. 1 (March 2004): 59–77.

Ivanhoe, Philip J., ed. *Chinese Language, Thought, and Culture: Nivison and his Critics*. Chicago and La Salle, Illinois: Open Court, 1996.

———. *Confucian Moral Self Cultivation*. Indianapolis: Hackett Publishing Company, 2000.

———. "Confucian Self Cultivation and Mengzi's Notion of Extension." In Liu and Ivanhoe, *Essays on the Moral Philosophy of Mengzi*.

———. "Mengzi's Conception of Courage." *Dao: A Journal of Comparative Philosophy* 5, no. 2 (June 2006): 221–34.

———. "Reweaving the 'One Thread' of the *Analects*." *Philosophy East and West* 40, no. 1 (January 1990): 17–33.

———. "Whose Confucius? Which *Analects*?" In Van Norden, *Confucius and the Analects*.

Jiang Nanhua 蔣南華, Luo Shuqin 羅書勤, and Yang Hanqing 楊寒清, eds. *Xunzi Quanyi* 荀子全譯. Guiyang: Guizhou Renmin Chubanshe, 1995.

Jingmenshi bowuguan 荊門市博物館. *Guodian Chumu zhujian* 郭店楚墓竹簡. Beijing: Wenwu chubanshe, 1998.

Kline, T. C., III, and Philip J. Ivanhoe, eds. *Virtue, Nature, and Moral Agency in the Xunzi*. Indianapolis: Hackett Publishing Company, 2000.

Knoblock, John, tr. *Xunzi: A Translation and Study of the Complete Works*. Vols.1–3. Stanford: Stanford University Press, 1988, 1990, 1994.

Knoblock, John, and Riegel, Jeffrey, trs. *The Annals of Lü Buwei*. Stanford: Stanford University Press, 2000.

Kupperman, Joel. *Learning from Asian Philosophy*. New York: Oxford University Press, 1999.

——. "Naturalness Revisited: Why Western Philosophers Should Study Confucius." In Van Norden, *Confucius and the Analects*.

Lai, Whalen. "Kao Tzu and Mencius on Mind: Analyzing a Paradigm Shift in Classical China." *Philosophy East and West* 34, no. 2 (April 1984): 147–60.

Lau, D. C., tr. *Confucius: The Analects*. Harmondsworth: Penguin, 1979.

——, tr. *Confucius: The Analects*. Hong Kong: The Chinese University Press, 1992.

——, tr. *Mencius*. 2 vols. Hong Kong: The Chinese University Press, 1984.

——. "On Mencius' Use of the Method of Analogy in Argument." In Lau, *Mencius*, vol. 2. (Originally published in *Asia Major*, N. S., vol. X [1963].)

——. "Theories of Human Nature in Mencius and Xunzi." In Kline and Ivanhoe, *Virtue, Nature, and Moral Agency in the Xunzi*. (Originally published in *Bulletin of the School of Oriental and African Studies* 15 [1953]: 541–65.)

Lau, D. C., and F. C. Chen, eds. *A Concordance to the Xunzi*. The Chinese University of Hong Kong Institute of Chinese Studies Ancient Chinese Texts Concordance Series. Hong Kong: The Commercial Press, 1996.

Legge, James, tr. *The Chinese Classics*. 2 vols. Taipei: Southern Materials Center, Inc., 1985.

Li Disheng 李滌生. *Xunzi Ji Shi* 荀子集釋. Taipei: Xuesheng Shuju, 1994.

Li Zehou 李澤厚. *Lunyu Jindu* 論語今讀. Hefei: Anhui Wenyi, 1998.

Liang Qixiong 梁啓雄. *Xunzi Jianshi* 荀子簡釋. Taipei: Taiwan Shangwu, 1978.

Lin, Pinshi 林品石, ed. *Lü shi chunqiu jin zhu jin yi* 呂氏春秋今註今譯. Taipei: Taiwan Shangwu yinshuguan, 1985.

Lin, Yizheng (Lin Yih-jing) 林義正. "*Chunqiu gongyang zhuan sixiang zhong daode juezhe de wenti* 春秋公羊傳思想中道德抉擇的問題." In *Proceedings of the International Conference on Chinese Philosophy*. National Taiwan University, Taipei, R.O.C., November 3–7, 1985.

Lin, Yü-sheng. "The Evolution of the Pre-Confucian Meaning of *Jen* 仁 and the Confucian Concept of Moral Autonomy." *Monumenta Serica (Journal of Oriental Studies)* 31 (1974-75): 172–204.

Liu Baonan 劉寶楠. *Lunyu Zhengyi* 論語正義. Beijing: Zhonghua Shuju, 1982.

Liu, Shu-hsien. "Sinological Torque: An observation." *Philosophy East and West* 28, no. 2 (April 1978): 199–207.

Liu, Xiusheng, and Philip J. Ivanhoe, eds. *Essays on the Moral Philosophy of Mengzi*. Indianapolis: Hackett Publishing Company, 2002.

Lo, Yuet Keung. "Finding the Self in the Analects: A Philological Approach." In Chong, Tan, and Ten, *The Moral Circle and the Self*.

Makeham, John. *Transmitters and Creators: Chinese Commentators and Commentaries on the Analects*. Cambridge: Harvard University Asia Center, 2003.

Marks, Joel, and Roger Ames, eds. *Emotions in Asian Thought: A Dialogue in Comparative Philosophy*. New York: State University of New York Press, 1995.

Mei, Yi-pao, tr. *The Works of Motze*. Taipei: Wenzhi Chubanshe (Confucius Publishing Co.), 1977.

Mou, Bo. "A Re-examination of the Structure and Content of Confucius's Version of the Golden Rule." *Philosophy East and West* 54, no. 2 (April 2004): 218–48.

——, ed. *Two Roads to Wisdom? Chinese and Analytic Philosophical Traditions*. Chicago: Open Court, 2001.

Munro, Donald J. *The Concept of Man in Contemporary China*. Ann Arbor: The University of Michigan Press, 1977.

——. "A Villain in the *Xunzi*." In Ivanhoe, *Chinese Language, Thought, and Culture*.

Nivison, David S. "Golden Rule Arguments in Chinese Moral Philosophy." In Nivison, *The Ways of Confucianism*.

——. "Mencius and Motivation." *Journal of the American Academy of Religion* 47, no. 3, Thematic Issue S (September 1980): 417–32.

——. "Mengzi: Just Not Doing It." In Liu and Ivanhoe, *Essays on the Moral Philosophy of Mengzi*.

——. "Motivation and Moral Action in Mencius." In Nivison, *The Ways of Confucianism*.

——. "The Paradox of Virtue." In Nivison, *The Ways of Confucianism*.

——. "Philosophical Voluntarism in Fourth-Century China." In Nivison, *The Ways of Confucianism*.

——. "Response to James Behuniak." *Philosophy East and West* 50, no. 1 (January 2000): 110–15.

——. *The Ways of Confucianism: Investigations in Chinese Philosophy*. Edited by Bryan Van Norden. Chicago: Open Court, 1996.

——. "Weakness of Will in Ancient Chinese Philosophy." In Nivison, *The Ways of Confucianism*.

——. "Xunzi on 'Human Nature'." In Nivison, *The Ways of Confucianism*.

Nuyen, A. T. "Confucianism and the Idea of Equality" *Asian Philosophy* 11, no. 2 (July 2001): 61–71.

Owen, Stephen. *Readings in Chinese Literary Thought*. Cambridge: Council on East Asian Studies, Harvard University, 1992.

Pang, Pu 龐樸. *Boshu Wuxingpian Yanjiu* 帛書五行篇研究. 2nd ed. Jinan: Qilu shushe, 1988.

——. "Yingyan Shushuo—Guodian Chujian Zhongshan sanqi xinpangzi shishuo 郢燕書說——郭店楚簡中山三器心旁字試說." Wuhandaxue zhongguowenhua yanjiuyuan 武漢大學中國文化研究院, ed. *Guodian Chujian guoji xueshu yantaohui bian wenji* 郭店楚簡國際學術研討會論文集. Hubei: Renmin Chubanshe, 2000.

Perrett, Roy. "Evil and Human Nature." *Monist* 85, no. 2 (April 2002): 304–19.

Pinker, Steven. *The Blank Slate: The Modern Denial of Human Nature*. New York: Viking, 2002.

Plaks, Andrew H., tr. *Ta Hsüeh and Chung Yung*. London: Penguin Books, 2003.

Qian Mu 錢穆. *Lunyu Xinjie* 論語新解. Taipei: Dongda, 1988.

Rachels, James. *The Elements of Moral Philosophy*. Boston: McGraw Hill, 2003.

Rawls, John. *A Theory of Justice*. New York: Oxford University Press, 1972.

Riegel, Jeffrey. "Reflections on an Unmoved Mind." *Journal of the American Academy of Religion* 47, no. 3, Thematic Issue S (September 1980): 433–57.

Robins, Dan. "The Development of Xunzi's Theory of Xing, Reconstructed on the Basis of a Textual Analysis of Xunzi 23, 'Xing E' 性惡 (Xing is Bad)." *Early China* 26-27 (2001-2002): 99–158.

Rosemont, Henry, Jr., ed. *Chinese Texts and Philosophical Contexts: Essays Dedicated to Angus C. Graham.* La Salle: Open Court, 1991.

Ryle, Gilbert. *The Concept of Mind.* London: Hutchinson, 1949.

Sato, Masayuki. *The Confucian Quest for Order: The Origin and Formation of the Political Thought of Xun Zi.* Leiden: Brill, 2003.

Scarpari, Maurizio. "The Debate on Human Nature in Early Confucian Literature." *Philosophy East and West* 53, no. 3 (July 2003): 323–39.

Schwartz, Benjamin. *The World of Thought in Ancient China.* Cambridge, Massachusetts: Harvard University Press, 1985.

Screech, M.A., tr. *The Essays of Michel de Montaigne.* Harmondsworth: The Penguin Press, 1991.

Searle, John. "How to Derive 'Ought' from 'Is'." *The Philosophical Review* 73, no. 1 (1964): 43–58.

Shen, Vincent. "Chen Daqi (Ch'en Ta-ch'i)." In Cua, *Encyclopedia of Chinese Philosophy.*

Shun, Kwong-loi. *Mencius and Early Chinese Thought.* Stanford: Stanford University Press, 1997.

———. "Moral Reasons in Confucian Ethics." *Journal of Chinese Philosophy* 16, no. 3/4 (September/December 1989): 317–43.

———. "*Ren* and *Li* in the *Analects*." *Philosophy East and West* 43, no. 3 (July 1993): 457–79. Reprinted in Van Norden, *Confucius and the Analects.*

———. "Self and Self-Cultivation in Early Confucian Thought." In Mou, *Two Roads to Wisdom?*

Slingerland, Edward. *Effortless Action: Wu-wei as Conceptual Metaphor and Spiritual Ideal in Early China.* New York: Oxford University Press, 2003.

Soothill, W. E., tr. *Analects.* London: Oxford World Classics, 1962.

Stalnaker, Aron. "Aspects of Xunzi's Engagement with Early Daoism." *Philosophy East and West* 53, no. 1 (January 2003): 87–129.

Stocker, Michael. "The Schizophrenia of Modern Ethical Theories." In Crisp and Slote, *Virtue Ethics.*

Sun Yirang 孫詒讓. *Mozi Xiangu* 墨子閒詁. Beijing: Zhonghua shuju, 1986.

Tan, Sor-hoon. *Confucian Democracy: A Deweyan Reconstruction.* Albany: State University of New York Press, 2004.

———. "Women's Virtues and the *Analects*." In Chong and Liu, *Conceptions of Virtue East and West.*

Tang Junyi 唐君毅. "Lun Zhongguo zhexue sixiangshi zhong (li) zhi liu yi 論中國哲學思想史中 (理) 之六義." In *Xinya Xuebao* 新亞學報, vol. 1, no. 1 (1995): 45–98.

———. *Zhongguo zhexue yuanlun : yuan xing pian : Zhongguo zhexue zhong renxing sixiang zhi fazhan*, 中國哲學原論: 原性篇: 中國哲學中人性思想之發展. Hong Kong: Xinya shuyuan yanjiusuo, 1974.

Tao, Julia Lai Po-Wah "Two Perspectives of Care: Confucian *Ren* and Feminist Care." *Journal of Chinese Philosophy* 27, no. 2 (June 2000): 215–40.

Ten, C. L. "The Moral Circle." In Chong, Tan, and Ten, *The Moral Circle and the Self*.

Tu, Wei-ming . *Confucian Thought: Selfhood as Creative Transformation*. New York: State University of New York Press, 1985.

———. "The Creative Tension Between *Jen* and *Li*." In Tu, *Humanity and Self-Cultivation*. (Originally published in *Philosophy East and West* 18, no. 1/2 [January/April 1968]: 29–39.)

———. *Humanity and Self-Cultivation: Essays in Confucian Thought*. Berkeley: Asian Humanities Press, 1979.

———. "*Jen* as a Living Metaphor in the Confucian *Analects*." In Tu, *Confucian Thought*.

Van Norden, Bryan W., ed. *Confucius and the Analects*: *New Essays*. New York: Oxford University Press, 2002.

———. "Kwong-loi Shun on Moral Reasons in Mencius." *Journal of Chinese Philosophy* 18, no. 4 (December 1991): 353–70.

———. "Mengzi and Xunzi: Two Views of Human Agency." In Kline and Ivanhoe, *Virtue, Nature, and Moral Agency in the Xunzi*.

———. "Unweaving the 'One Thread' of *Analects* 4:15." In Van Norden, *Confucius and the Analects*.

Van Zoeren, Steven Jay. *Poetry and Personality: Reading, Exegesis, and Hermeneutics in Traditional China*. Stanford: Stanford University Press, 1991.

Waley, Arthur. *Three Ways of Thought in Ancient China*. London: Allen and Unwin, 1939. Reprinted New York: Doubleday, 1956.

———. *The Analects of Confucius*. New York: Vintage Books, 1989.

Wang Chong 王充 (Huang Hui 黃暉, ed.) *Lunheng Jiaoshi* 論衡校釋. Beijing: Zhonghua Shuju, 1996.

Watson, Burton, tr. *Basic Writings of Mo Tzu, Hsün Tzu, and Han Fei Tzu*. New York: Columbia University Press, 1963.

———, tr. *Hsün Tzu: Basic Writings*. New York: Columbia University Press, 1963.

———, tr. *Mo Tzu: Basic Writings*. New York: Columbia University Press, 1963.

Wittgenstein, Ludwig. *Culture and Value*. Tr. Peter Winch. Chicago: University of Chicago Press, 1980.

Wolf, Susan. "Moral Saints." *Journal of Philosophy* 79, no. 8 (August 1982): 419–39.

Wong, David B . "Is There a Distinction Between Reason and Emotion in Mencius?" *Philosophy East and West* 41, no. 1 (January 1991): 31–44.

———. "Reasons and Analogical Reasoning in Mengzi." In Liu and Ivanhoe, *Essays on the Moral Philosophy of Mengzi*.

———. "Universalism versus Love With Distinctions: An Ancient Debate Revived." *Journal of Chinese Philosophy* 16 (September/December 1989): 251–72.

———. "Xunzi on Moral Motivation." In Ivanhoe, *Chinese Language, Thought, and Culture*. Reprinted in Kline and Ivanhoe, *Virtue, Nature, and Moral Agency in the Xunzi*.

Xiao, Yang. "When Political Philosophy Meets Moral Psychology: Expressivism in the *Mencius*. *Dao: A Journal of Comparative Philosophy* 5, no. 2 (June 2006): 257–71.

Xue, Ke 雪克, ed. *Xin yi Gongyang Zhuan* 新譯公羊傳. Taipei: Sanmin shuju, 1998.

Yang Bojun 楊伯峻. *Lunyu Yizhu* 論語譯注. Taizhong, Taiwan: Landeng Wenhua, 1987.

———. *Mengzi Yizhu* 孟子譯注. Hong Kong: Zhonghua Zhuju, 1984.

Yao, Xinzhong. "*Jen*, Love and Universality: Three Arguments Concerning *Jen* in Confucianism." *Asian Philosophy* 5, no. 2 (July 1995): 185–95.

Zhu Xi 朱熹. *Sishu Zhangju Jizhu* 四書章句集注. Taipei: Changan, 1990.

Index